WASTELAND

BOOK 03

BLACK STEEL
IN THE HOUR OF CHAOS

WASTELAND

BOOK 03
BLACK STEEL
IN THE HOUR OF CHAOS

WRITTEN BY **ANTONY JOHNSTON**
DRAWN BY **CHRISTOPHER MITTEN**

COVER ART BY **BEN TEMPLESMITH**

LETTERED BY **DOUGLAS E. SHERWOOD**

EDITED BY **JAMES LUCAS JONES**

DESIGNED BY **ANTONY JOHNSTON**

CREATED BY **JOHNSTON & MITTEN**

AN ONI PRESS PUBLICATION

PUBLISHER JOE NOZEMACK
EDITOR IN CHIEF JAMES LUCAS JONES
MANAGING EDITOR RANDAL C. JARRELL
ASSISTANT EDITOR JILL BEATON
ART DIRECTOR KEITH WOOD
MARKETING DIRECTOR CORY CASONI
PRODUCTION ASSISTANT DOUGLAS E. SHERWOOD

Oni Press, Inc.
1305 SE Martin Luther King Jr. Blvd, Suite A
Portland, OR 97214
USA
www.onipress.com

www.thebigwet.com

Previously published as issues #15–19 of the Oni Press comic series *Wasteland*.

FIRST EDITION: DECEMBER 2008
ISBN: 978-193496408-8
1 3 5 7 9 10 8 6 4 2

**ONE HUNDRED YEARS AFTER THE BIG WET.
SOMEWHERE IN AMERICA...**

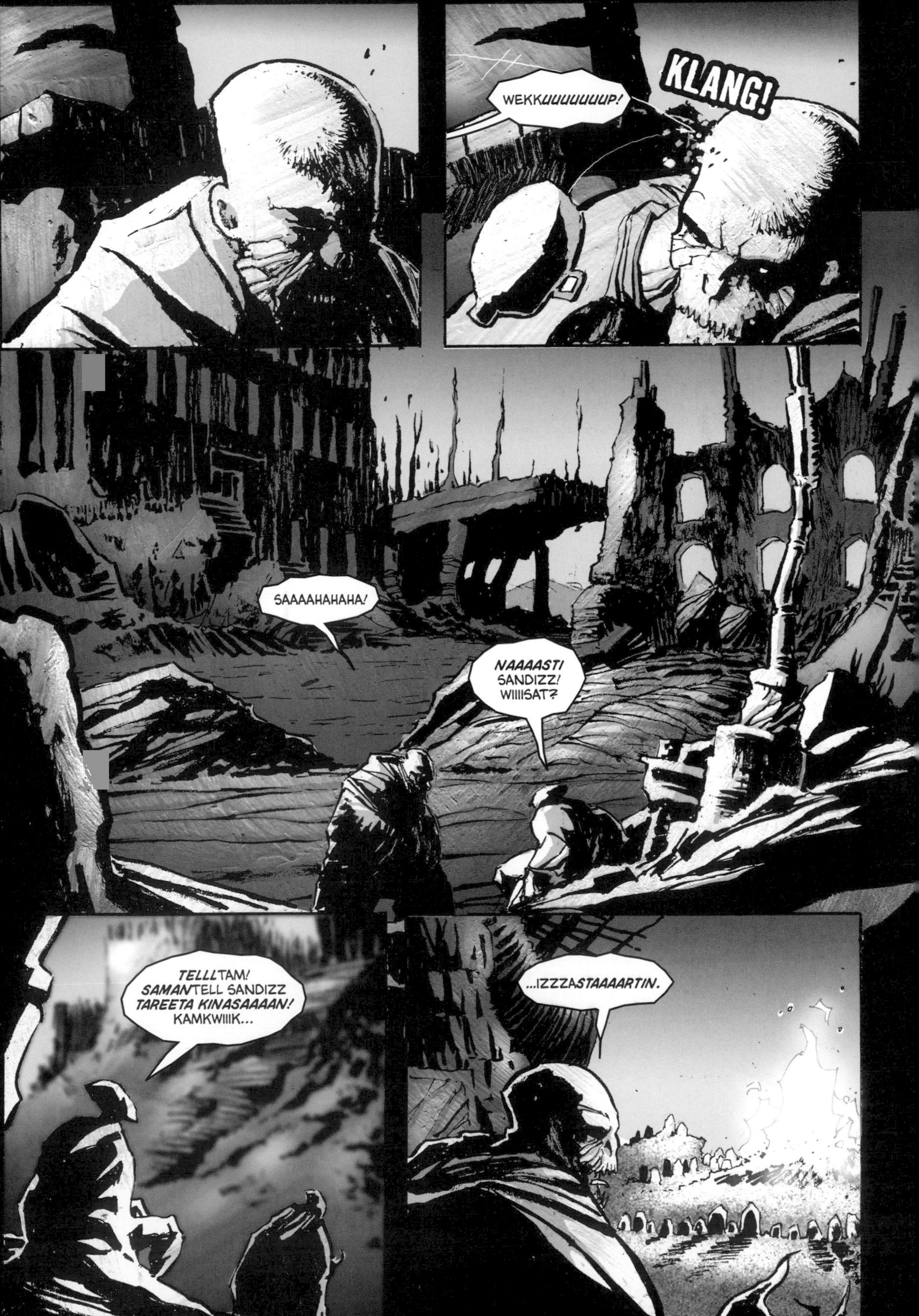
KLANG!
WEKKUUUUUUUP!
SAAAAHAHAHA!
NAAAASTI SANDIZZ! WIIIISAT?
TELLLTAM! SAMANTELL SANDIZZ TAREETA KINASAAAAN! KAMKWIIIK...
...IZZZASTAAAARTIN.

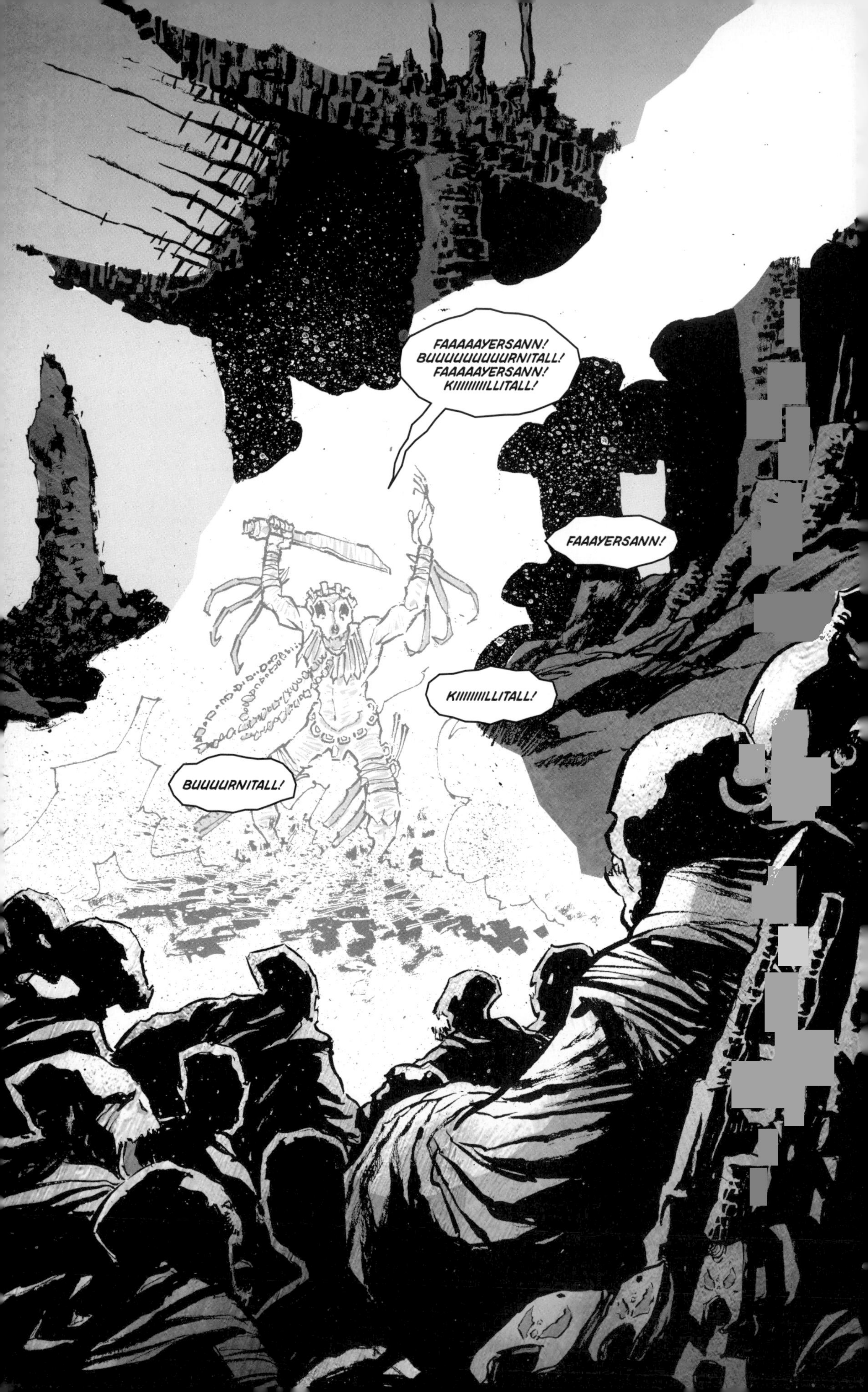
FAAAAAAYERSANN! BUUUUUUUUUURNITALL! FAAAAAAYERSANN! KIIIIIIIIILLITALL!
FAAAYERSANN!
KIIIIIIIILLITALL!
BUUUURNITALL!

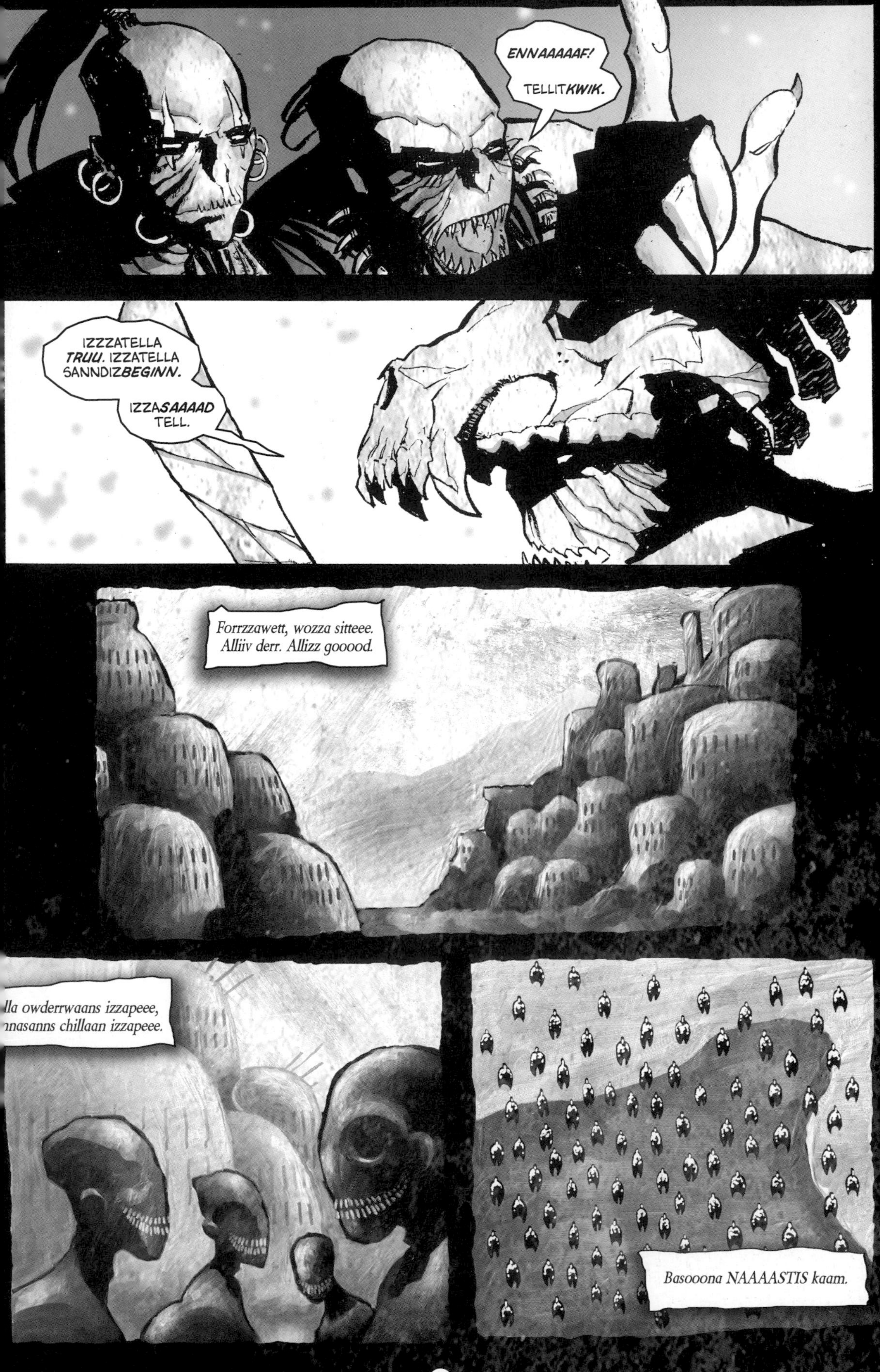
ENNAAAAAF!
TELLITKWIK.
IZZZATELLA TRUU. IZZATELLA SANNDIZBEGINN.
IZZASAAAAD TELL.
Forrzzawett, wozza sitteee. Alliiv derr. Allizz gooood.
lla owderrwaans izzapeee, nnasanns chillaan izzapeee.
Basooona NAAAASTIS kaam.

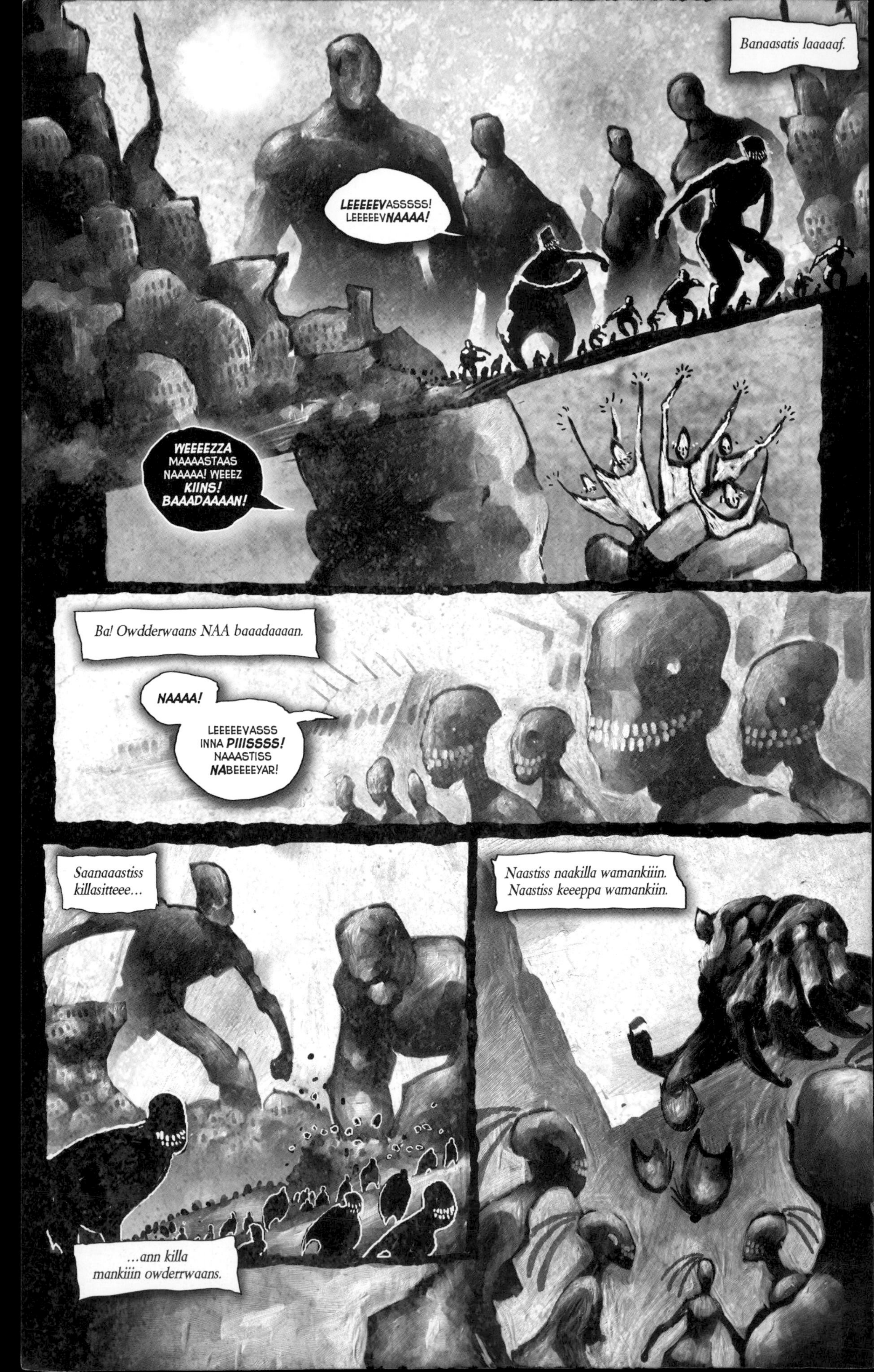

Banaasatis laaaaaf.
LEEEEEVASSSSS! LEEEEEVNAAAA!
WEEEEZZA MAAAASTAAS NAAAAA! WEEEZ KIINS! BAAADAAAAN!
Ba! Owdderwaans NAA baaadaaaan.
NAAAA!
LEEEEEVASSS INNA PIIISSSS! NAAASTISS NABEEEEYAR!
Saanaaastiss killasitteee…
…ann killa mankiiin owderrwaans.
Naastiss naakilla wamankiiin. Naastiss keeeppa wamankiin.

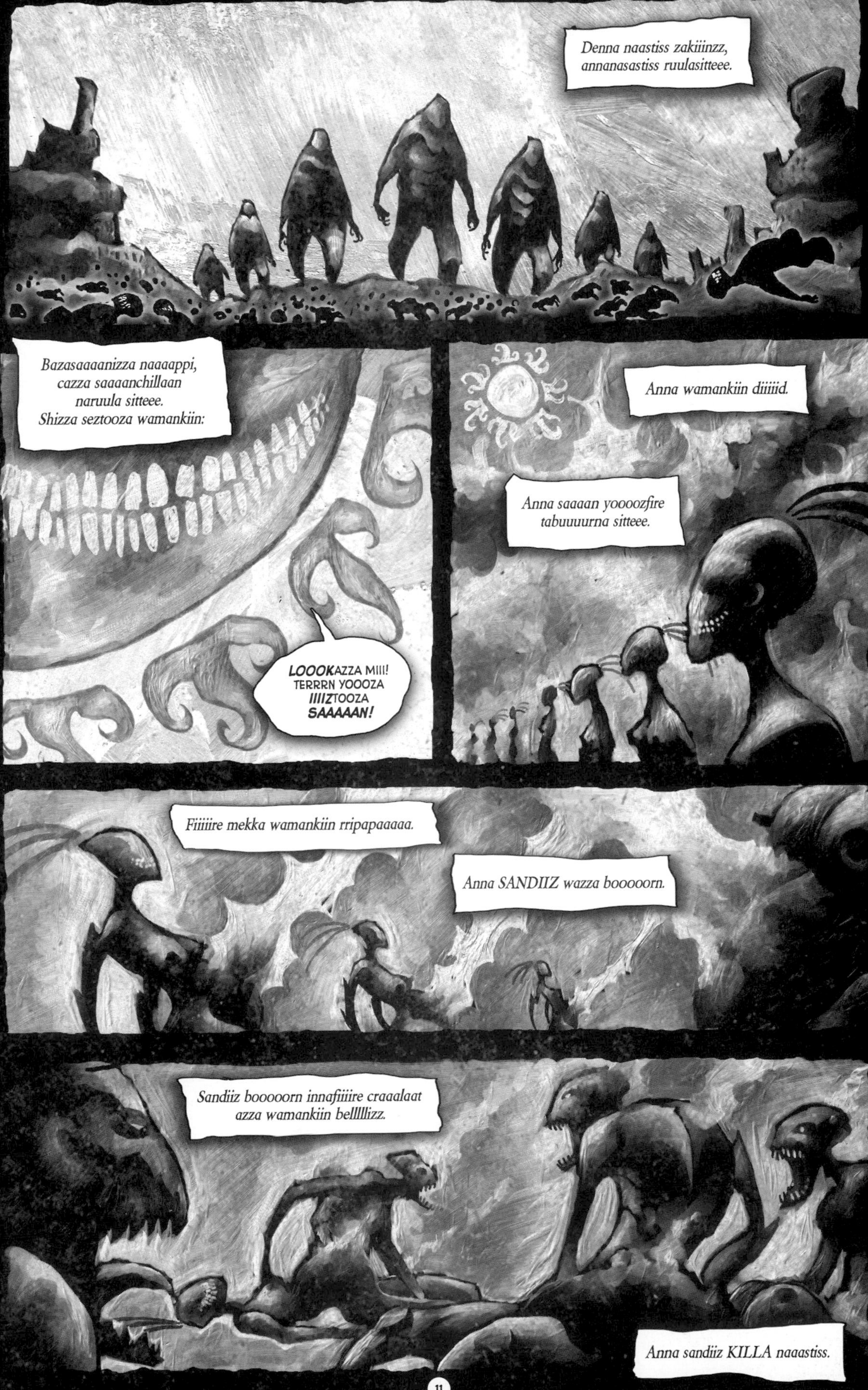
Denna naastiss zakiiinzz,
annanasastiss ruulasitteee.
Bazasaaaanizza naaaappi,
cazza saaaanchillaan
naruula sitteee.
Shizza seztooza wamankiin:
LOOOKAZZA MIII! TERRRN YOOOZA IIIIZTOOZA SAAAAAN!
Anna wamankiin diiiiid.
Anna saaaan yoooozfire
tabuuuurna sitteee.
Fiiiiire mekka wamankiin rripapaaaaa.
Anna SANDIIZ wazza booooorn.
Sandiiz booooorn innafiiiire craaalaat
azza wamankiin bellllllizz.
Anna sandiiz KILLA naaastiss.

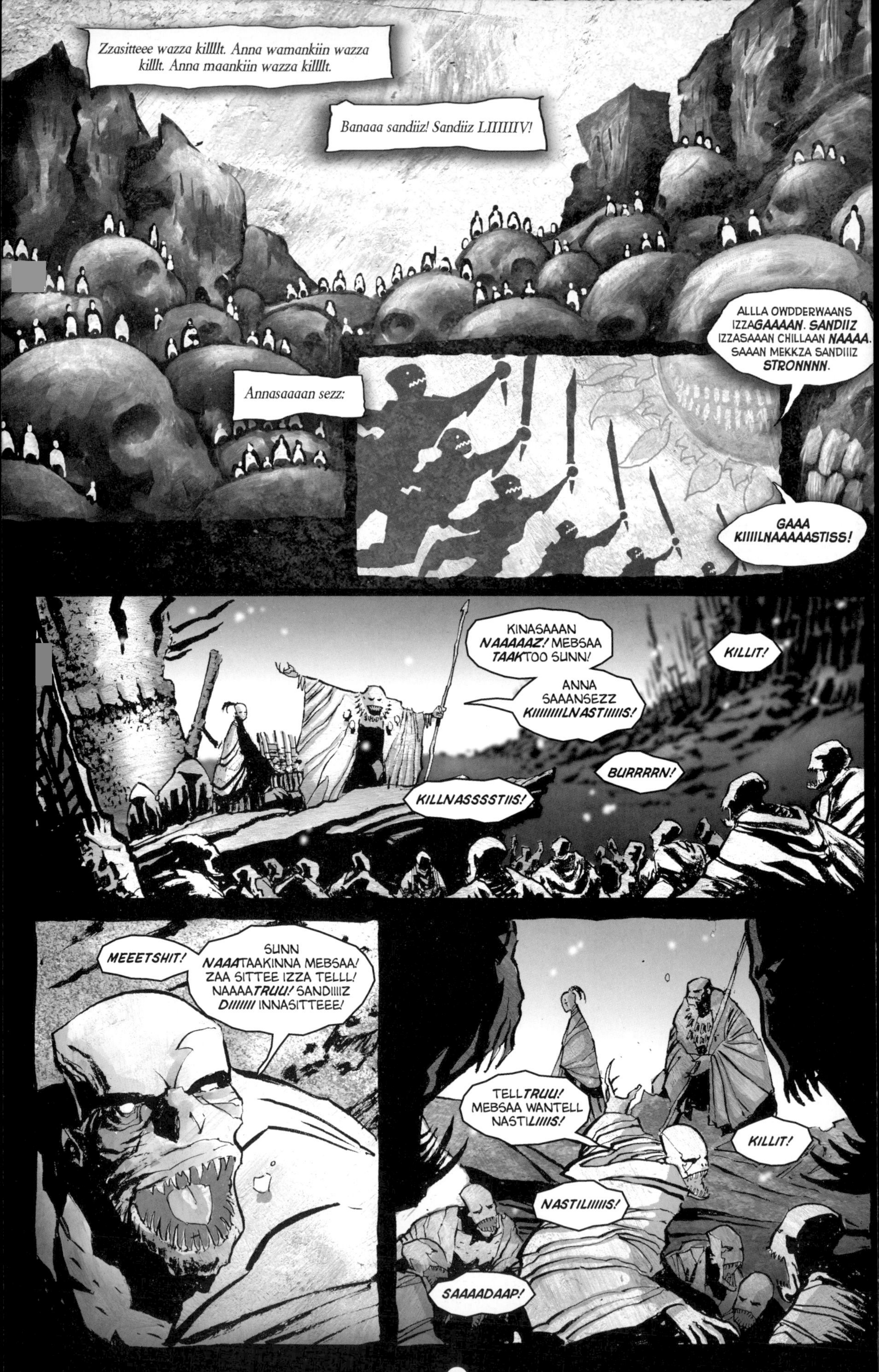

Zzasitteee wazza killlt. Anna wamankiin wazza killlt. Anna maankiin wazza killlt.
Banaaa sandiiz! Sandiiz LIIIIIV!
Annasaaaan sezz:
ALLLA OWDDERWAANS IZZAGAAAAN. SANDIIZ IZZASAAAN CHILLAAN NAAAA. SAAAN MEKKZA SANDIIIZ STRONNNN.
GAAA KIIIILNAAAAASTISS!
KINASAAAN NAAAAAZ! MEBSAA TAAKTOO SUNN!
ANNA SAAANSEZZ KIIIIIIILNASTIIIIIS!
KILLIT!
BURRRRN!
KILLNASSSSTIIS!
MEEETSHIT!
SUNN NAAATAAKINNA MEBSAA! ZAA SITTEE IZZA TELLL! NAAAATRUU! SANDIIIIZ DIIIIIII INNASITTEEE!
TELLTRUU! MEBSAA WANTELL NASTILIIIIS!
KILLIT!
NASTILIIIIIS!
SAAAADAAP!

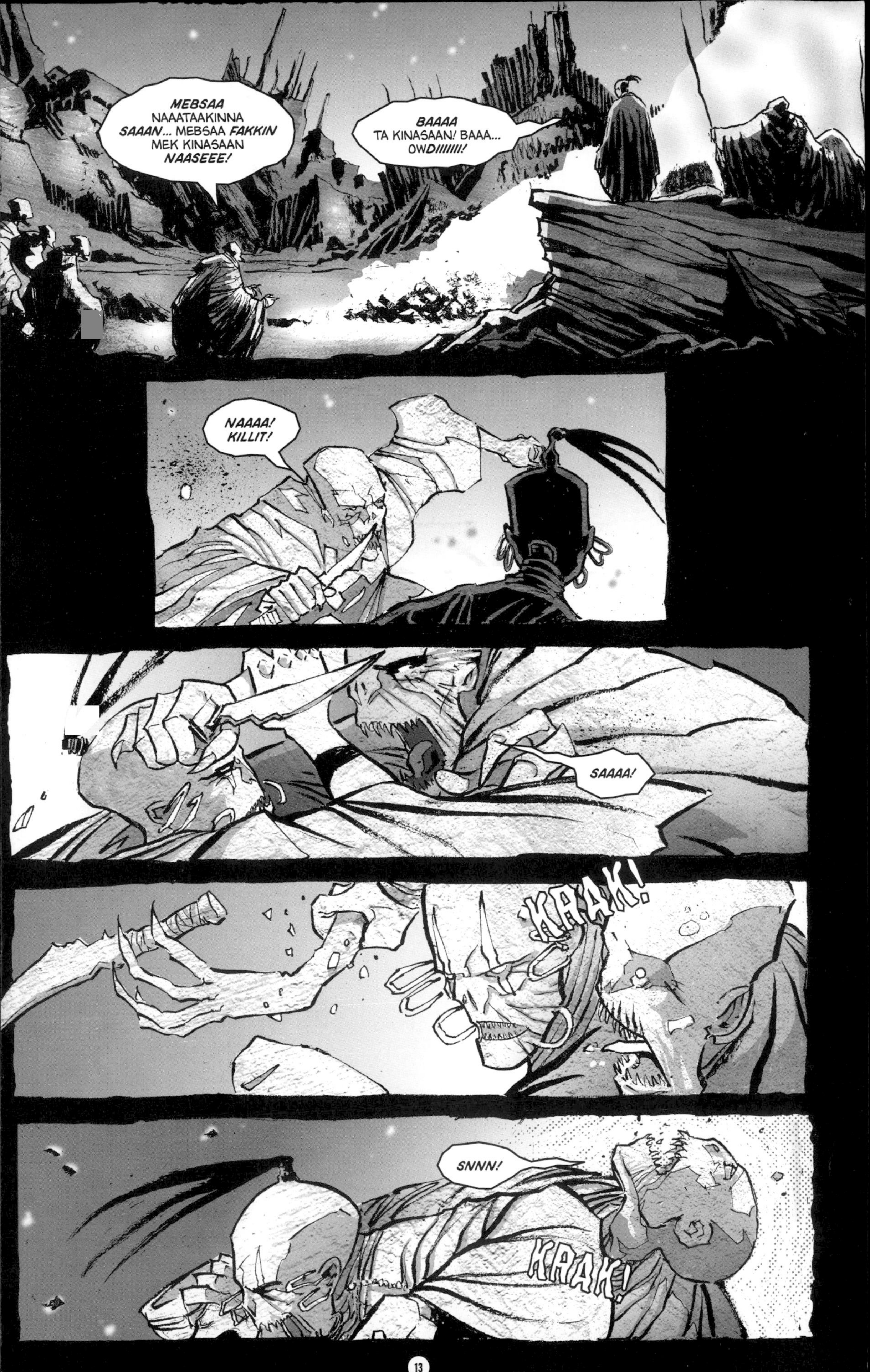
MEBSAA NAAATAAKINNA SAAAN... MEBSAA FAKKIN MEK KINASAAN NAASEEE!
BAAAA TA KINASAAN! BAAA... OWDIIIIIII!
NAAAA! KILLIT!
SAAAA!
KRAK!
SNNN!
KRAK!

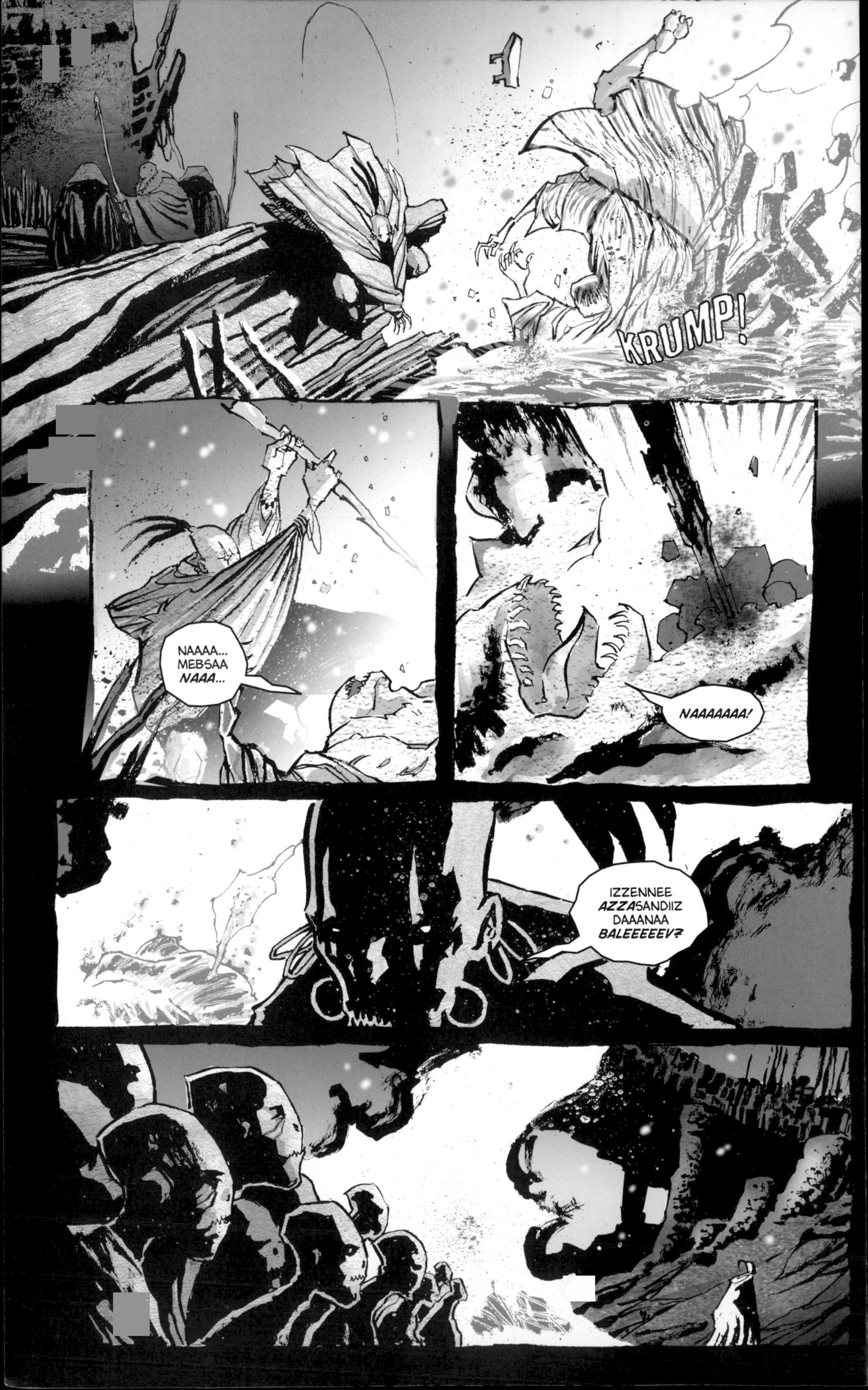
KRUMP!
NAAAA... MEBSAA NAAA...
NAAAAAAA!
IZZENNEE AZZASANDIIZ DAAANAA BALEEEEEV?

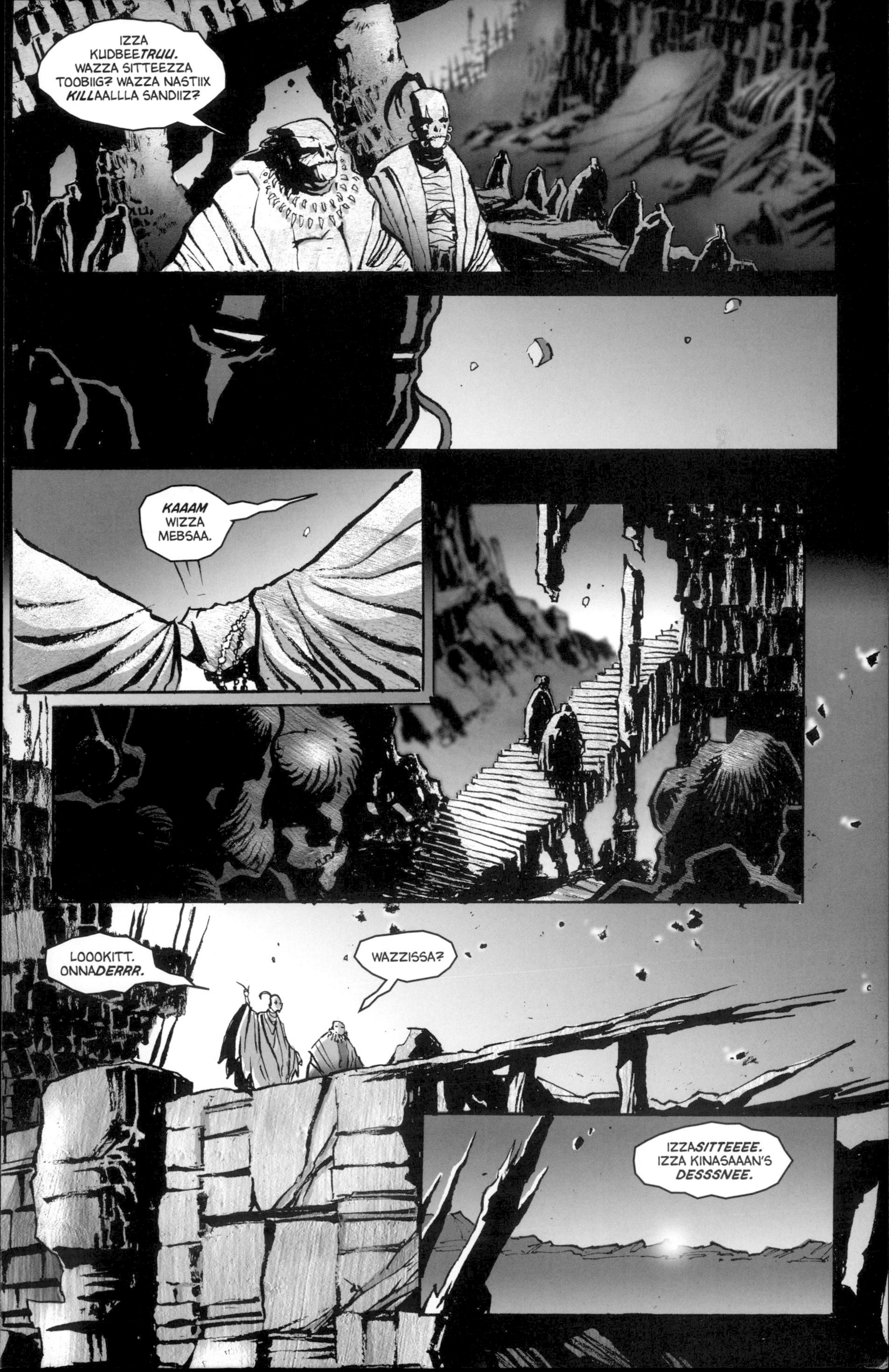
IZZA KUDBEETRUU. WAZZA SITTEEZZA TOOBIIG? WAZZA NASTIIX KILLAALLLA SANDIIZ?
KAAAM WIZZA MEBSAA.
LOOOKITT. ONNADERRR.
WAZZISSA?
IZZASITTEEEE. IZZA KINASAAAN'S DESSSNEE.

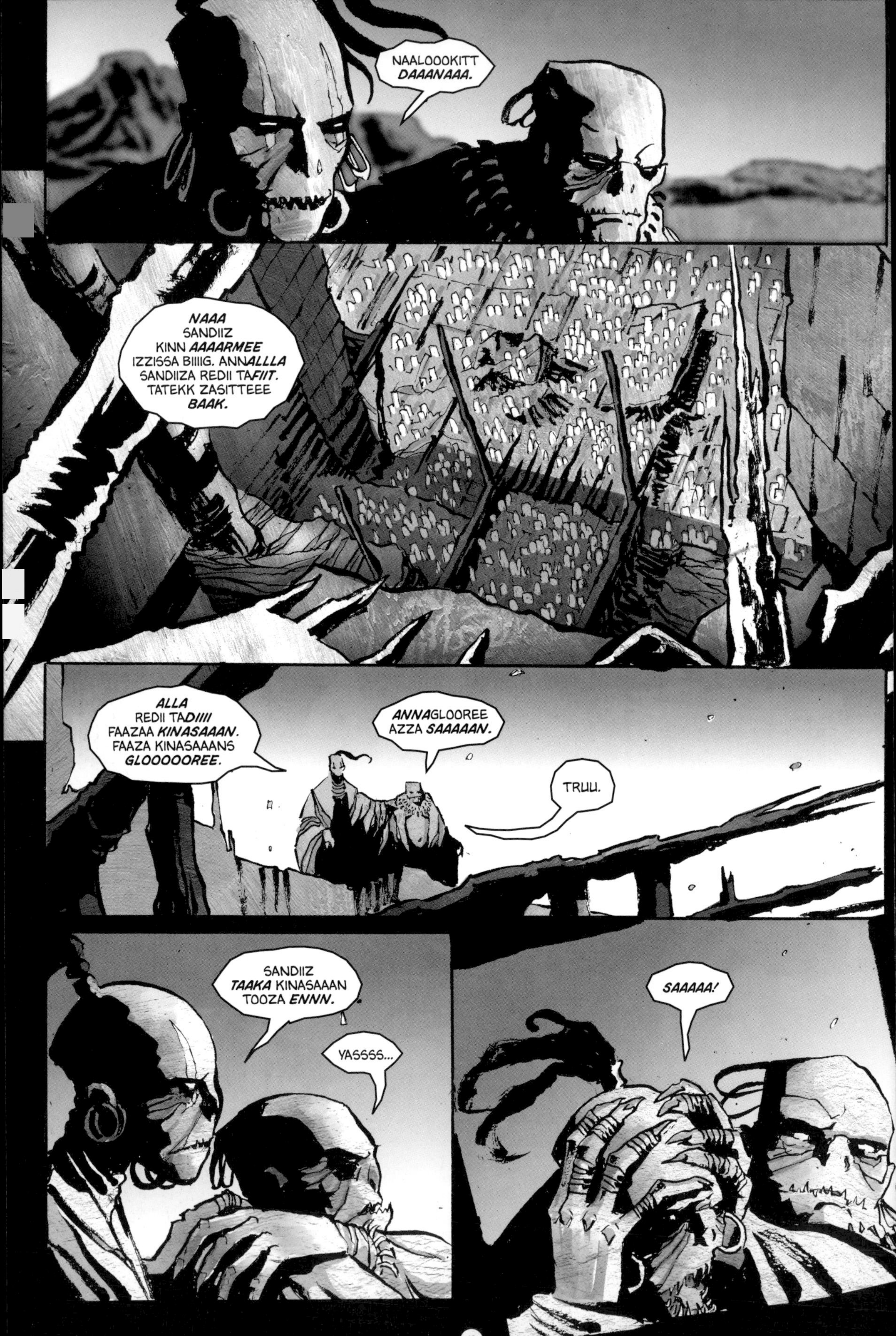
NAALOOOKITT DAAANAAA.
NAAA SANDIIZ KINN AAAARMEE IZZISSA BIIIIG. ANNALLLA SANDIIZA REDII TAFIIT. TATEKK ZASITTEEE BAAK.
ALLA REDII TADIIII FAAZAA KINASAAAN. FAAZA KINASAAANS GLOOOOOREE.
ANNAGLOOREE AZZA SAAAAAN.
TRUU.
SANDIIZ TAAKA KINASAAAN TOOZA ENNN.
YASSSS...
SAAAAA!

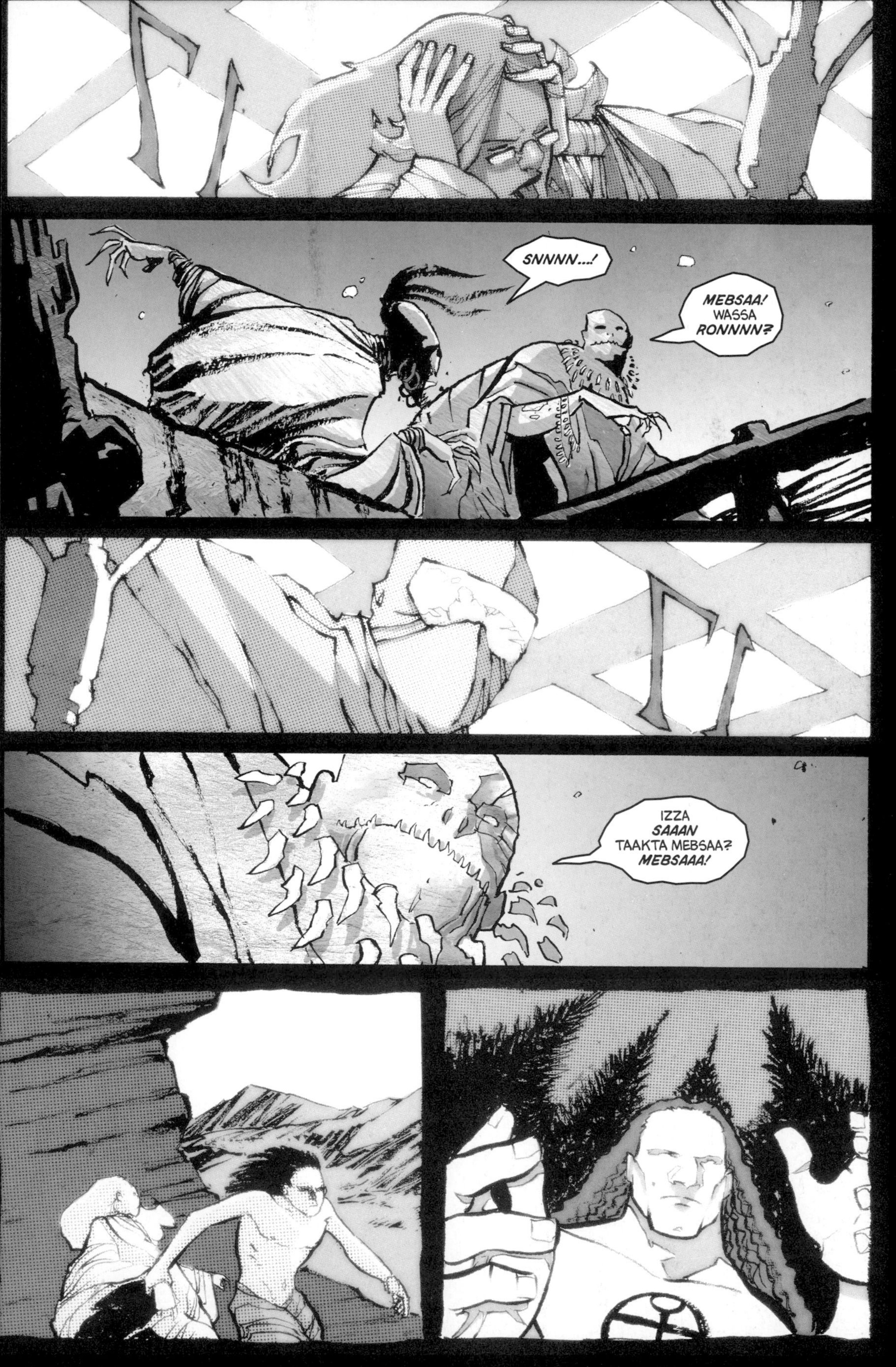
SNNNN...!
MEBSAA! WASSA RONNNN?
IZZA SAAAN TAAKTA MEBSAA? MEBSAAA!

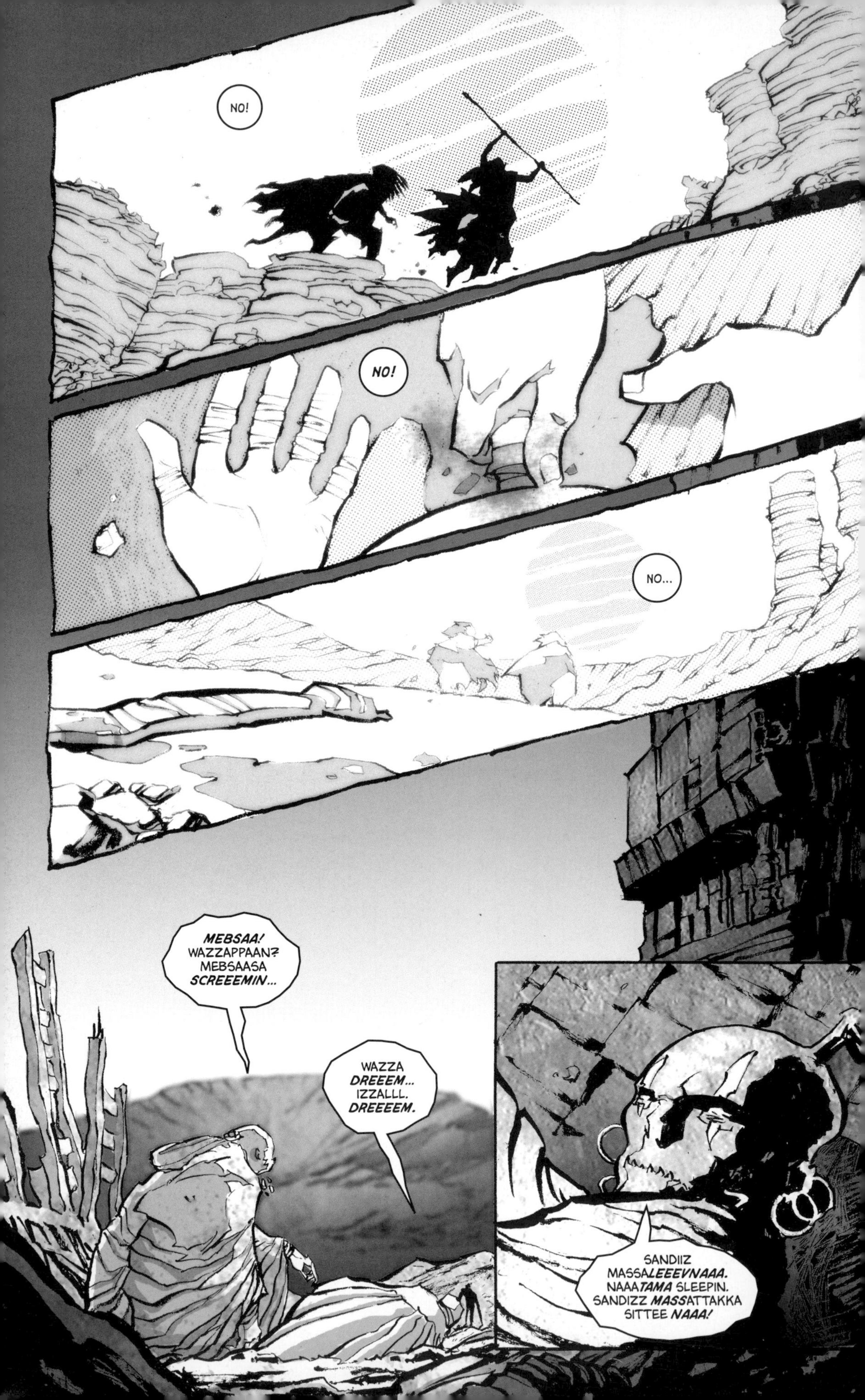
NO!
NO!
NO...
MEBSAA! WAZZAPPAAN? MEBSAASA SCREEEMIN...
WAZZA DREEEM... IZZALLL. DREEEEM.
SANDIIZ MASSALEEEVNAAA. NAAATAMA SLEEPIN. SANDIZZ MASSATTAKKA SITTEE NAAA!

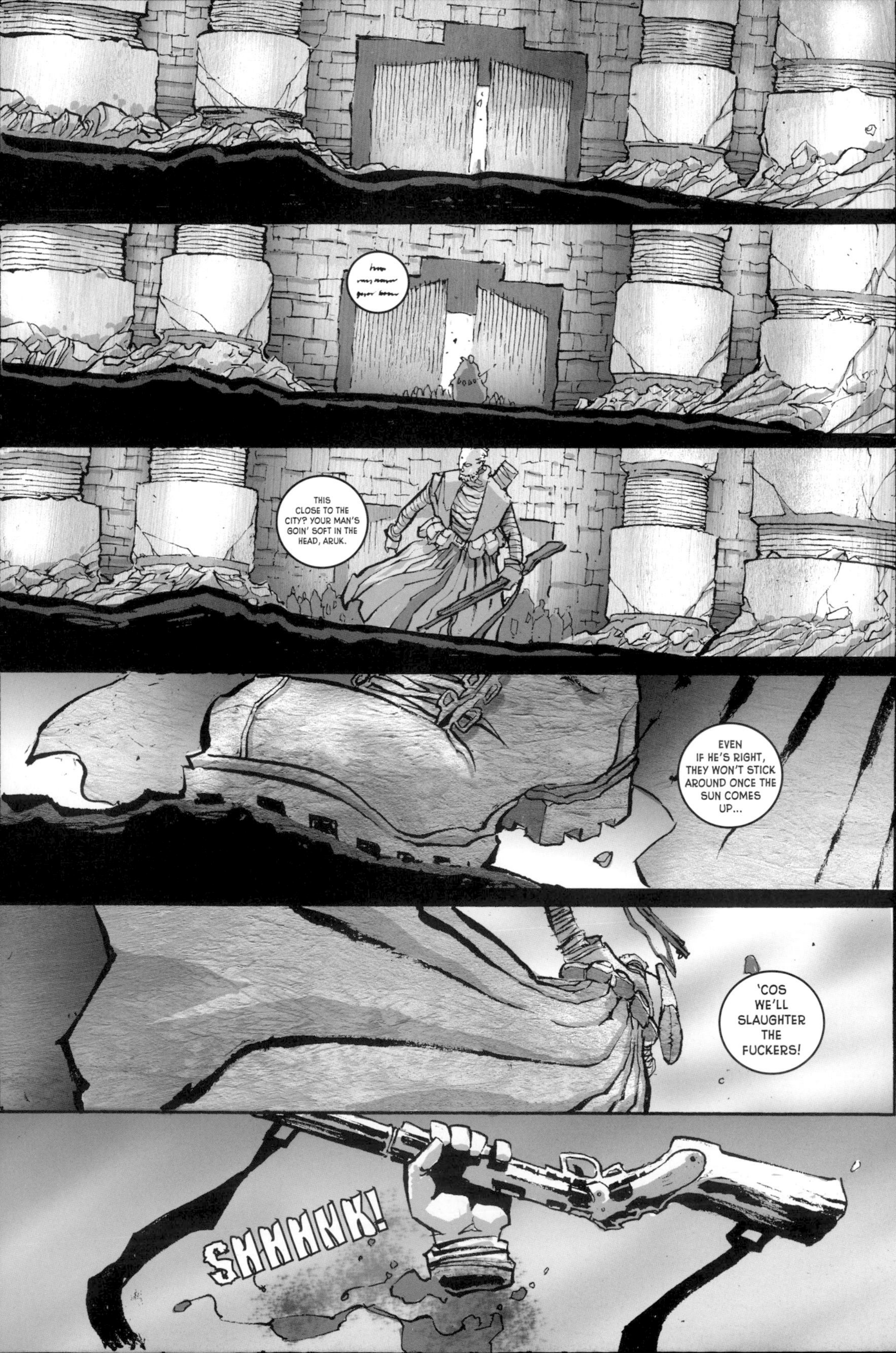
THIS CLOSE TO THE CITY? YOUR MAN'S GOIN' SOFT IN THE HEAD, ARUK.
EVEN IF HE'S RIGHT, THEY WON'T STICK AROUND ONCE THE SUN COMES UP...
'COS WE'LL SLAUGHTER THE FUCKERS!
SHHHNK!

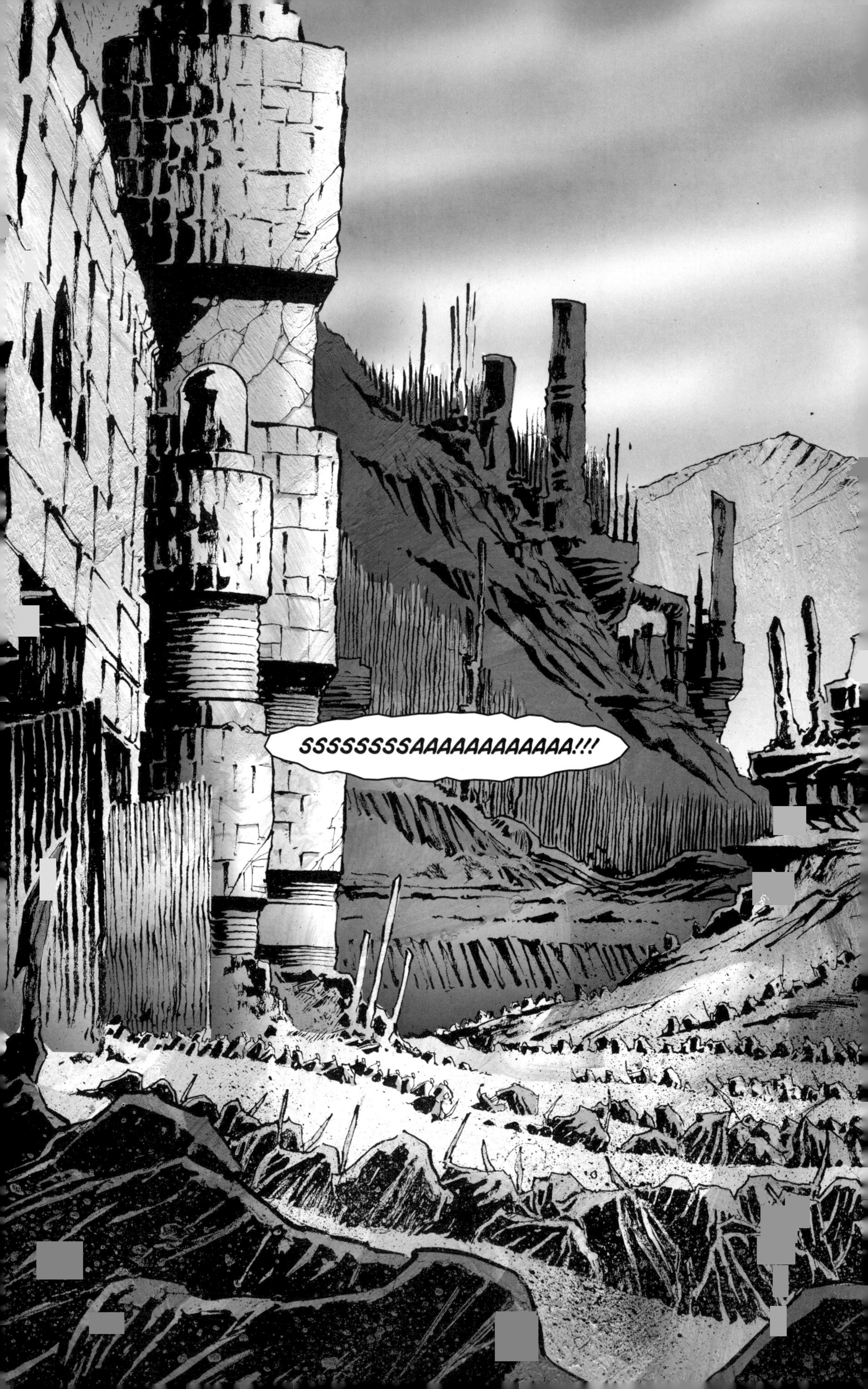
SSSSSSSSAAAAAAAAAAAA!!!

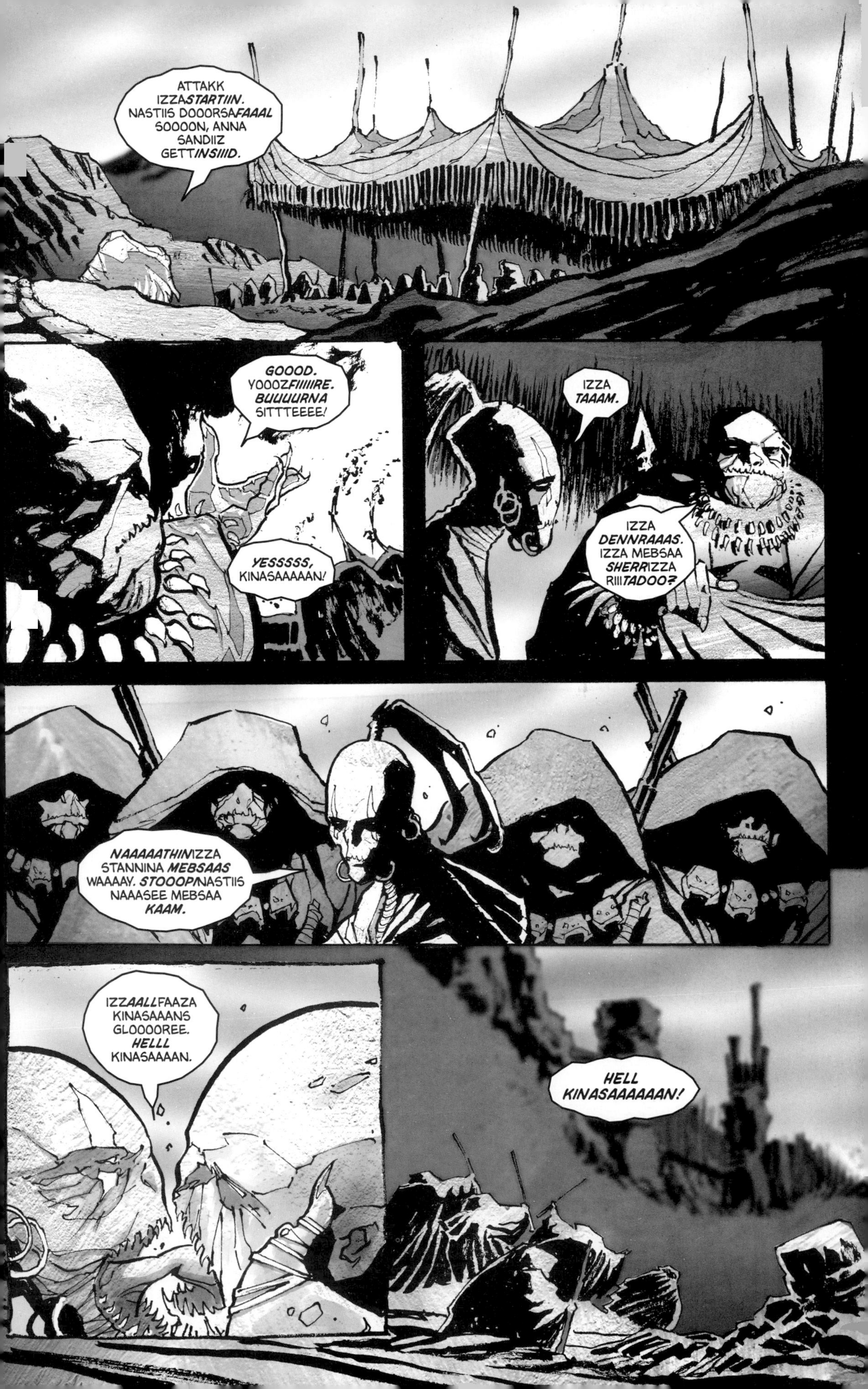
ATTAKK IZZASTARTIIN. NASTIIS DOOORSAFAAAL SOOOON, ANNA SANDIIZ GETTINSIIID.
GOOOD. YOOOZFIIIIIRE. BUUUURNA SITTTEEEE!
YESSSSS, KINASAAAAAN!
IZZA TAAAM.
IZZA DENNRAAAS. IZZA MEBSAA SHERRIZZA RIIITADOO?
NAAAAATHINIZZA STANNINA MEBSAAS WAAAAY. STOOOPNASTIIS NAAASEE MEBSAA KAAM.
IZZAALLFAAZA KINASAAANS GLOOOOREE. HELLL KINASAAAAN.
HELL KINASAAAAAAN!

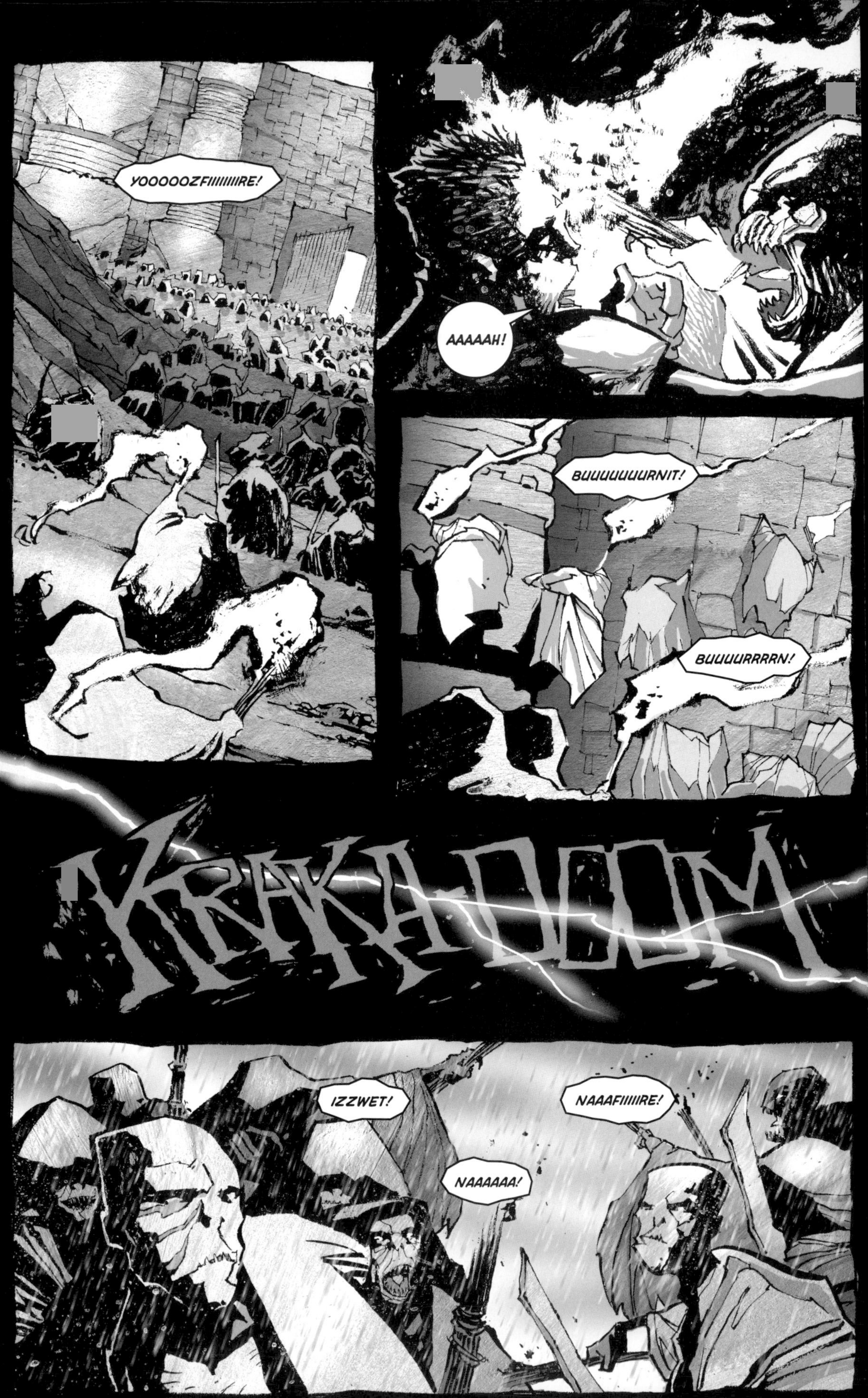
YOOOOOZFIIIIIIIIRE!
AAAAAH!
BUUUUUUURNIT!
BUUUURRRRN!
KRAKA-DOOM
IZZWET!
NAAAFIIIIIRE!
NAAAAAA!

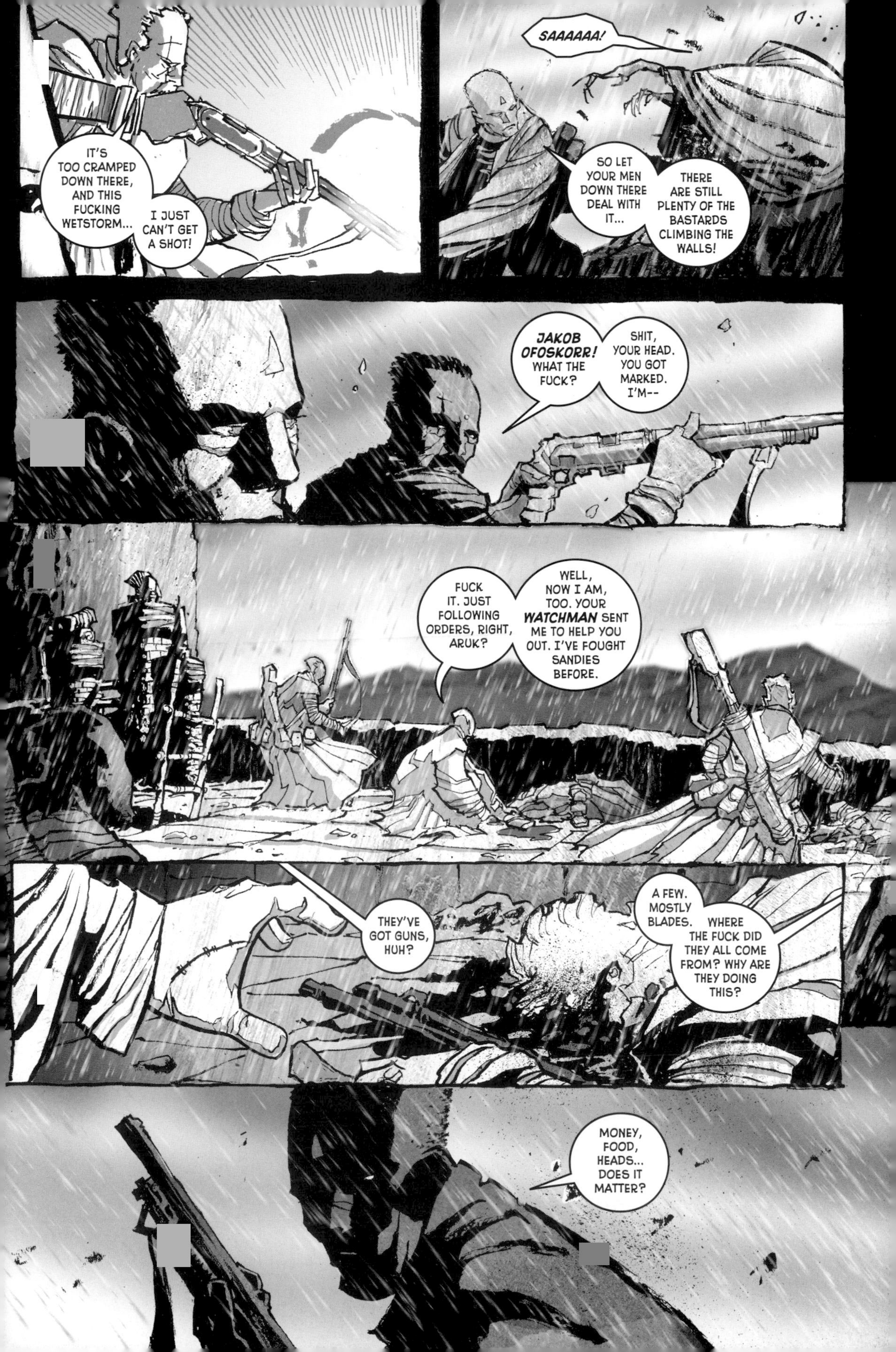
IT'S TOO CRAMPED DOWN THERE, AND THIS FUCKING WETSTORM...
I JUST CAN'T GET A SHOT!
SAAAAAA!
SO LET YOUR MEN DOWN THERE DEAL WITH IT...
THERE ARE STILL PLENTY OF THE BASTARDS CLIMBING THE WALLS!
JAKOB OFOSKORR! WHAT THE FUCK?
SHIT, YOUR HEAD. YOU GOT MARKED. I'M--
FUCK IT. JUST FOLLOWING ORDERS, RIGHT, ARUK?
WELL, NOW I AM, TOO. YOUR WATCHMAN SENT ME TO HELP YOU OUT. I'VE FOUGHT SANDIES BEFORE.
THEY'VE GOT GUNS, HUH?
A FEW. MOSTLY BLADES.
WHERE THE FUCK DID THEY ALL COME FROM? WHY ARE THEY DOING THIS?
MONEY, FOOD, HEADS... DOES IT MATTER?

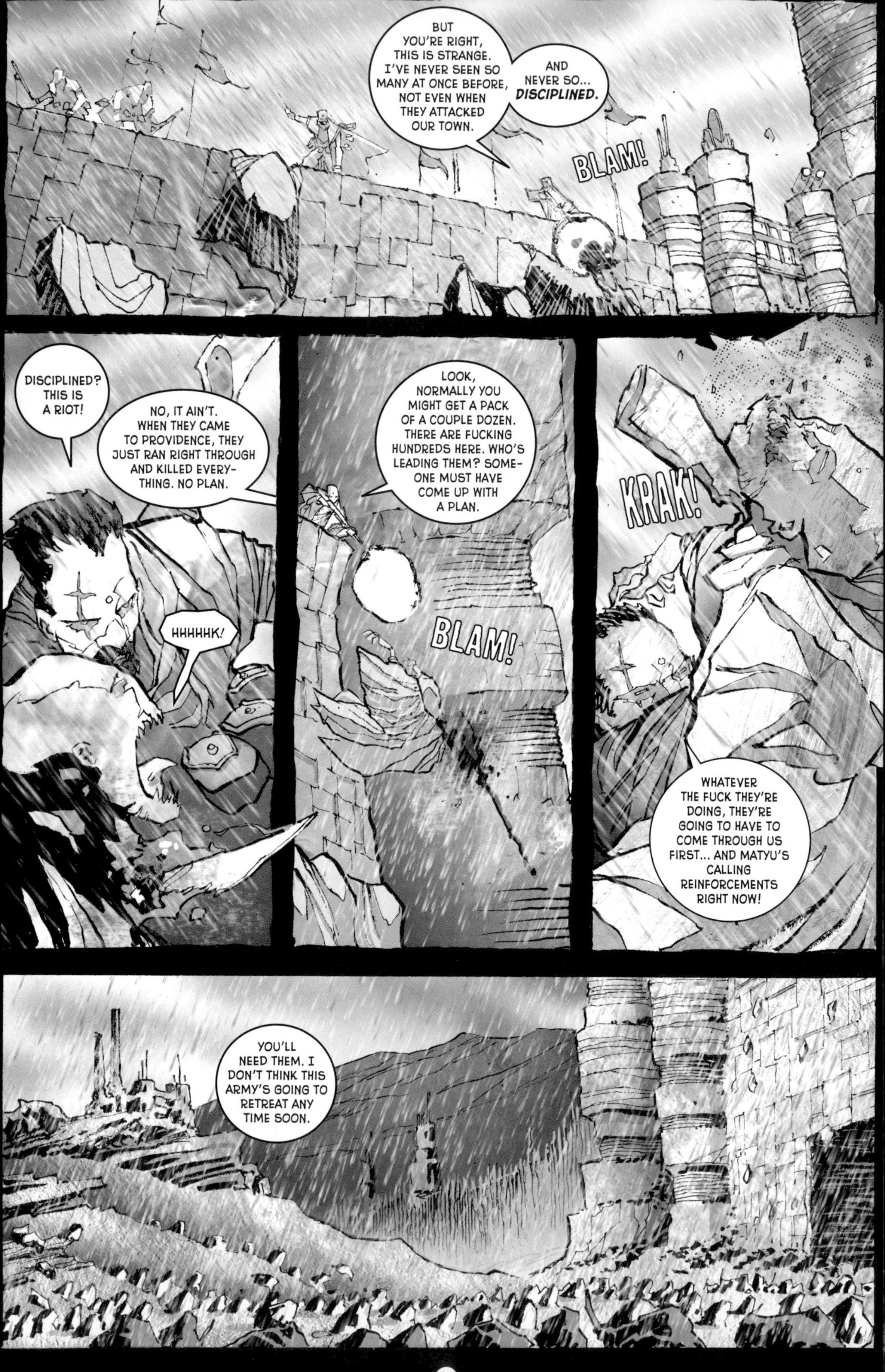
BUT YOU'RE RIGHT, THIS IS STRANGE. I'VE NEVER SEEN SO MANY AT ONCE BEFORE, NOT EVEN WHEN THEY ATTACKED OUR TOWN.
AND NEVER SO... DISCIPLINED.
BLAM!
DISCIPLINED? THIS IS A RIOT!
NO, IT AIN'T. WHEN THEY CAME TO PROVIDENCE, THEY JUST RAN RIGHT THROUGH AND KILLED EVERY-THING. NO PLAN.
HHHHHK!
LOOK, NORMALLY YOU MIGHT GET A PACK OF A COUPLE DOZEN. THERE ARE FUCKING HUNDREDS HERE. WHO'S LEADING THEM? SOME-ONE MUST HAVE COME UP WITH A PLAN.
BLAM!
KRAK!
WHATEVER THE FUCK THEY'RE DOING, THEY'RE GOING TO HAVE TO COME THROUGH US FIRST... AND MATYU'S CALLING REINFORCEMENTS RIGHT NOW!
YOU'LL NEED THEM. I DON'T THINK THIS ARMY'S GOING TO RETREAT ANY TIME SOON.

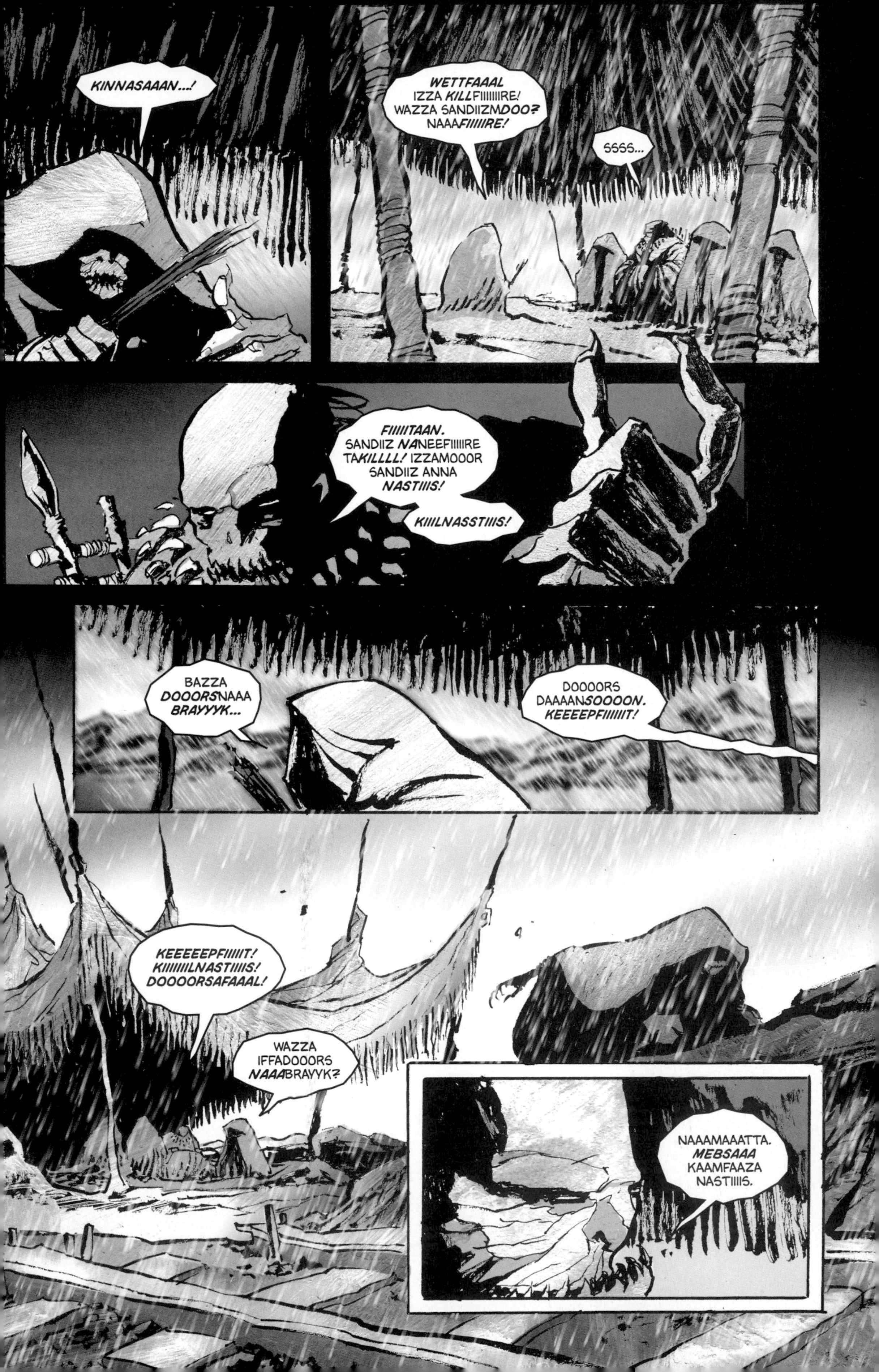
KINNASAAAN...!
WETTFAAAL IZZA KILLFIIIIIIRE! WAZZA SANDIIZMDOO? NAAAFIIIIRE!
SSSS...
FIIIITAAN. SANDIIZ NANEEFIIIIRE TAKILLLL! IZZAMOOOR SANDIIZ ANNA NASTIIIS!
KIIILNASSTIIIS!
BAZZA DOOORSNAAA BRAYYYK...
DOOOORS DAAAANSOOOON. KEEEEPFIIIIIIT!
KEEEEEPFIIIIIT! KIIIIIILNASTIIIIS! DOOOORSAFAAAL!
WAZZA IFFADOOORS NAAABRAYYK?
NAAAMAAATTA. MEBSAAA KAAMFAAZA NASTIIIIS.

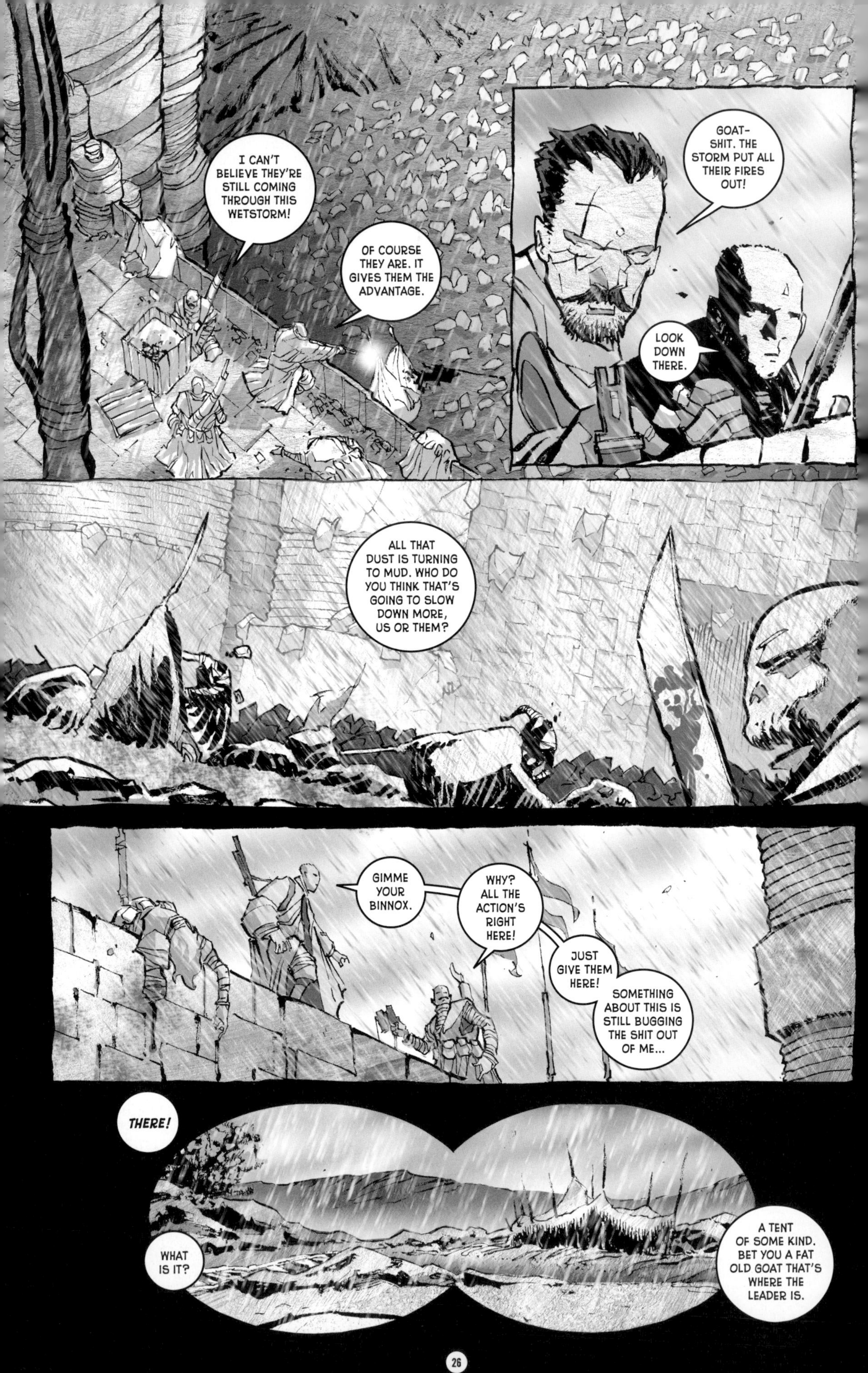

I CAN'T BELIEVE THEY'RE STILL COMING THROUGH THIS WETSTORM!
OF COURSE THEY ARE. IT GIVES THEM THE ADVANTAGE.
GOAT-SHIT. THE STORM PUT ALL THEIR FIRES OUT!
LOOK DOWN THERE.
ALL THAT DUST IS TURNING TO MUD. WHO DO YOU THINK THAT'S GOING TO SLOW DOWN MORE, US OR THEM?
GIMME YOUR BINNOX.
WHY? ALL THE ACTION'S RIGHT HERE!
JUST GIVE THEM HERE!
SOMETHING ABOUT THIS IS STILL BUGGING THE SHIT OUT OF ME...
THERE!
WHAT IS IT?
A TENT OF SOME KIND. BET YOU A FAT OLD GOAT THAT'S WHERE THE LEADER IS.

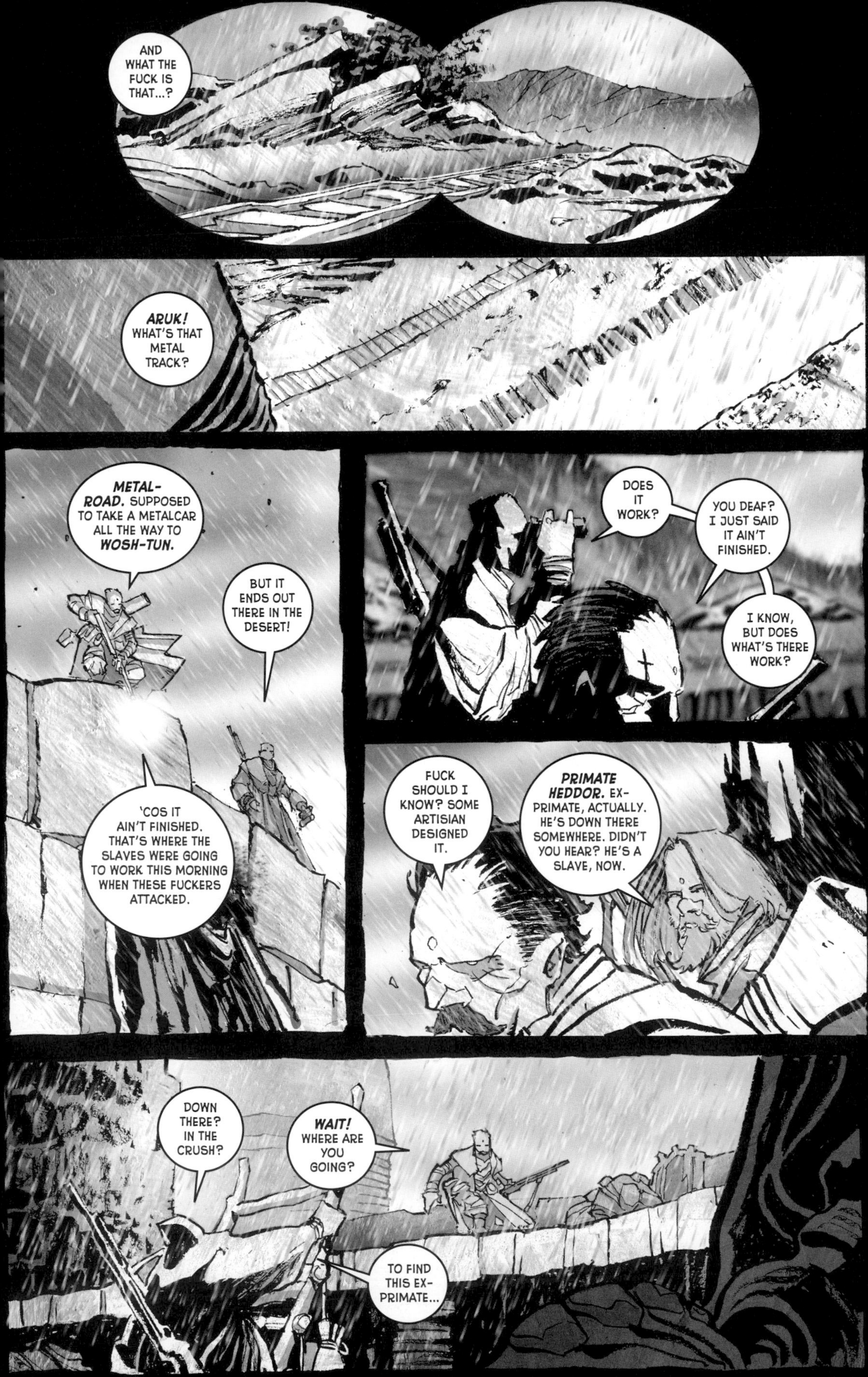
AND WHAT THE FUCK IS THAT...?
ARUK! WHAT'S THAT METAL TRACK?
METAL-ROAD. SUPPOSED TO TAKE A METALCAR ALL THE WAY TO WOSH-TUN.
BUT IT ENDS OUT THERE IN THE DESERT!
'COS IT AIN'T FINISHED. THAT'S WHERE THE SLAVES WERE GOING TO WORK THIS MORNING WHEN THESE FUCKERS ATTACKED.
DOES IT WORK?
YOU DEAF? I JUST SAID IT AIN'T FINISHED.
I KNOW, BUT DOES WHAT'S THERE WORK?
FUCK SHOULD I KNOW? SOME ARTISIAN DESIGNED IT.
PRIMATE HEDDOR. EX-PRIMATE, ACTUALLY. HE'S DOWN THERE SOMEWHERE. DIDN'T YOU HEAR? HE'S A SLAVE, NOW.
DOWN THERE? IN THE CRUSH?
WAIT! WHERE ARE YOU GOING?
TO FIND THIS EX-PRIMATE...

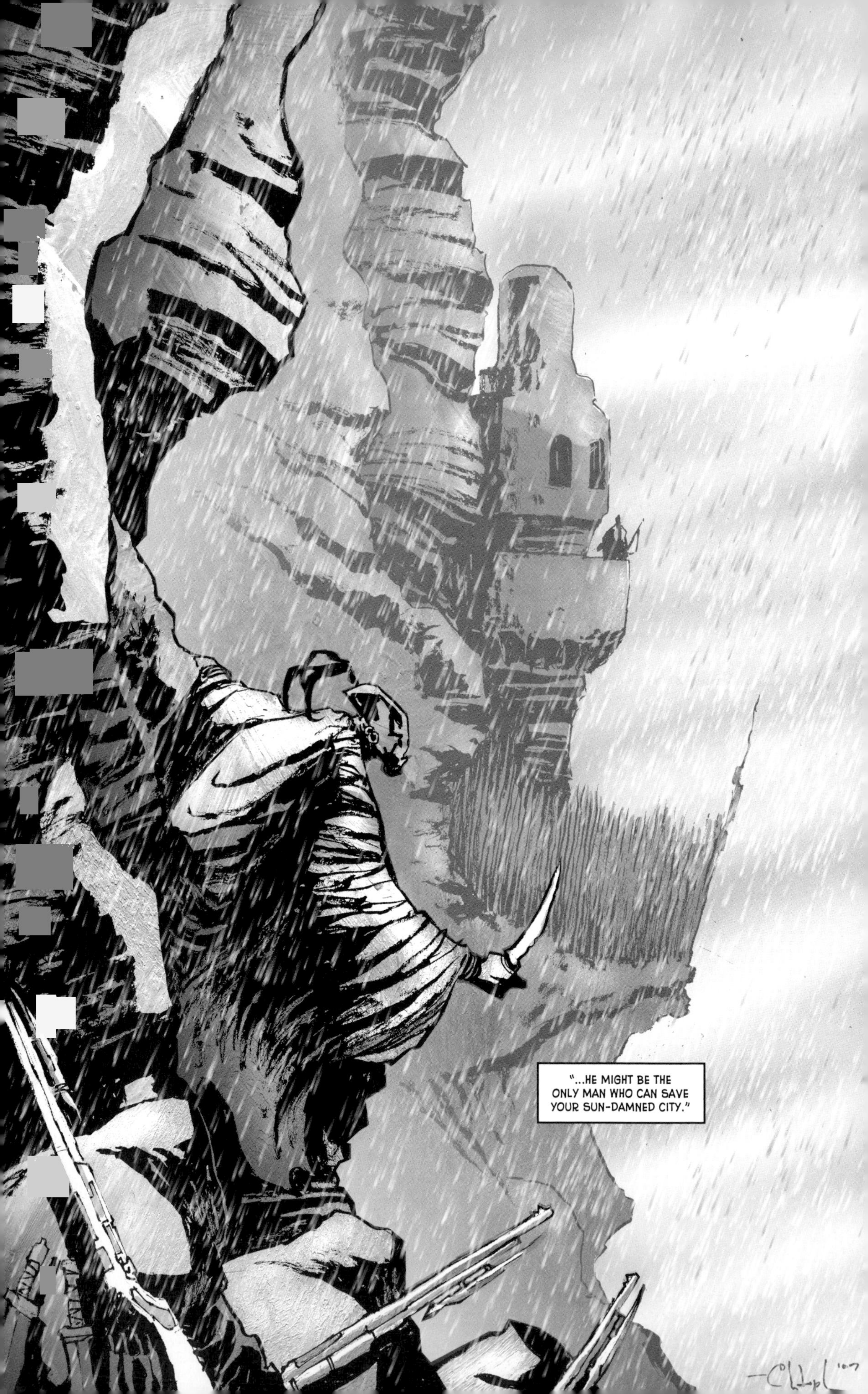
"...HE MIGHT BE THE ONLY MAN WHO CAN SAVE YOUR SUN-DAMNED CITY."

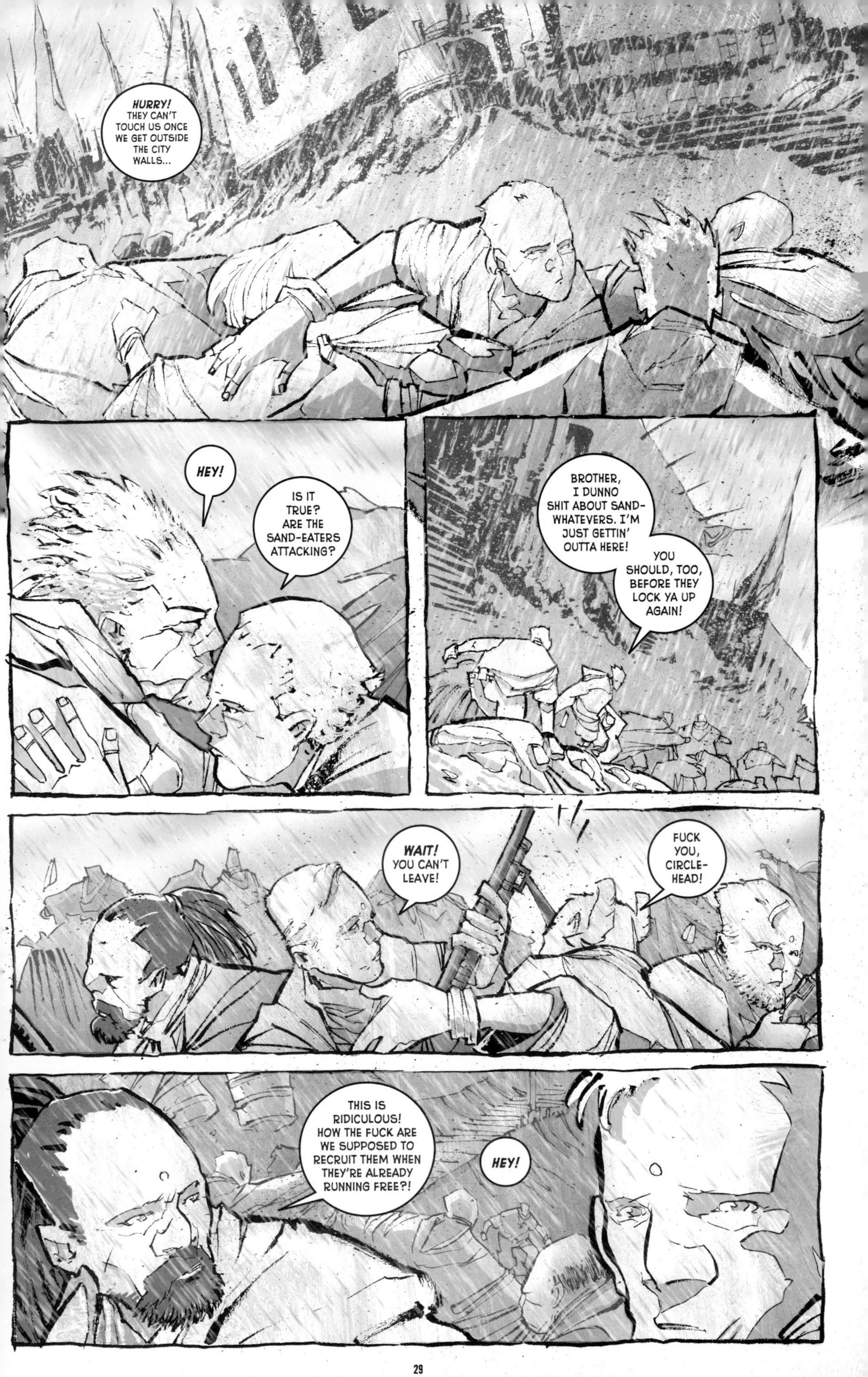
HURRY! THEY CAN'T TOUCH US ONCE WE GET OUTSIDE THE CITY WALLS...
HEY!
IS IT TRUE? ARE THE SAND-EATERS ATTACKING?
BROTHER, I DUNNO SHIT ABOUT SAND-WHATEVERS. I'M JUST GETTIN' OUTTA HERE!
YOU SHOULD, TOO, BEFORE THEY LOCK YA UP AGAIN!
WAIT! YOU CAN'T LEAVE!
FUCK YOU, CIRCLE-HEAD!
THIS IS RIDICULOUS! HOW THE FUCK ARE WE SUPPOSED TO RECRUIT THEM WHEN THEY'RE ALREADY RUNNING FREE?!
HEY!

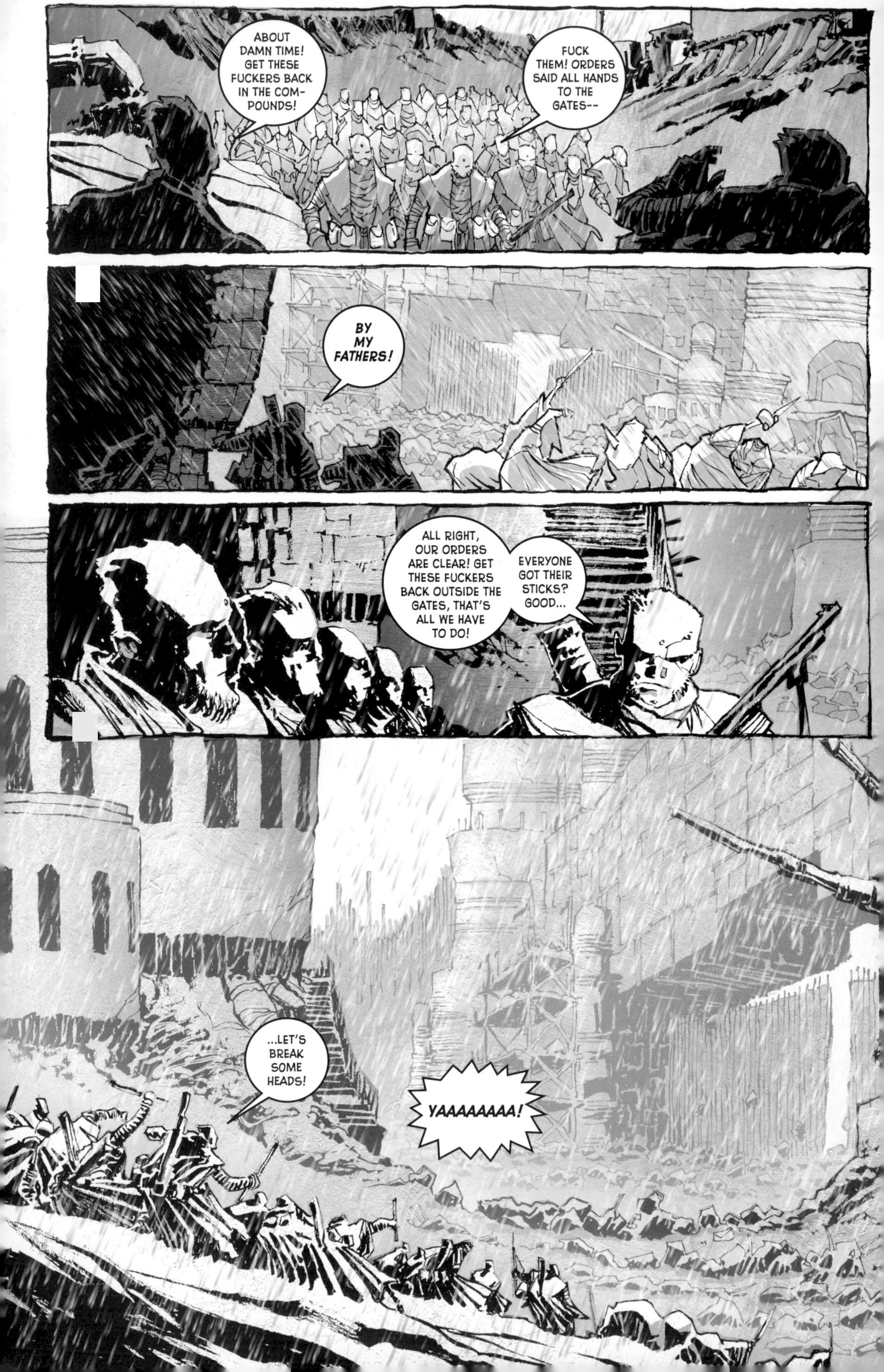
ABOUT DAMN TIME! GET THESE FUCKERS BACK IN THE COM-POUNDS!
FUCK THEM! ORDERS SAID ALL HANDS TO THE GATES--
BY MY FATHERS!
ALL RIGHT, OUR ORDERS ARE CLEAR! GET THESE FUCKERS BACK OUTSIDE THE GATES, THAT'S ALL WE HAVE TO DO!
EVERYONE GOT THEIR STICKS? GOOD...
...LET'S BREAK SOME HEADS!
YAAAAAAAA!

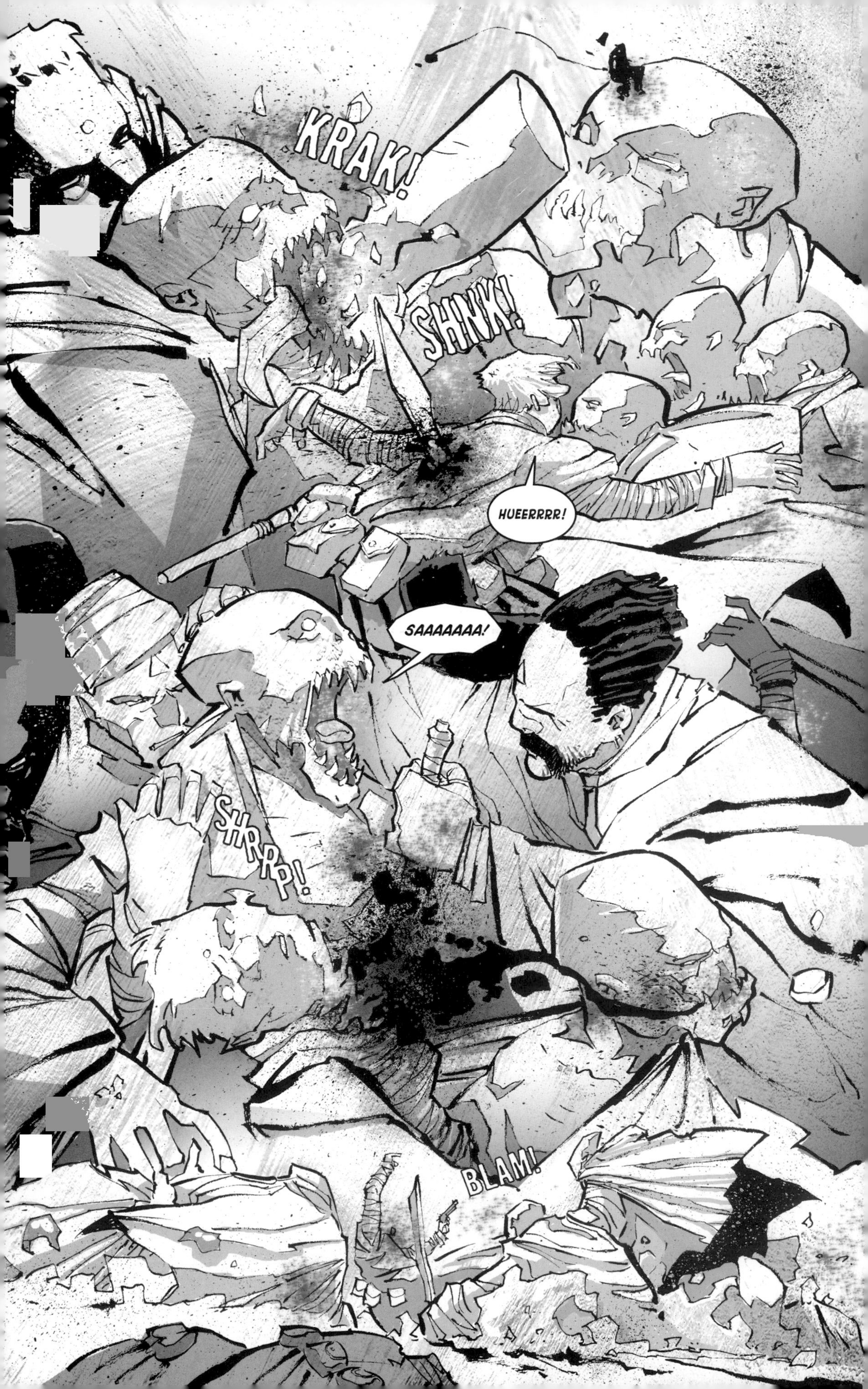
KRAK!
SHNK!
HUEERRRR!
SAAAAAAA!
SHRRP!
BLAM!

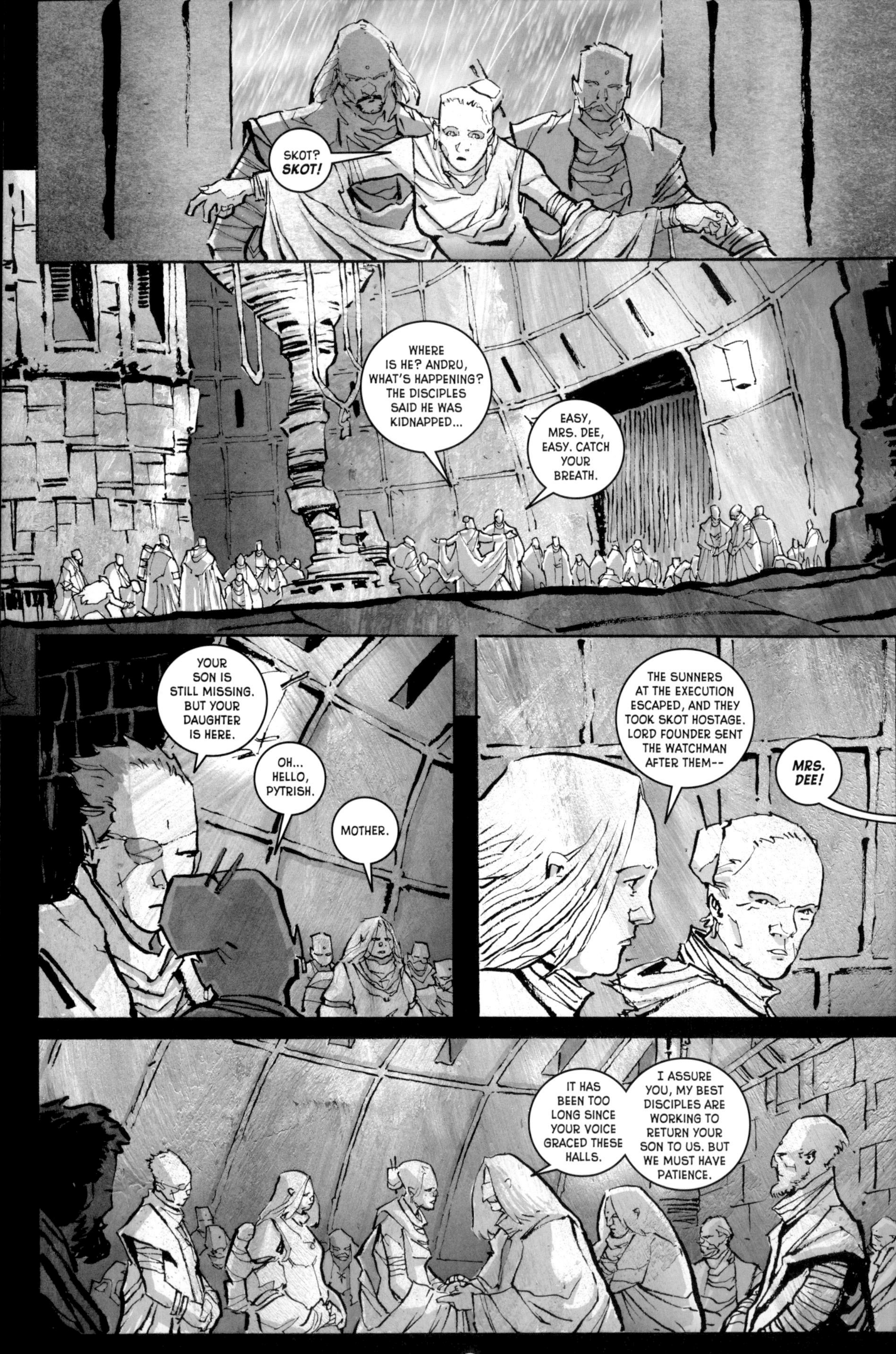
SKOT? SKOT!
WHERE IS HE? ANDRU, WHAT'S HAPPENING? THE DISCIPLES SAID HE WAS KIDNAPPED...
EASY, MRS. DEE, EASY. CATCH YOUR BREATH.
YOUR SON IS STILL MISSING. BUT YOUR DAUGHTER IS HERE.
OH... HELLO, PYTRISH.
MOTHER.
THE SUNNERS AT THE EXECUTION ESCAPED, AND THEY TOOK SKOT HOSTAGE. LORD FOUNDER SENT THE WATCHMAN AFTER THEM--
MRS. DEE!
IT HAS BEEN TOO LONG SINCE YOUR VOICE GRACED THESE HALLS.
I ASSURE YOU, MY BEST DISCIPLES ARE WORKING TO RETURN YOUR SON TO US. BUT WE MUST HAVE PATIENCE.

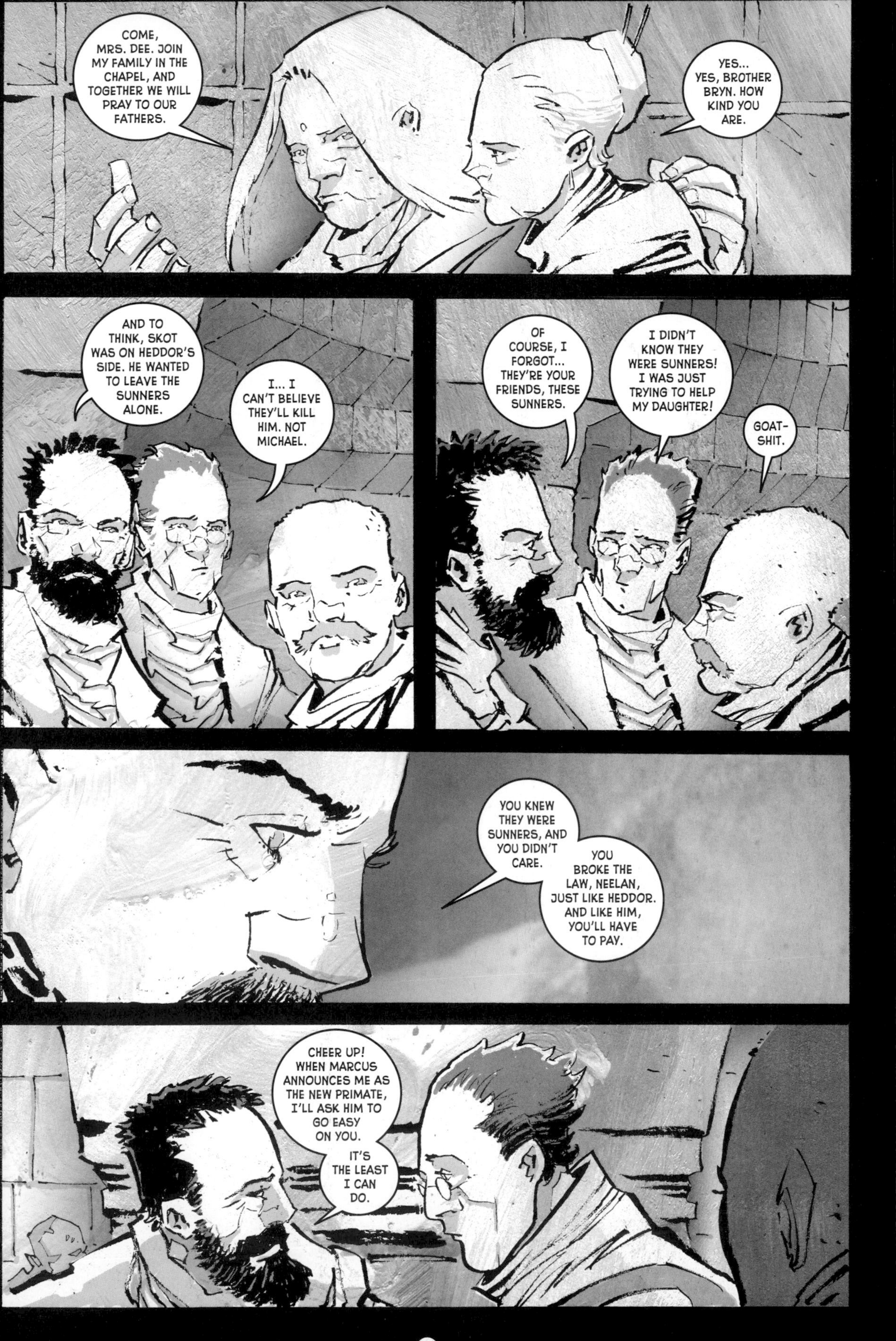
COME, MRS. DEE. JOIN MY FAMILY IN THE CHAPEL, AND TOGETHER WE WILL PRAY TO OUR FATHERS.
YES... YES, BROTHER BRYN. HOW KIND YOU ARE.
AND TO THINK, SKOT WAS ON HEDDOR'S SIDE. HE WANTED TO LEAVE THE SUNNERS ALONE.
I... I CAN'T BELIEVE THEY'LL KILL HIM. NOT MICHAEL.
OF COURSE, I FORGOT... THEY'RE YOUR FRIENDS, THESE SUNNERS.
I DIDN'T KNOW THEY WERE SUNNERS! I WAS JUST TRYING TO HELP MY DAUGHTER!
GOAT-SHIT.
YOU KNEW THEY WERE SUNNERS, AND YOU DIDN'T CARE.
YOU BROKE THE LAW, NEELAN, JUST LIKE HEDDOR. AND LIKE HIM, YOU'LL HAVE TO PAY.
CHEER UP! WHEN MARCUS ANNOUNCES ME AS THE NEW PRIMATE, I'LL ASK HIM TO GO EASY ON YOU.
IT'S THE LEAST I CAN DO.

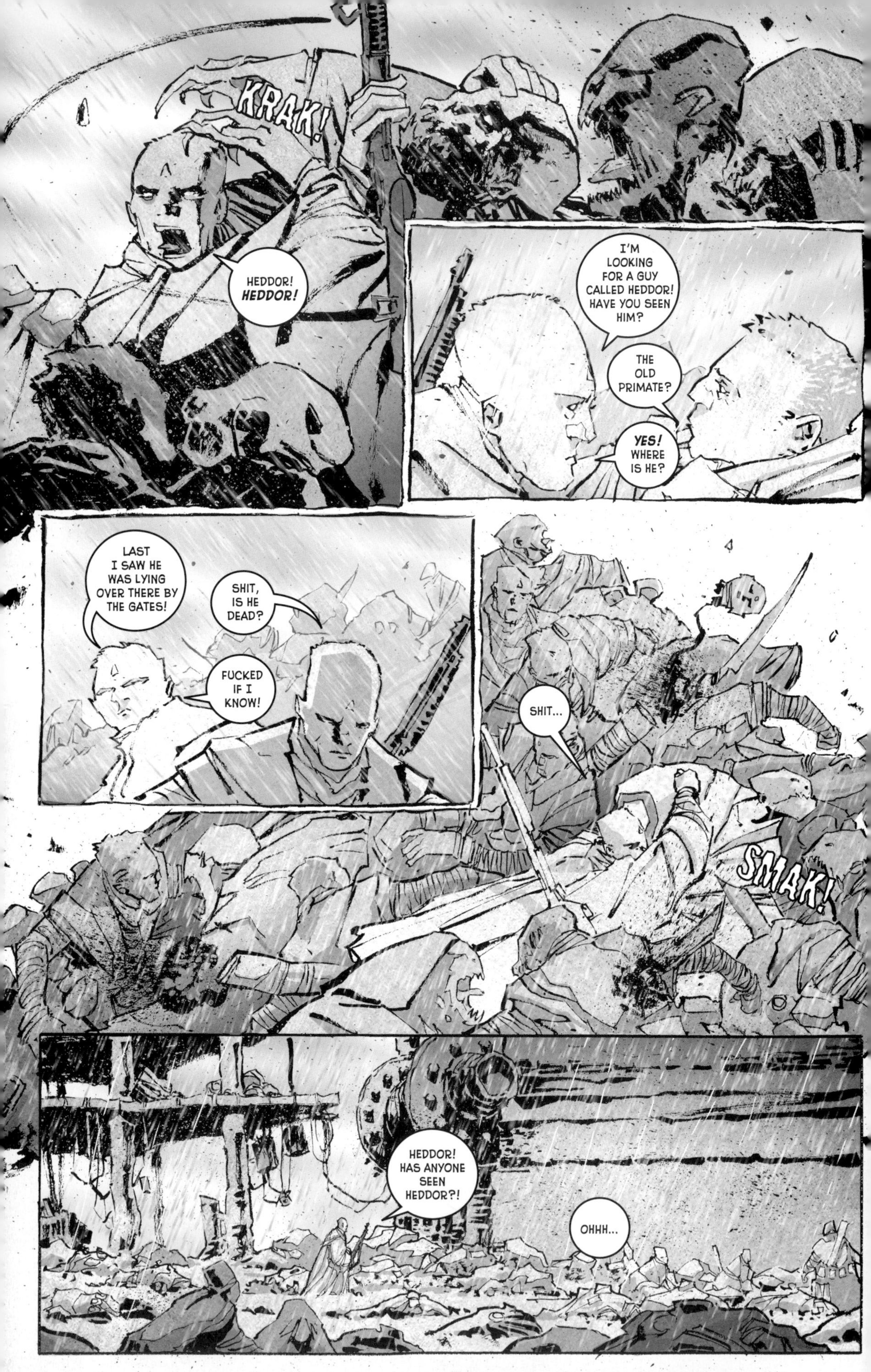
KRAK!
HEDDOR! HEDDOR!
I'M LOOKING FOR A GUY CALLED HEDDOR! HAVE YOU SEEN HIM?
THE OLD PRIMATE?
YES! WHERE IS HE?
LAST I SAW HE WAS LYING OVER THERE BY THE GATES!
SHIT, IS HE DEAD?
FUCKED IF I KNOW!
SHIT...
SMAK!
HEDDOR! HAS ANYONE SEEN HEDDOR?!
OHHH...

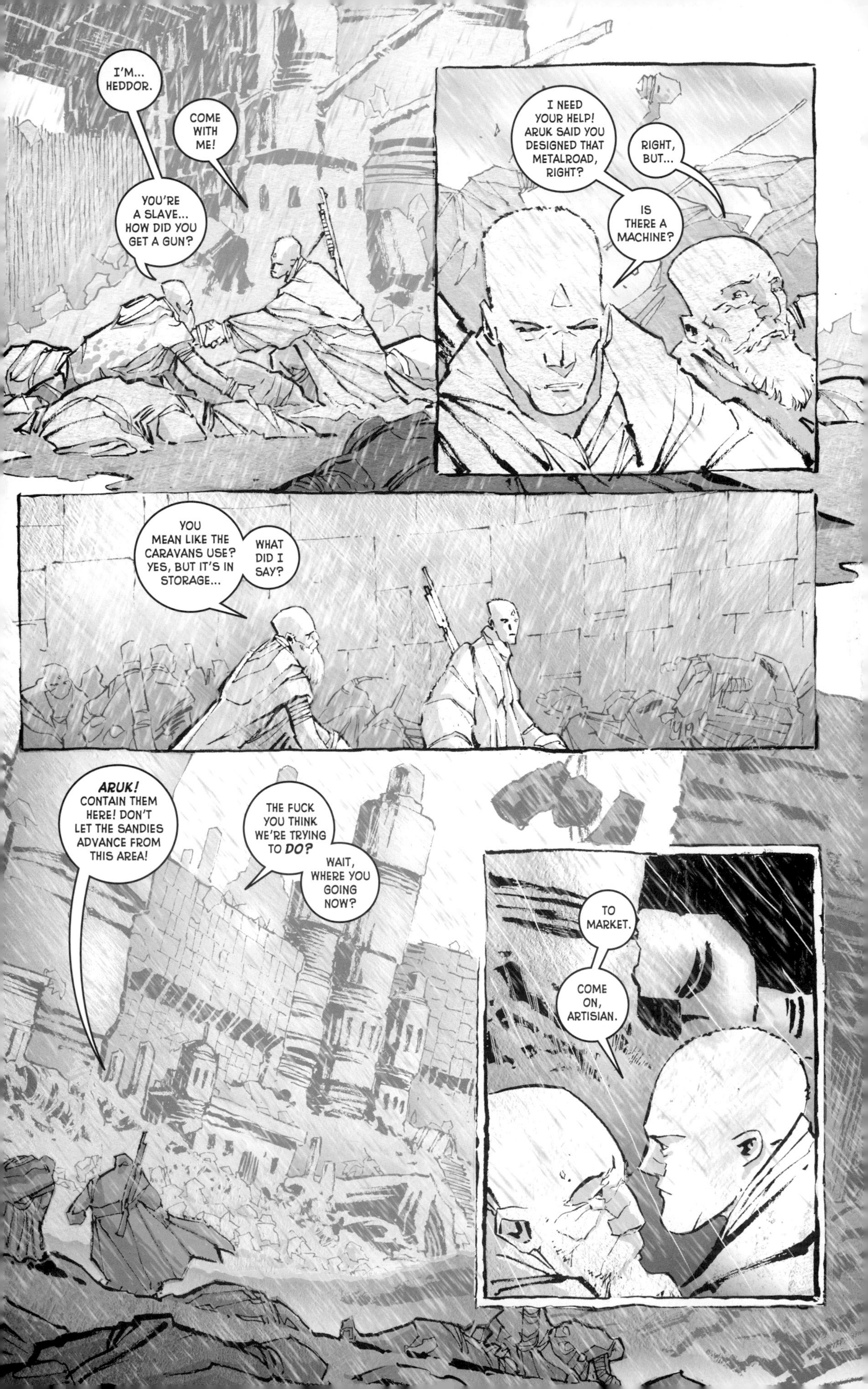
I'M... HEDDOR.
COME WITH ME!
YOU'RE A SLAVE... HOW DID YOU GET A GUN?
I NEED YOUR HELP! ARUK SAID YOU DESIGNED THAT METALROAD, RIGHT?
RIGHT, BUT...
IS THERE A MACHINE?
YOU MEAN LIKE THE CARAVANS USE? YES, BUT IT'S IN STORAGE...
WHAT DID I SAY?
ARUK! CONTAIN THEM HERE! DON'T LET THE SANDIES ADVANCE FROM THIS AREA!
THE FUCK YOU THINK WE'RE TRYING TO DO?
WAIT, WHERE YOU GOING NOW?
TO MARKET.
COME ON, ARTISIAN.

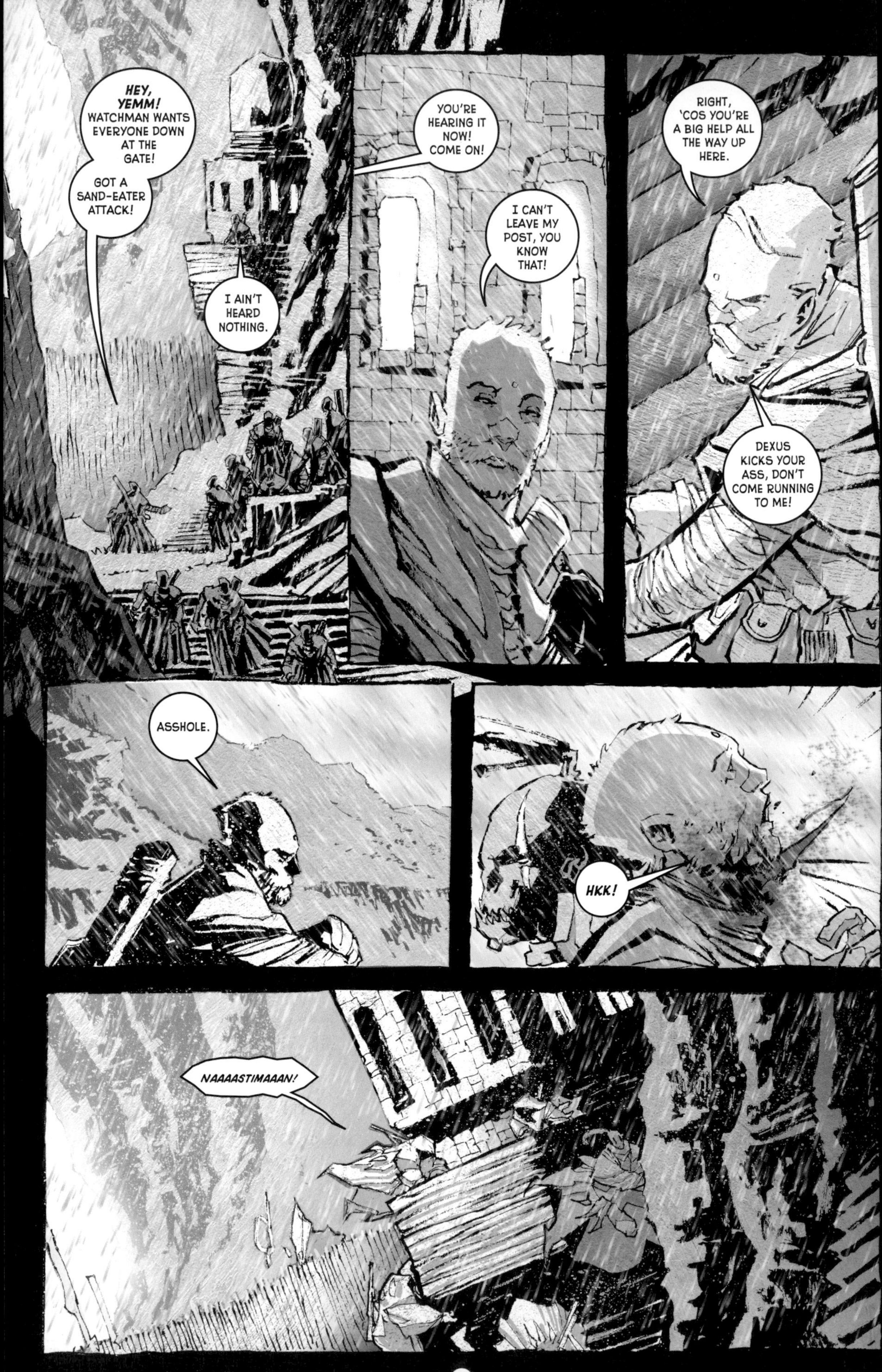
HEY, YEMM! WATCHMAN WANTS EVERYONE DOWN AT THE GATE!
GOT A SAND-EATER ATTACK!
I AIN'T HEARD NOTHING.
YOU'RE HEARING IT NOW! COME ON!
I CAN'T LEAVE MY POST, YOU KNOW THAT!
RIGHT, 'COS YOU'RE A BIG HELP ALL THE WAY UP HERE.
DEXUS KICKS YOUR ASS, DON'T COME RUNNING TO ME!
ASSHOLE.
HKK!
NAAAASTIMAAAN!

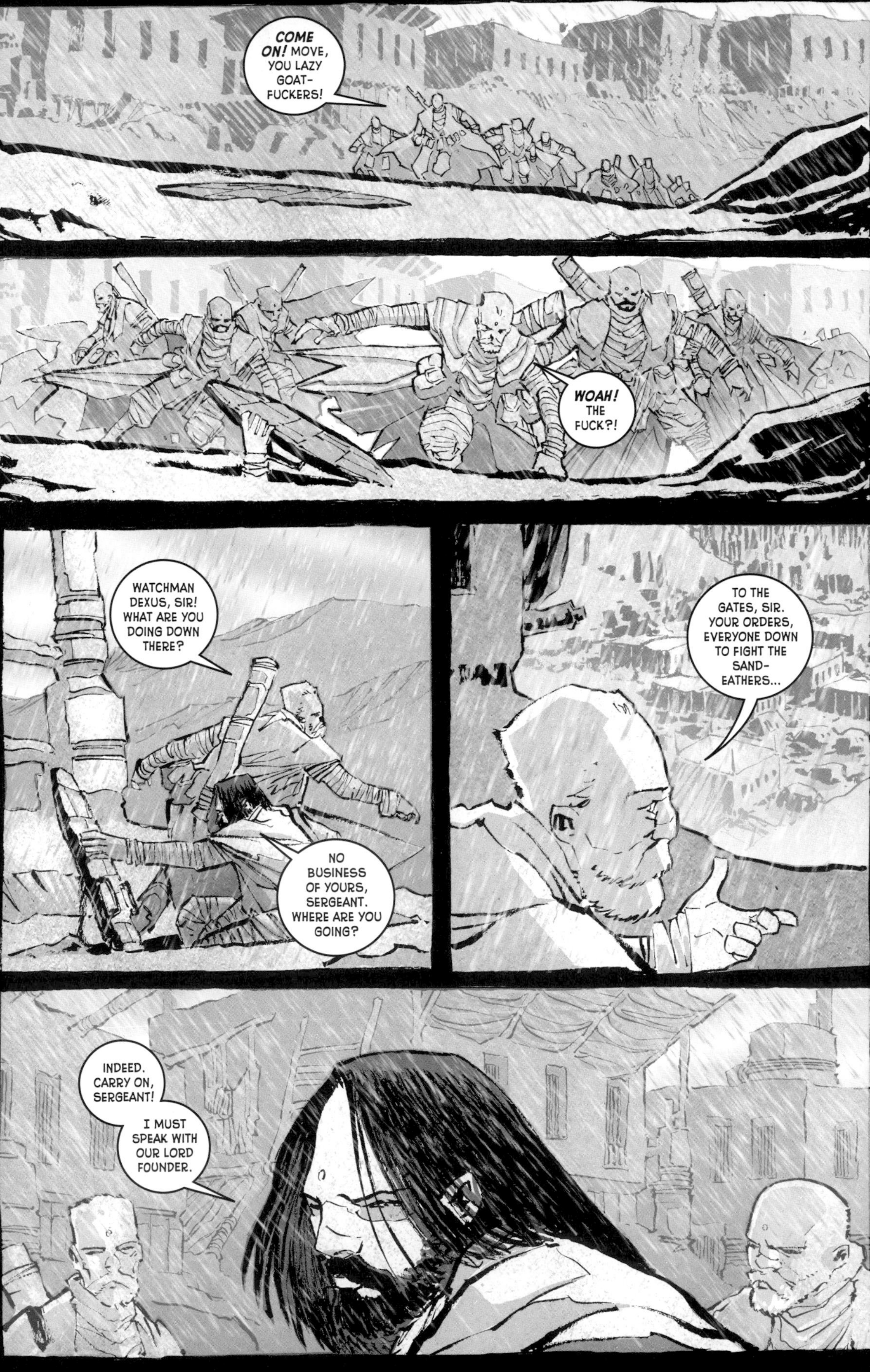
COME ON! MOVE, YOU LAZY GOAT-FUCKERS!
WOAH! THE FUCK?!
WATCHMAN DEXUS, SIR! WHAT ARE YOU DOING DOWN THERE?
NO BUSINESS OF YOURS, SERGEANT. WHERE ARE YOU GOING?
TO THE GATES, SIR. YOUR ORDERS, EVERYONE DOWN TO FIGHT THE SAND-EATHERS...
INDEED. CARRY ON, SERGEANT!
I MUST SPEAK WITH OUR LORD FOUNDER.

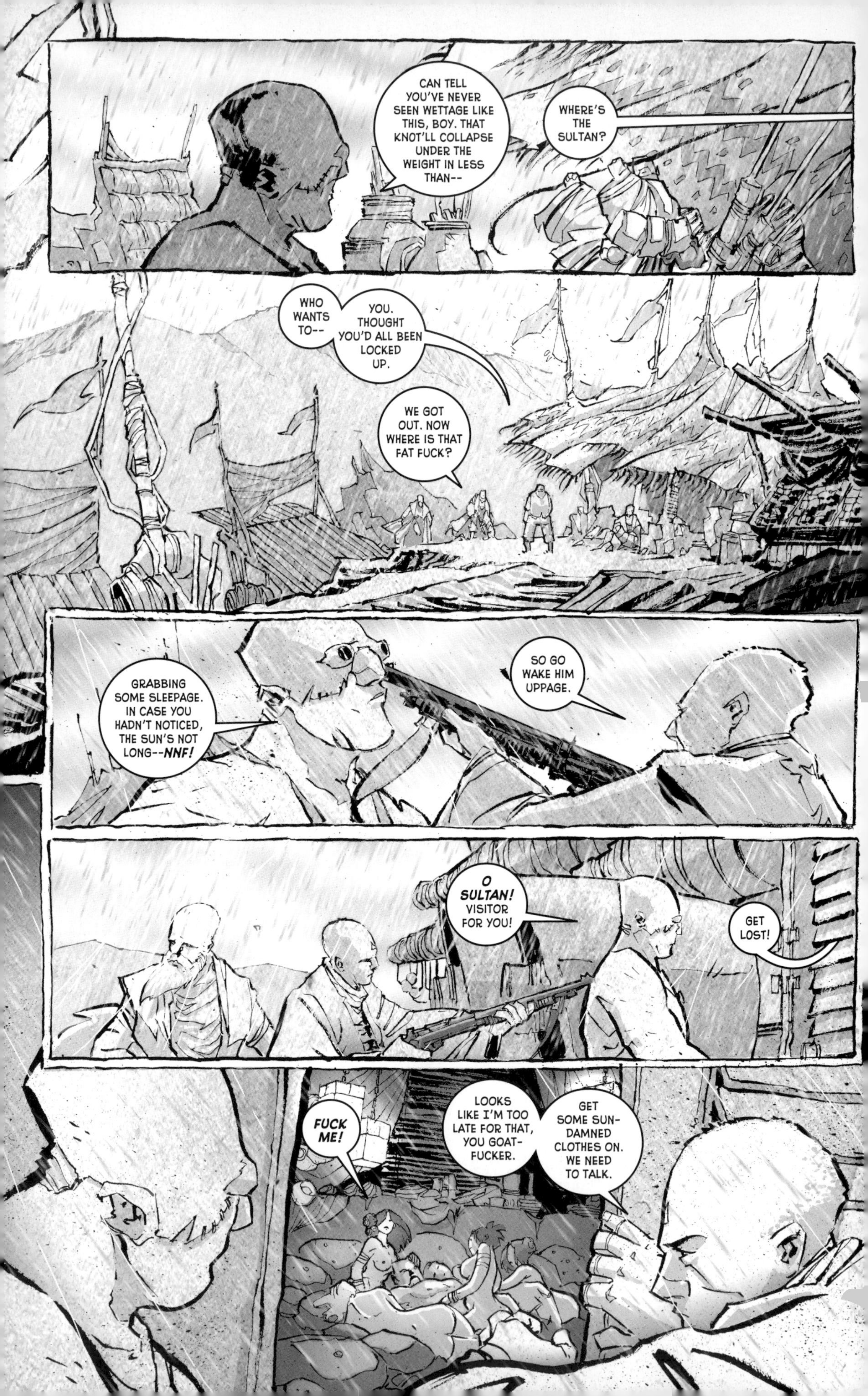
CAN TELL YOU'VE NEVER SEEN WETTAGE LIKE THIS, BOY. THAT KNOT'LL COLLAPSE UNDER THE WEIGHT IN LESS THAN--
WHERE'S THE SULTAN?
WHO WANTS TO--
YOU. THOUGHT YOU'D ALL BEEN LOCKED UP.
WE GOT OUT. NOW WHERE IS THAT FAT FUCK?
GRABBING SOME SLEEPAGE. IN CASE YOU HADN'T NOTICED, THE SUN'S NOT LONG--NNF!
SO GO WAKE HIM UPPAGE.
O SULTAN! VISITOR FOR YOU!
GET LOST!
FUCK ME!
LOOKS LIKE I'M TOO LATE FOR THAT, YOU GOAT-FUCKER.
GET SOME SUN-DAMNED CLOTHES ON. WE NEED TO TALK.

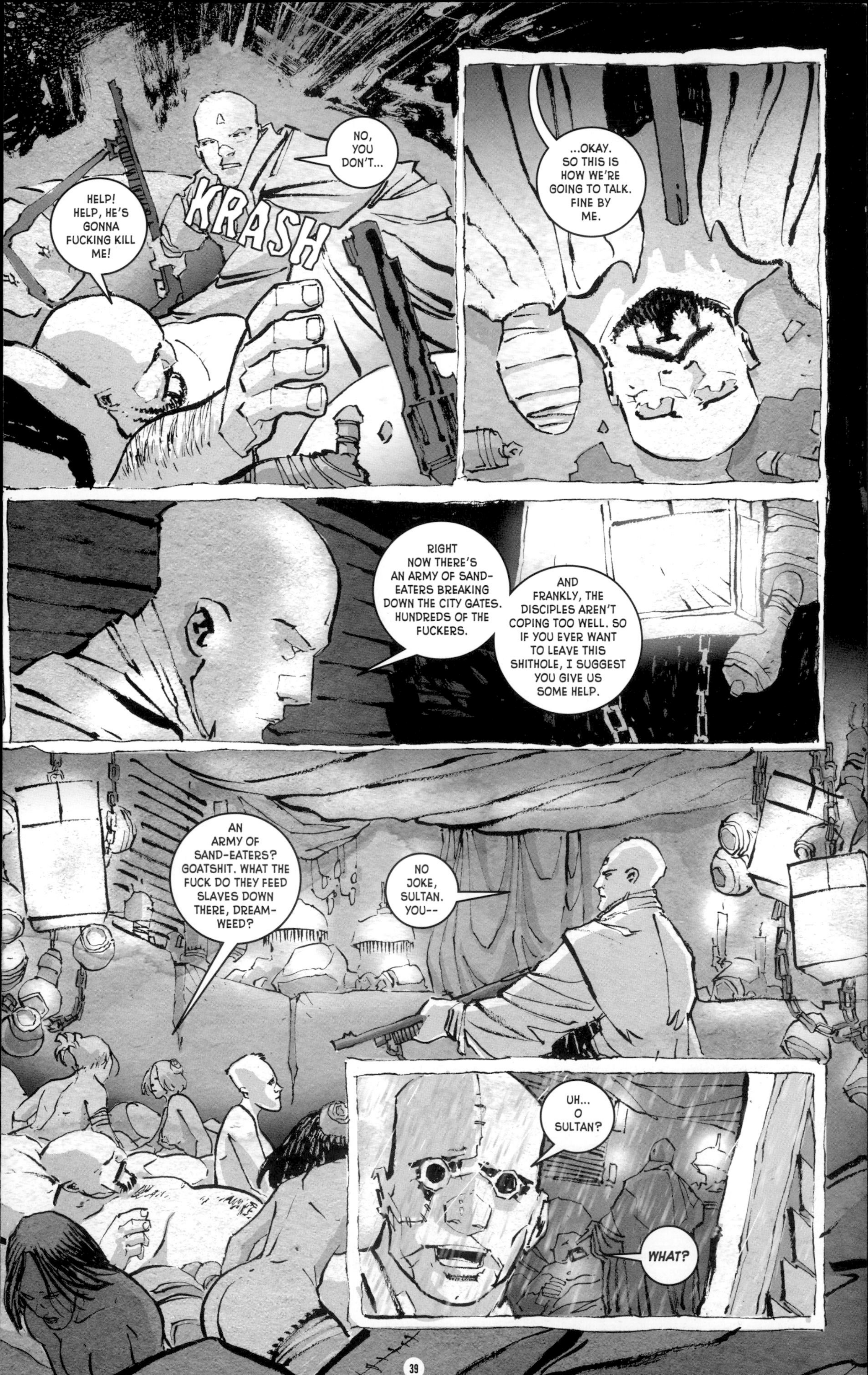
NO, YOU DON'T...
KRASH
HELP! HELP, HE'S GONNA FUCKING KILL ME!
...OKAY. SO THIS IS HOW WE'RE GOING TO TALK. FINE BY ME.
RIGHT NOW THERE'S AN ARMY OF SAND-EATERS BREAKING DOWN THE CITY GATES. HUNDREDS OF THE FUCKERS.
AND FRANKLY, THE DISCIPLES AREN'T COPING TOO WELL. SO IF YOU EVER WANT TO LEAVE THIS SHITHOLE, I SUGGEST YOU GIVE US SOME HELP.
AN ARMY OF SAND-EATERS? GOATSHIT. WHAT THE FUCK DO THEY FEED SLAVES DOWN THERE, DREAM-WEED?
NO JOKE, SULTAN. YOU--
UH... O SULTAN?
WHAT?

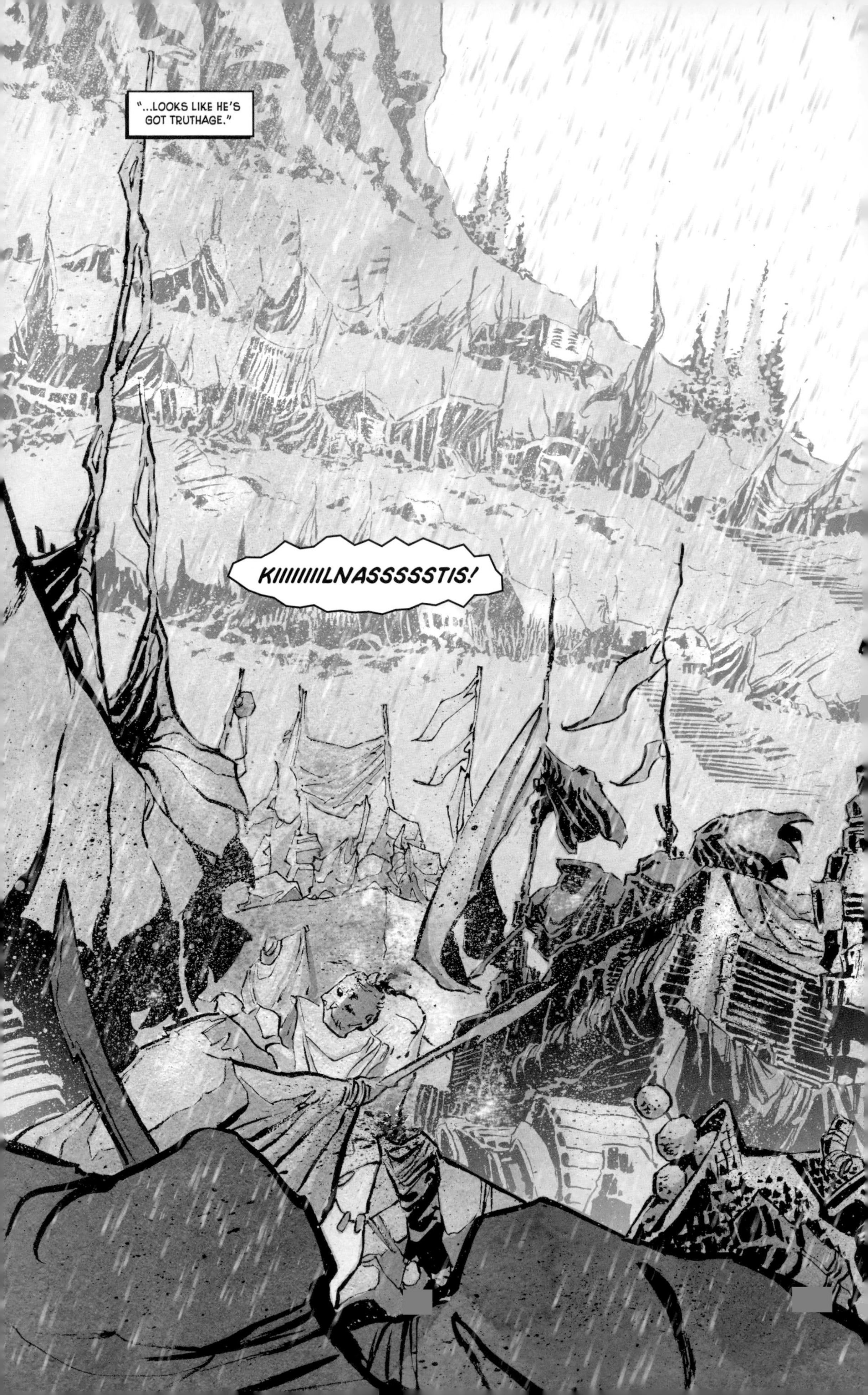
"...LOOKS LIKE HE'S GOT TRUTHAGE."
KIIIIIIIILNASSSSSTIS!

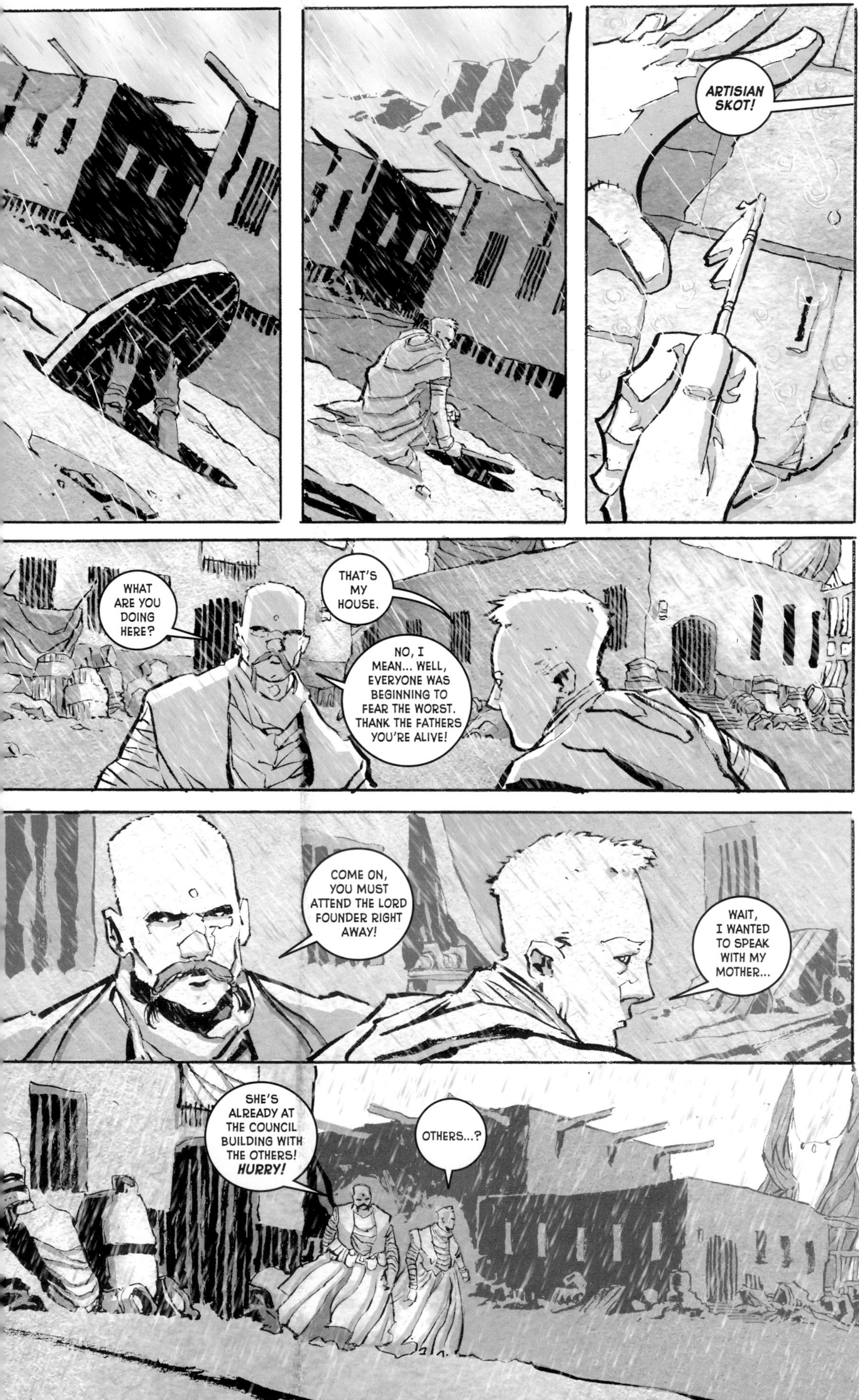
ARTISIAN SKOT!
WHAT ARE YOU DOING HERE?
THAT'S MY HOUSE.
NO, I MEAN... WELL, EVERYONE WAS BEGINNING TO FEAR THE WORST. THANK THE FATHERS YOU'RE ALIVE!
COME ON, YOU MUST ATTEND THE LORD FOUNDER RIGHT AWAY!
WAIT, I WANTED TO SPEAK WITH MY MOTHER...
SHE'S ALREADY AT THE COUNCIL BUILDING WITH THE OTHERS! *HURRY!*
OTHERS...?

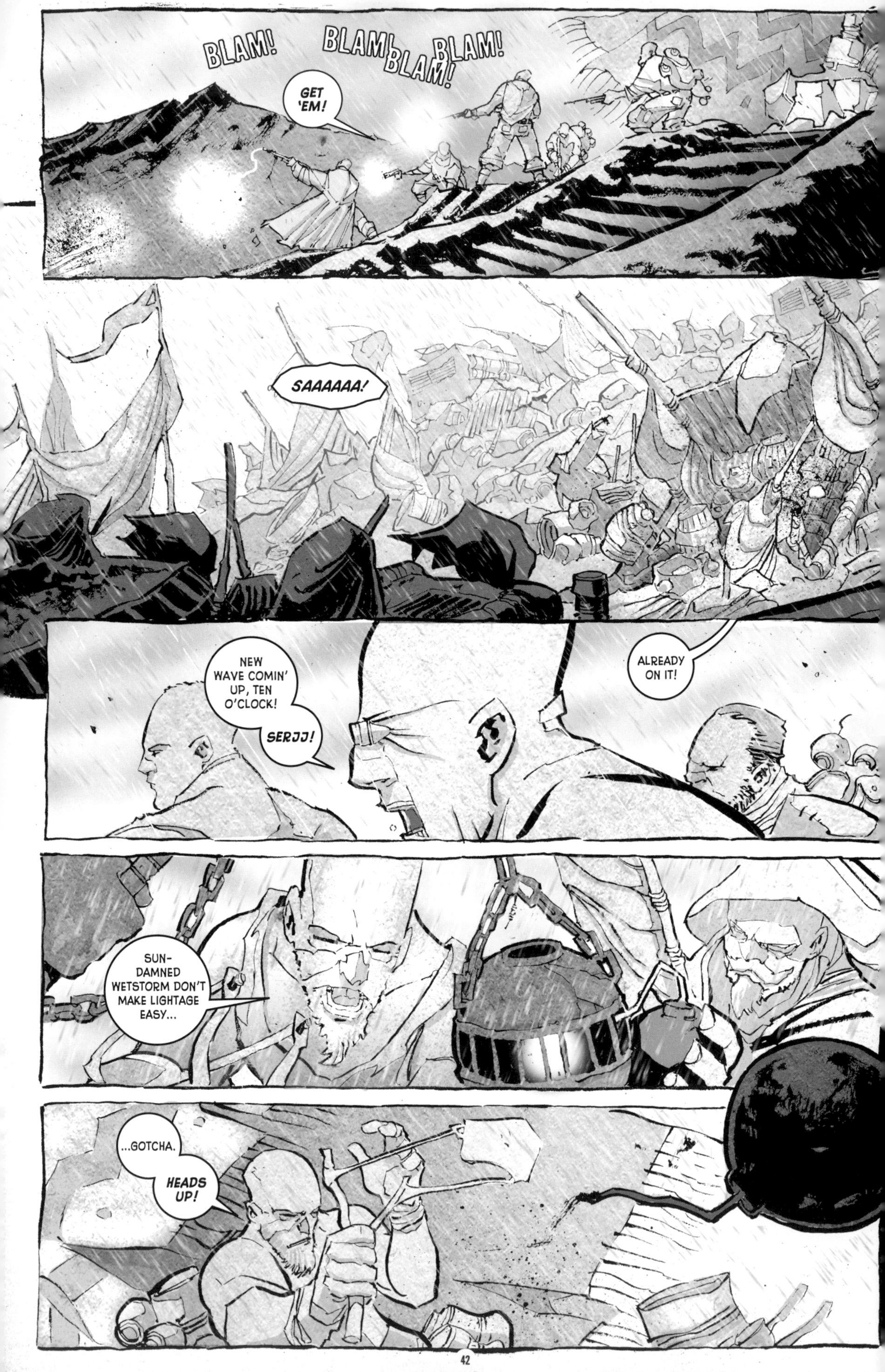
BLAM!
BLAM! BLAM! BLAM!
GET 'EM!
SAAAAAA!
NEW WAVE COMIN' UP, TEN O'CLOCK!
SERJJ!
ALREADY ON IT!
SUN-DAMNED WETSTORM DON'T MAKE LIGHTAGE EASY...
...GOTCHA.
HEADS UP!

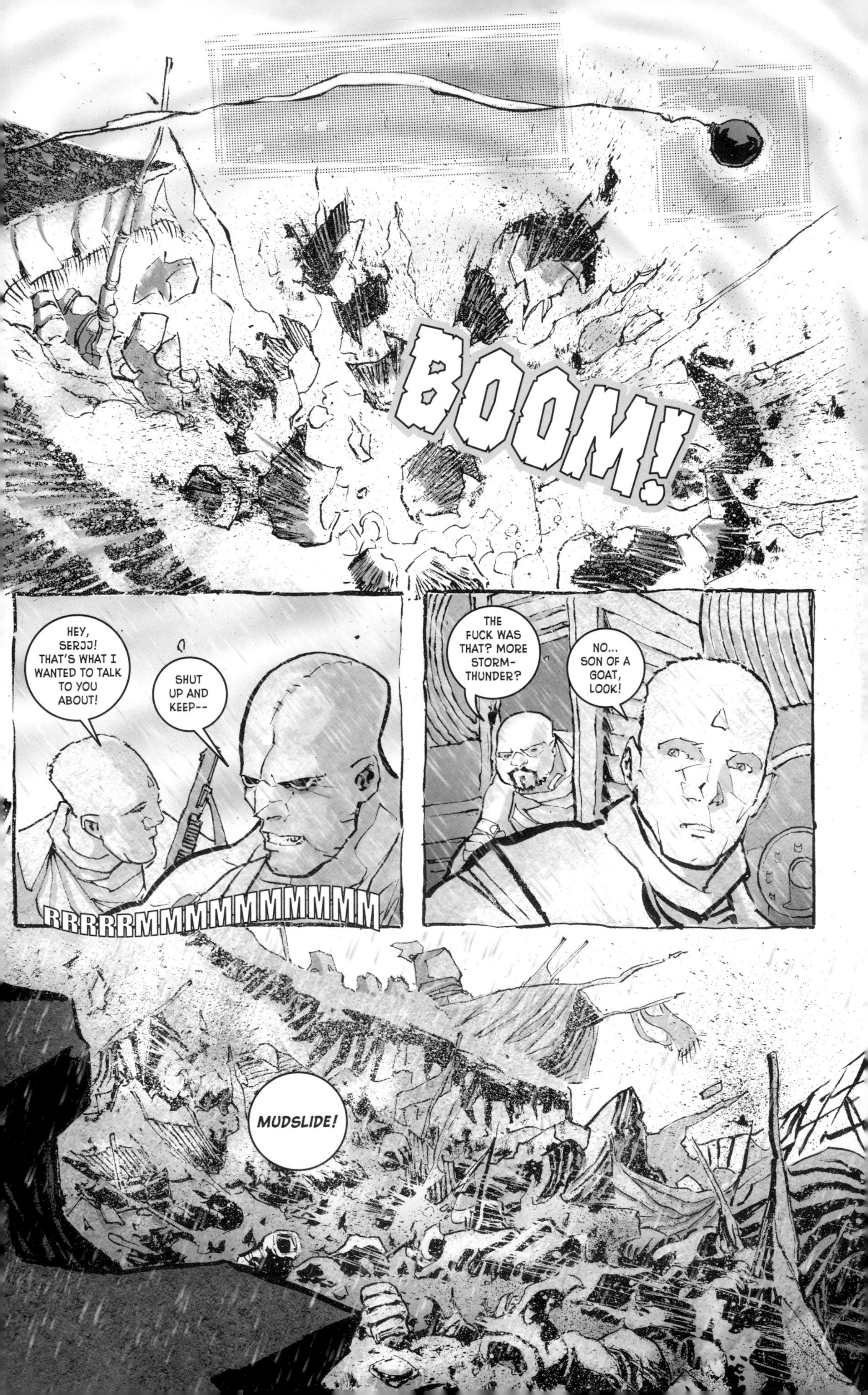
BOOM!
HEY, SERJJ! THAT'S WHAT I WANTED TO TALK TO YOU ABOUT!
SHUT UP AND KEEP--
RRRRRMMMMMMMMMMMM
THE FUCK WAS THAT? MORE STORM-THUNDER?
NO... SON OF A GOAT, LOOK!
MUDSLIDE!

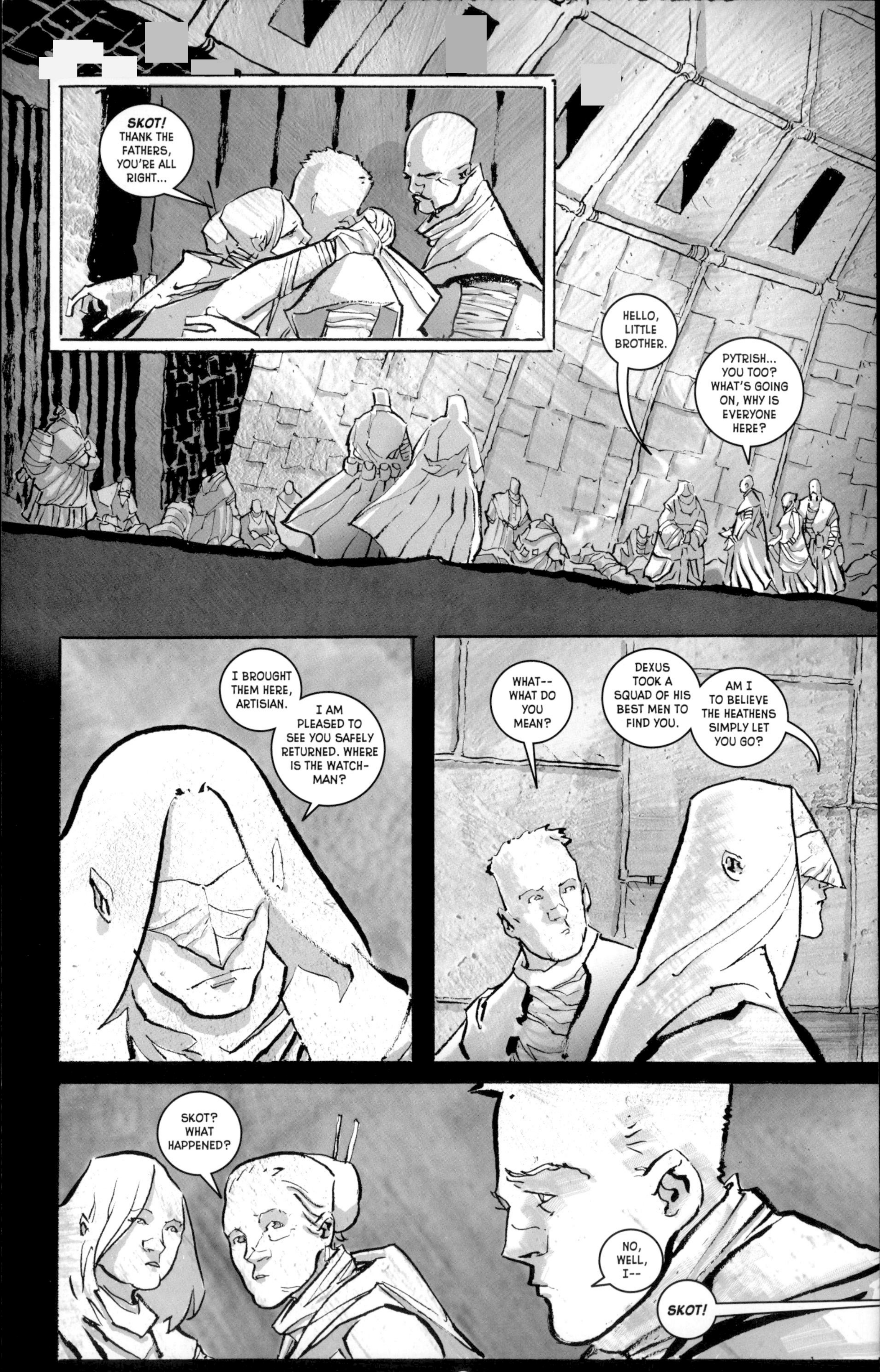
SKOT! THANK THE FATHERS, YOU'RE ALL RIGHT...
HELLO, LITTLE BROTHER.
PYTRISH... YOU TOO? WHAT'S GOING ON, WHY IS EVERYONE HERE?
I BROUGHT THEM HERE, ARTISIAN.
I AM PLEASED TO SEE YOU SAFELY RETURNED. WHERE IS THE WATCH-MAN?
WHAT-- WHAT DO YOU MEAN?
DEXUS TOOK A SQUAD OF HIS BEST MEN TO FIND YOU.
AM I TO BELIEVE THE HEATHENS SIMPLY LET YOU GO?
SKOT? WHAT HAPPENED?
NO, WELL, I--
SKOT!

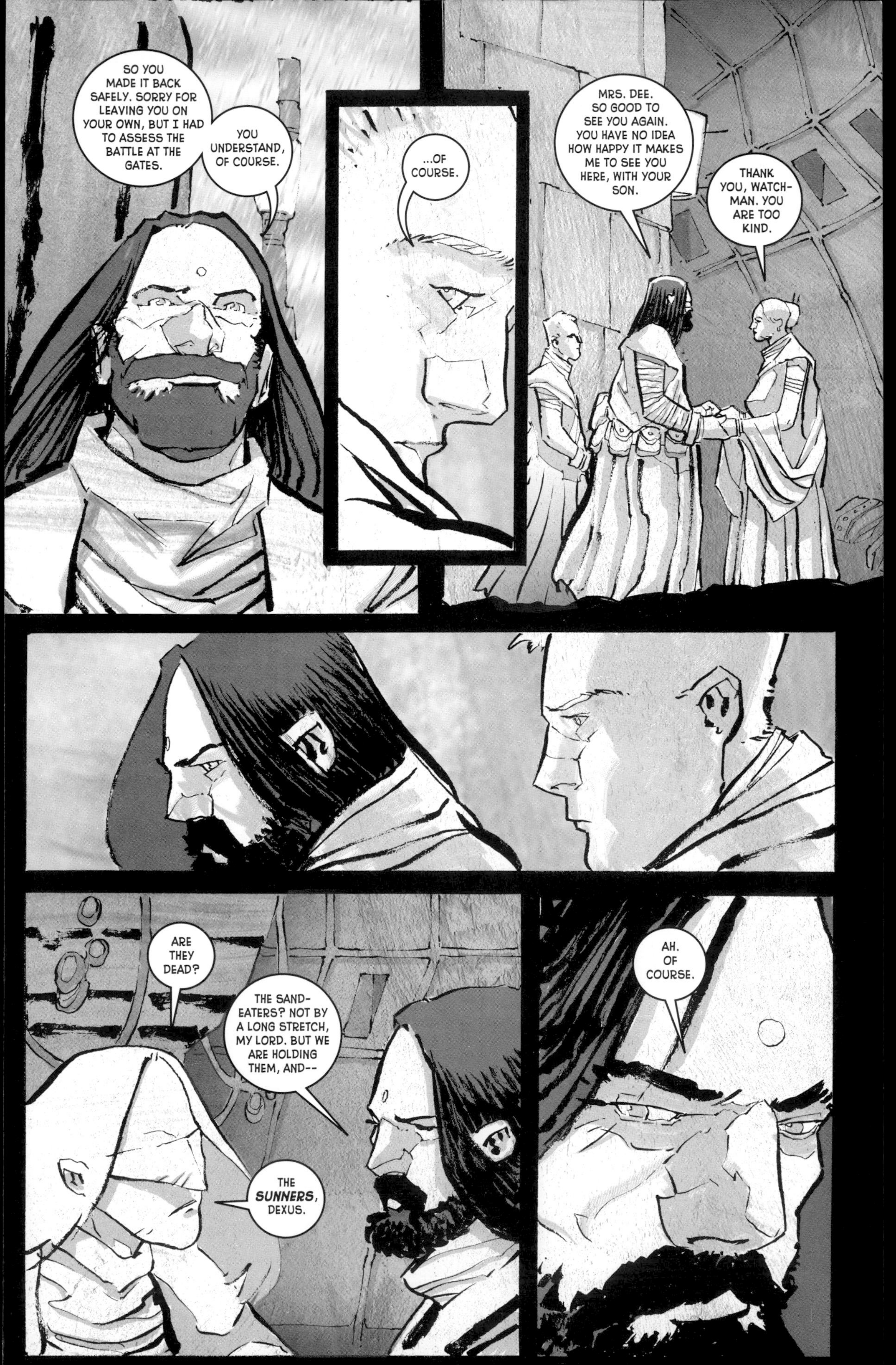
SO YOU MADE IT BACK SAFELY. SORRY FOR LEAVING YOU ON YOUR OWN, BUT I HAD TO ASSESS THE BATTLE AT THE GATES.
YOU UNDERSTAND, OF COURSE.
...OF COURSE.
MRS. DEE. SO GOOD TO SEE YOU AGAIN. YOU HAVE NO IDEA HOW HAPPY IT MAKES ME TO SEE YOU HERE, WITH YOUR SON.
THANK YOU, WATCH-MAN. YOU ARE TOO KIND.
ARE THEY DEAD?
THE SAND-EATERS? NOT BY A LONG STRETCH, MY LORD. BUT WE ARE HOLDING THEM, AND--
THE **SUNNERS**, DEXUS.
AH. OF COURSE.

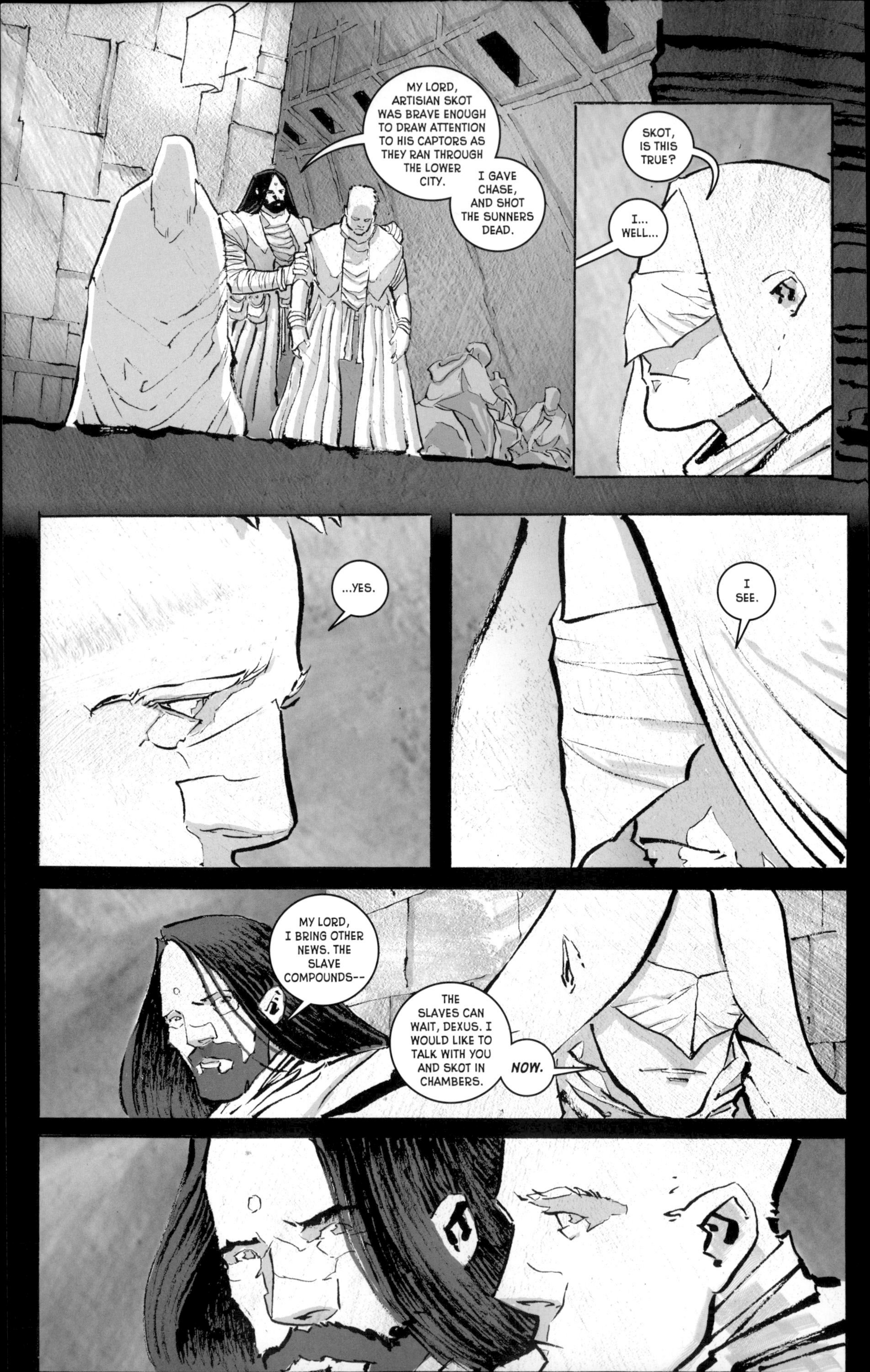
MY LORD, ARTISIAN SKOT WAS BRAVE ENOUGH TO DRAW ATTENTION TO HIS CAPTORS AS THEY RAN THROUGH THE LOWER CITY.
I GAVE CHASE, AND SHOT THE SUNNERS DEAD.
SKOT, IS THIS TRUE?
I... WELL...
...YES.
I SEE.
MY LORD, I BRING OTHER NEWS. THE SLAVE COMPOUNDS--
THE SLAVES CAN WAIT, DEXUS. I WOULD LIKE TO TALK WITH YOU AND SKOT IN CHAMBERS.
NOW.

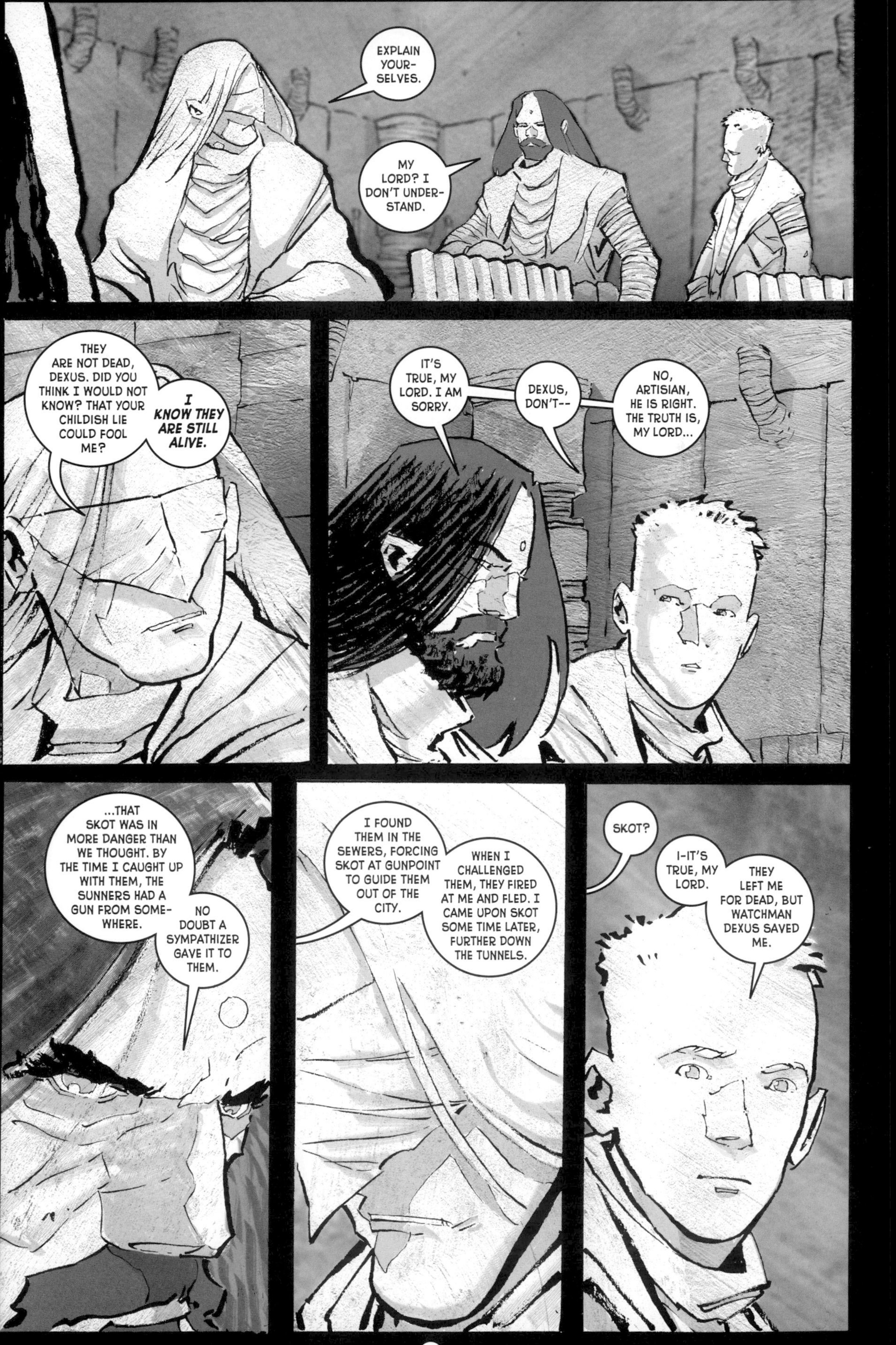
EXPLAIN YOURSELVES.
MY LORD? I DON'T UNDERSTAND.
THEY ARE NOT DEAD, DEXUS. DID YOU THINK I WOULD NOT KNOW? THAT YOUR CHILDISH LIE COULD FOOL ME?
I KNOW THEY ARE STILL ALIVE.
IT'S TRUE, MY LORD. I AM SORRY.
DEXUS, DON'T--
NO, ARTISIAN, HE IS RIGHT. THE TRUTH IS, MY LORD...
...THAT SKOT WAS IN MORE DANGER THAN WE THOUGHT. BY THE TIME I CAUGHT UP WITH THEM, THE SUNNERS HAD A GUN FROM SOMEWHERE.
NO DOUBT A SYMPATHIZER GAVE IT TO THEM.
I FOUND THEM IN THE SEWERS, FORCING SKOT AT GUNPOINT TO GUIDE THEM OUT OF THE CITY.
WHEN I CHALLENGED THEM, THEY FIRED AT ME AND FLED. I CAME UPON SKOT SOME TIME LATER, FURTHER DOWN THE TUNNELS.
SKOT?
I-IT'S TRUE, MY LORD.
THEY LEFT ME FOR DEAD, BUT WATCHMAN DEXUS SAVED ME.

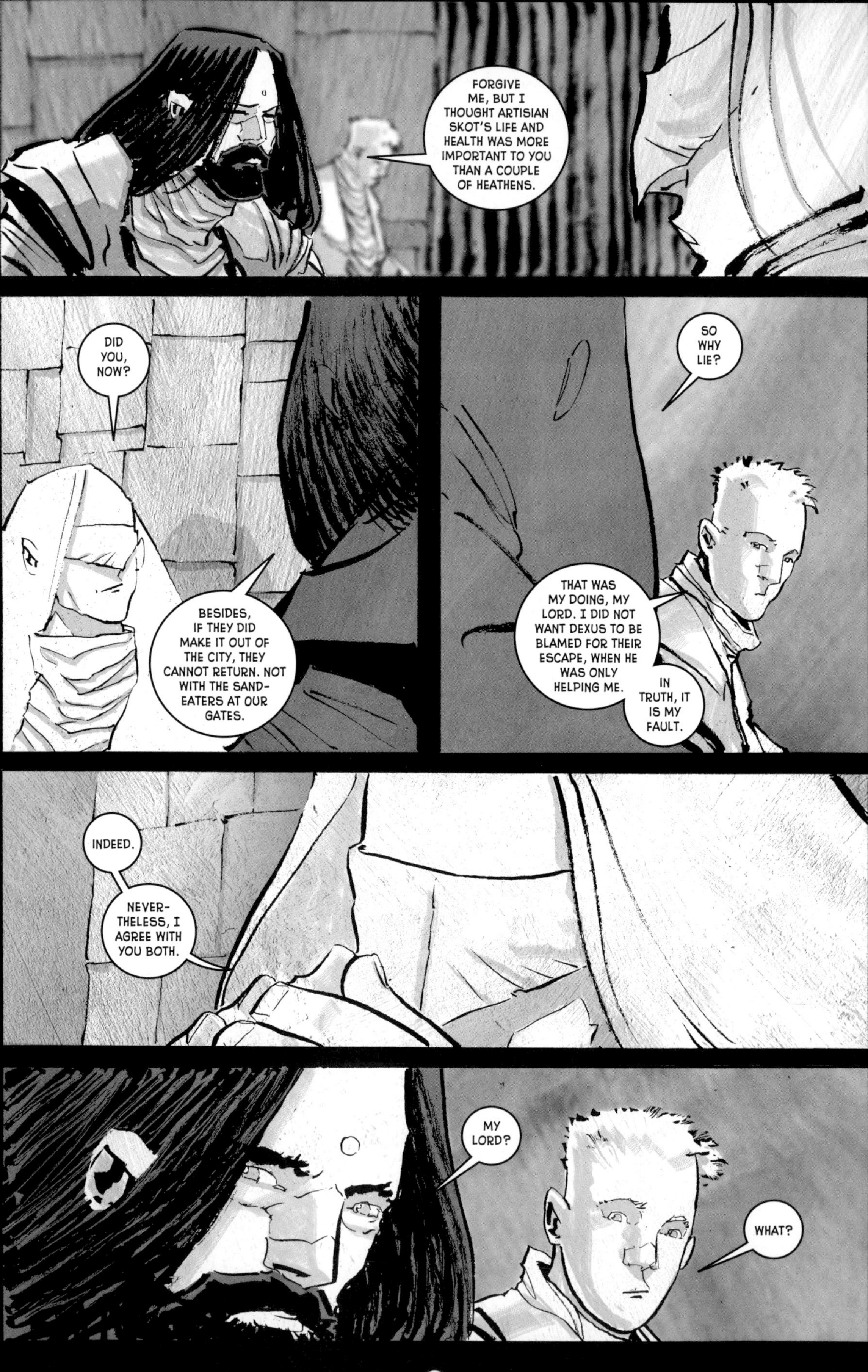
FORGIVE ME, BUT I THOUGHT ARTISIAN SKOT'S LIFE AND HEALTH WAS MORE IMPORTANT TO YOU THAN A COUPLE OF HEATHENS.
DID YOU, NOW?
BESIDES, IF THEY DID MAKE IT OUT OF THE CITY, THEY CANNOT RETURN. NOT WITH THE SAND-EATERS AT OUR GATES.
SO WHY LIE?
THAT WAS MY DOING, MY LORD. I DID NOT WANT DEXUS TO BE BLAMED FOR THEIR ESCAPE, WHEN HE WAS ONLY HELPING ME.
IN TRUTH, IT IS MY FAULT.
INDEED.
NEVER-THELESS, I AGREE WITH YOU BOTH.
MY LORD?
WHAT?

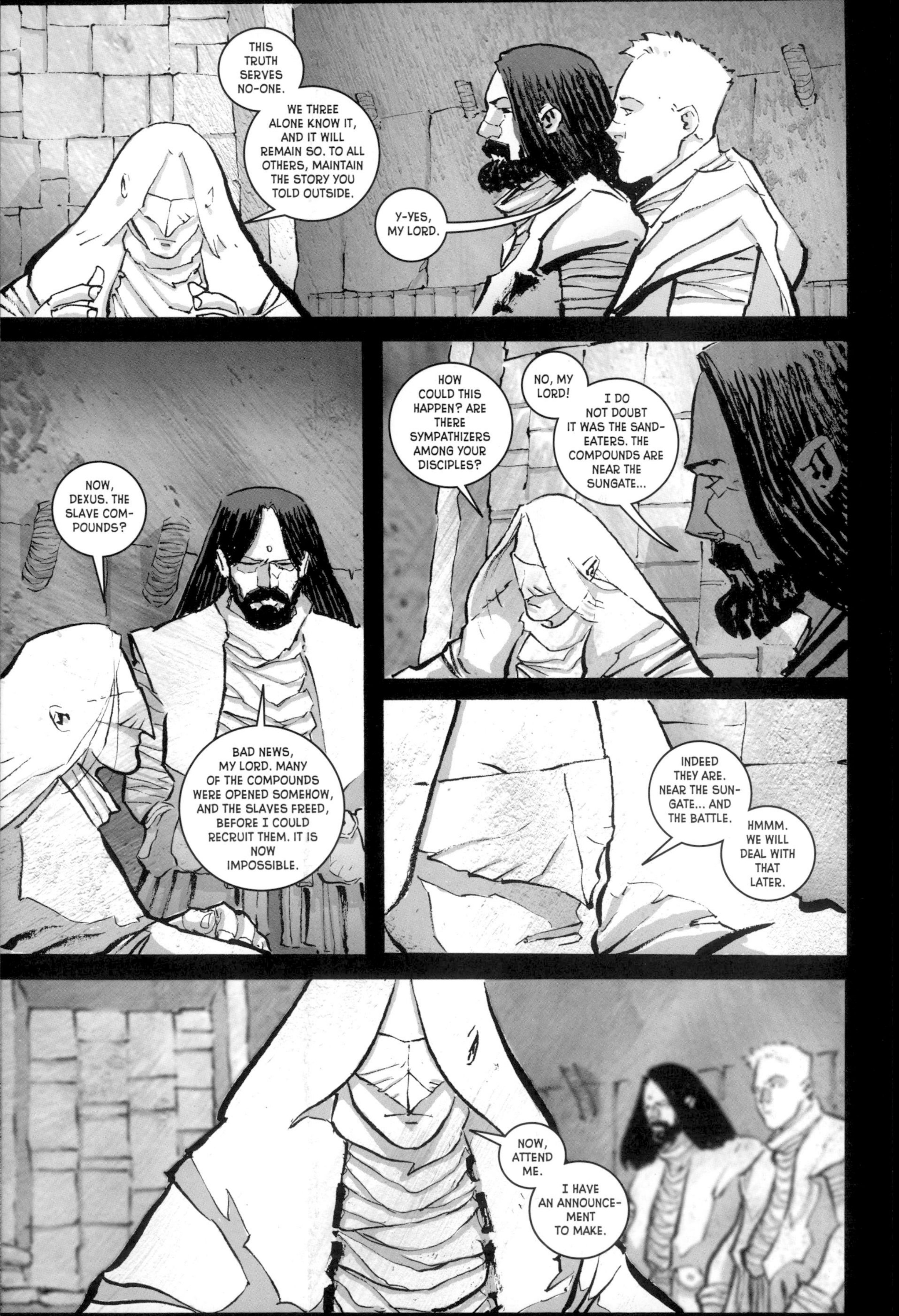
THIS TRUTH SERVES NO-ONE.
WE THREE ALONE KNOW IT, AND IT WILL REMAIN SO. TO ALL OTHERS, MAINTAIN THE STORY YOU TOLD OUTSIDE.
Y-YES, MY LORD.
NOW, DEXUS. THE SLAVE COMPOUNDS?
BAD NEWS, MY LORD. MANY OF THE COMPOUNDS WERE OPENED SOMEHOW, AND THE SLAVES FREED, BEFORE I COULD RECRUIT THEM. IT IS NOW IMPOSSIBLE.
HOW COULD THIS HAPPEN? ARE THERE SYMPATHIZERS AMONG YOUR DISCIPLES?
NO, MY LORD!
I DO NOT DOUBT IT WAS THE SAND-EATERS. THE COMPOUNDS ARE NEAR THE SUNGATE...
INDEED THEY ARE. NEAR THE SUN-GATE... AND THE BATTLE.
HMMM. WE WILL DEAL WITH THAT LATER.
NOW, ATTEND ME.
I HAVE AN ANNOUNCE-MENT TO MAKE.

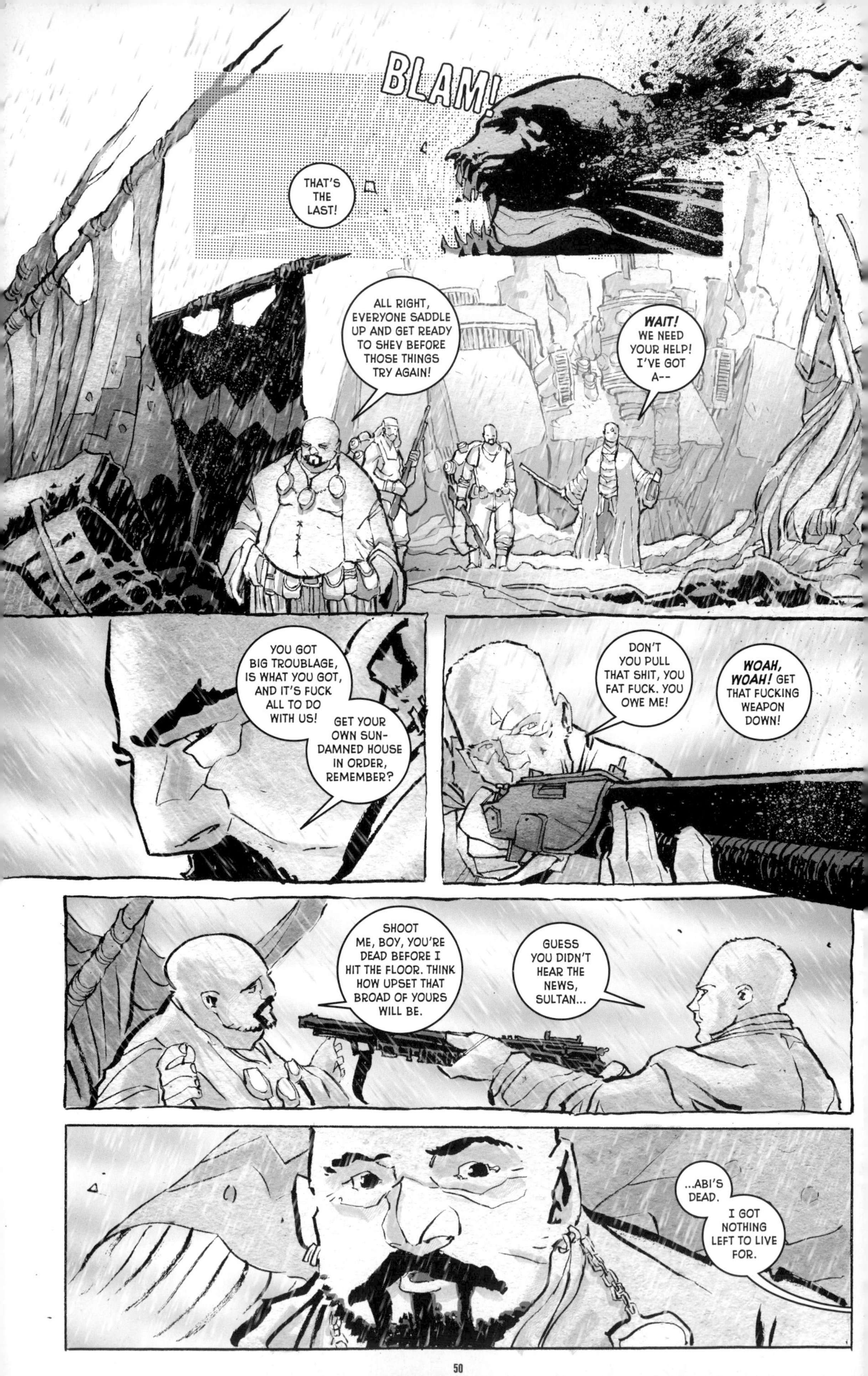
BLAM!
THAT'S THE LAST!
ALL RIGHT, EVERYONE SADDLE UP AND GET READY TO SHEV BEFORE THOSE THINGS TRY AGAIN!
WAIT! WE NEED YOUR HELP! I'VE GOT A--
YOU GOT BIG TROUBLAGE, IS WHAT YOU GOT, AND IT'S FUCK ALL TO DO WITH US!
GET YOUR OWN SUN-DAMNED HOUSE IN ORDER, REMEMBER?
DON'T YOU PULL THAT SHIT, YOU FAT FUCK. YOU OWE ME!
WOAH, WOAH! GET THAT FUCKING WEAPON DOWN!
SHOOT ME, BOY, YOU'RE DEAD BEFORE I HIT THE FLOOR. THINK HOW UPSET THAT BROAD OF YOURS WILL BE.
GUESS YOU DIDN'T HEAR THE NEWS, SULTAN...
...ABI'S DEAD.
I GOT NOTHING LEFT TO LIVE FOR.

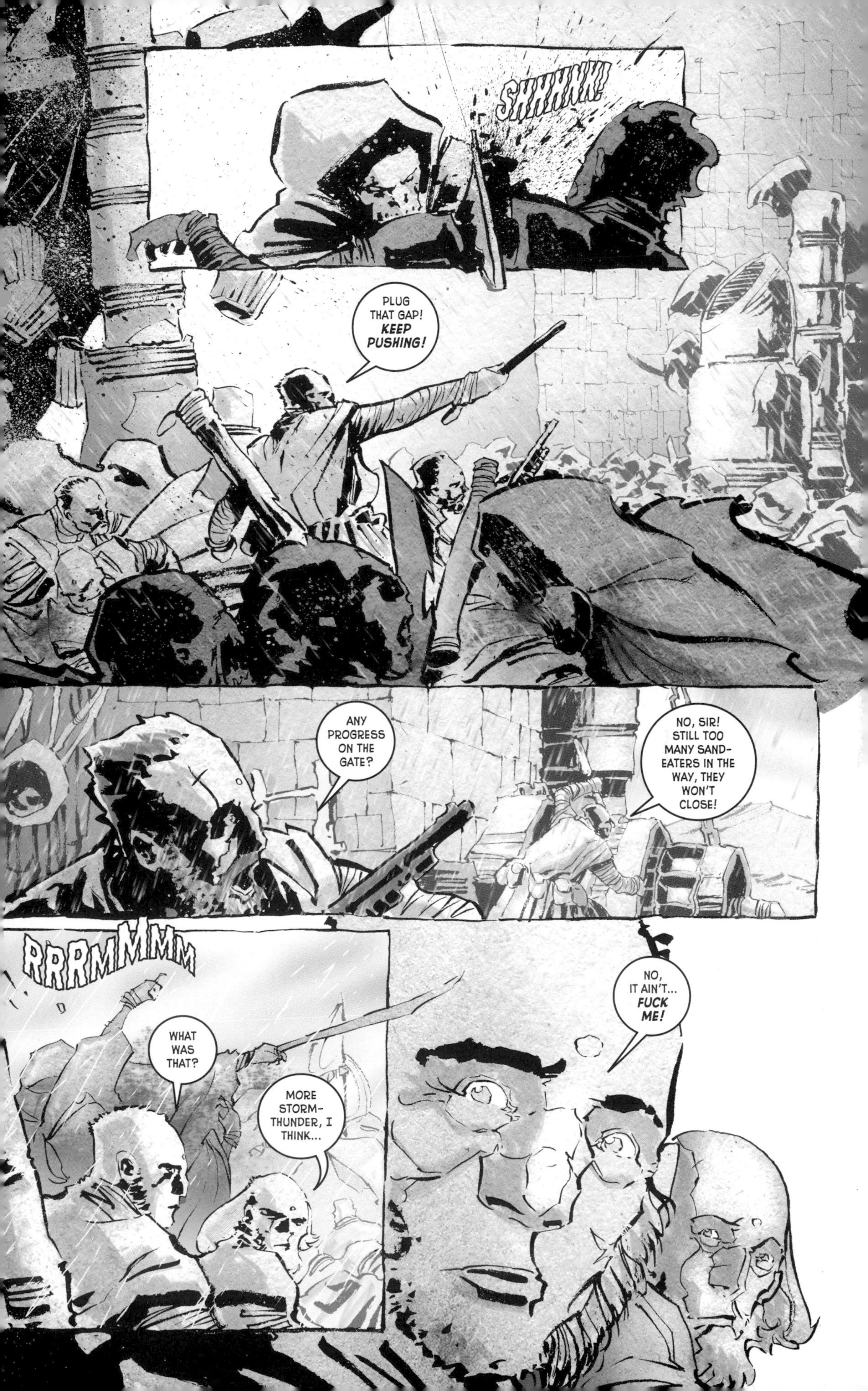
SHHHKK!
PLUG THAT GAP! KEEP PUSHING!
ANY PROGRESS ON THE GATE?
NO, SIR! STILL TOO MANY SAND-EATERS IN THE WAY, THEY WON'T CLOSE!
RRRMMMM
WHAT WAS THAT?
MORE STORM-THUNDER, I THINK...
NO, IT AIN'T... FUCK ME!

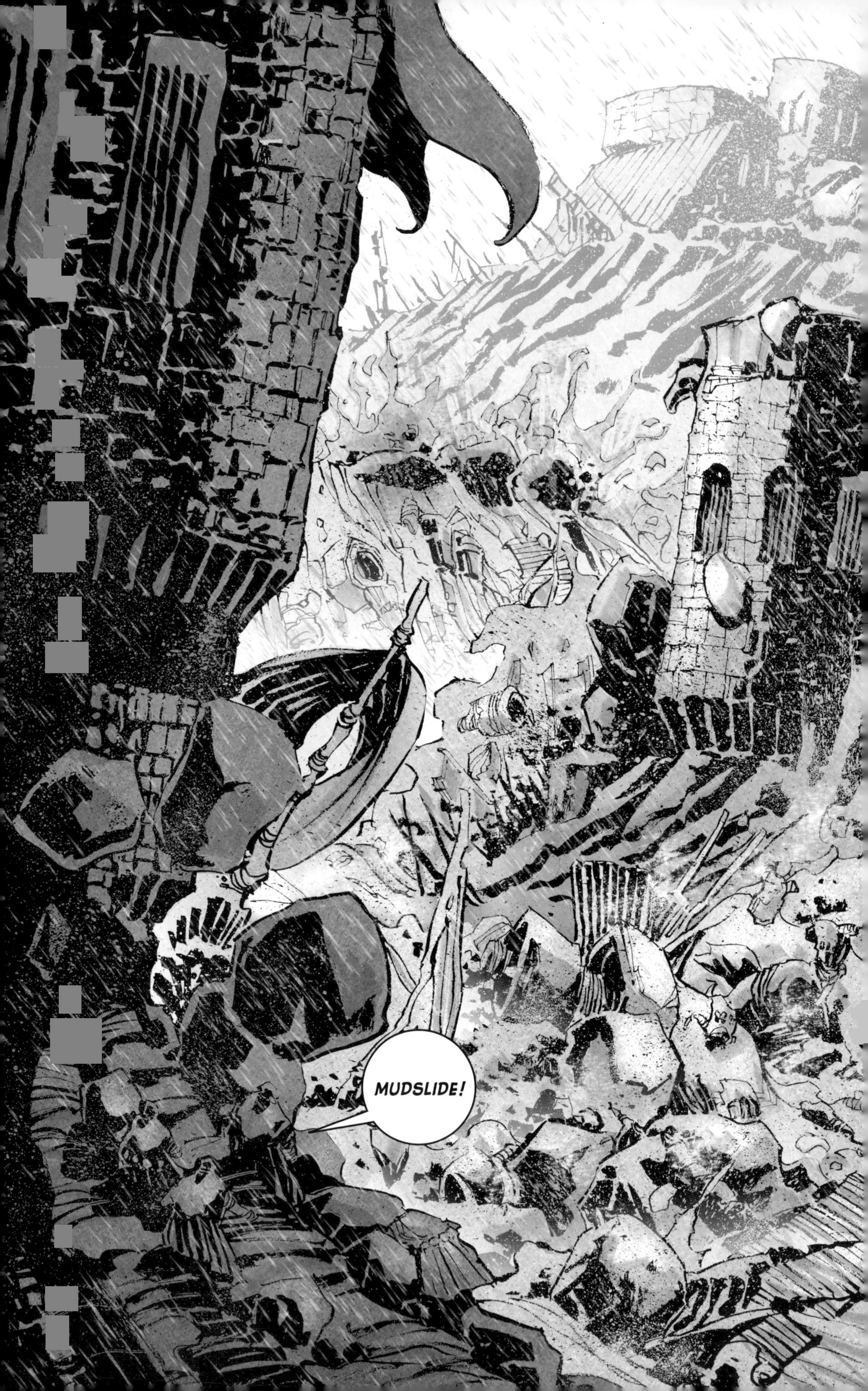
MUDSLIDE!

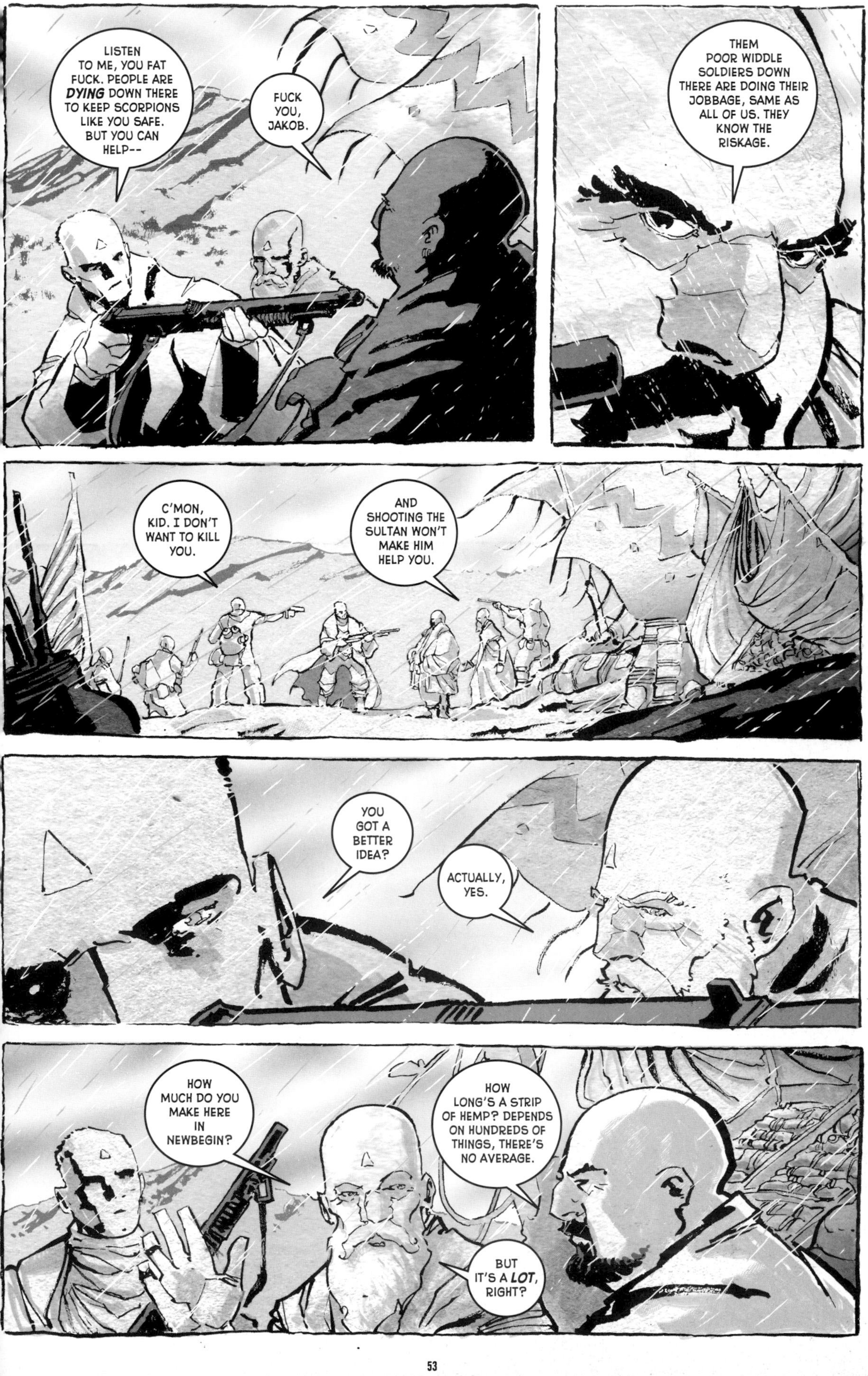
LISTEN TO ME, YOU FAT FUCK. PEOPLE ARE *DYING* DOWN THERE TO KEEP SCORPIONS LIKE YOU SAFE. BUT YOU CAN HELP--
FUCK YOU, JAKOB.
THEM POOR WIDDLE SOLDIERS DOWN THERE ARE DOING THEIR JOBBAGE, SAME AS ALL OF US. THEY KNOW THE RISKAGE.
C'MON, KID. I DON'T WANT TO KILL YOU.
AND SHOOTING THE SULTAN WON'T MAKE HIM HELP YOU.
YOU GOT A BETTER IDEA?
ACTUALLY, YES.
HOW MUCH DO YOU MAKE HERE IN NEWBEGIN?
HOW LONG'S A STRIP OF HEMP? DEPENDS ON HUNDREDS OF THINGS, THERE'S NO AVERAGE.
BUT IT'S A *LOT*, RIGHT?

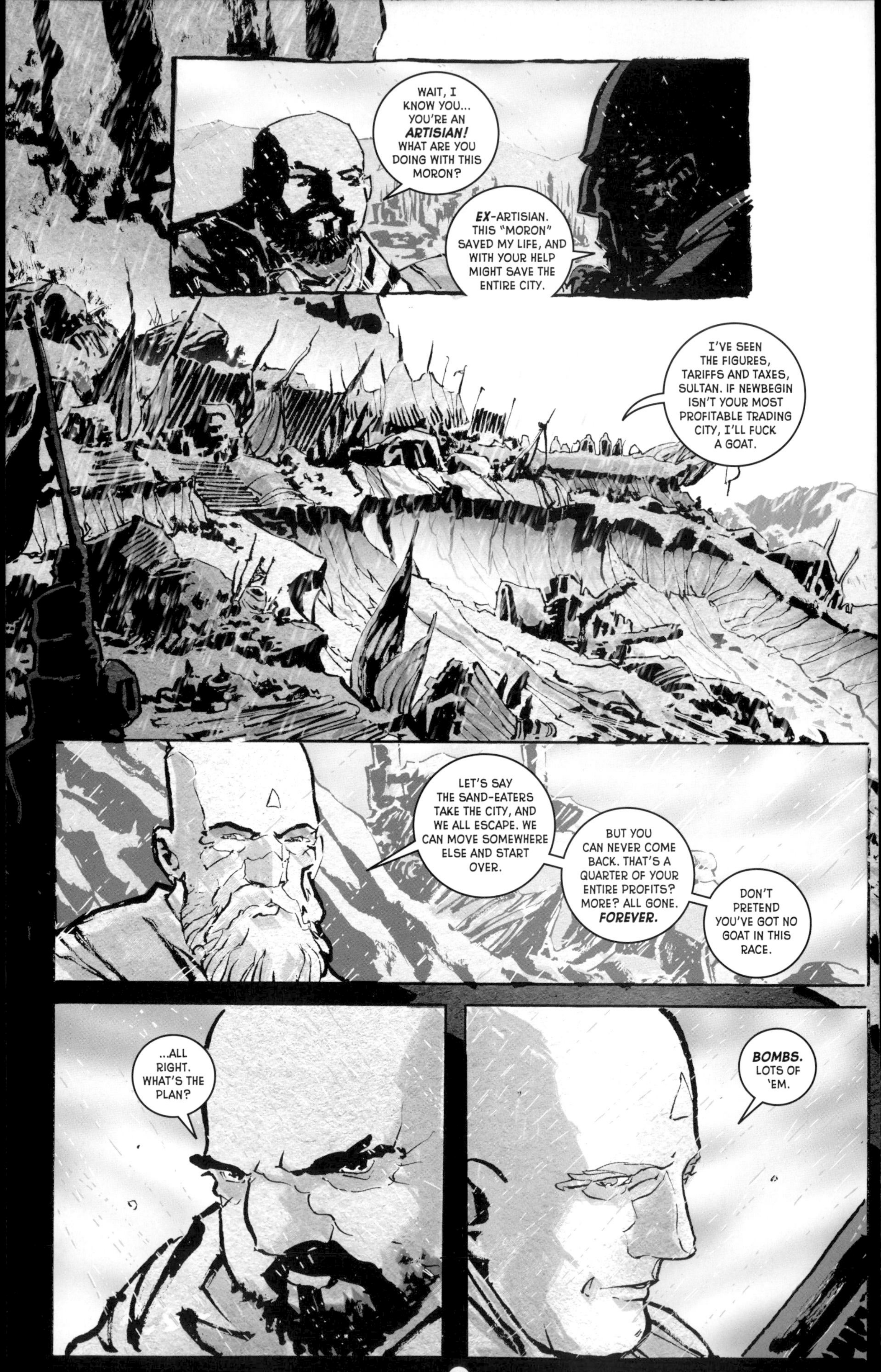
WAIT, I KNOW YOU... YOU'RE AN ARTISIAN! WHAT ARE YOU DOING WITH THIS MORON?
EX-ARTISIAN. THIS "MORON" SAVED MY LIFE, AND WITH YOUR HELP MIGHT SAVE THE ENTIRE CITY.
I'VE SEEN THE FIGURES, TARIFFS AND TAXES, SULTAN. IF NEWBEGIN ISN'T YOUR MOST PROFITABLE TRADING CITY, I'LL FUCK A GOAT.
LET'S SAY THE SAND-EATERS TAKE THE CITY, AND WE ALL ESCAPE. WE CAN MOVE SOMEWHERE ELSE AND START OVER.
BUT YOU CAN NEVER COME BACK. THAT'S A QUARTER OF YOUR ENTIRE PROFITS? MORE? ALL GONE. FOREVER.
DON'T PRETEND YOU'VE GOT NO GOAT IN THIS RACE.
...ALL RIGHT. WHAT'S THE PLAN?
BOMBS. LOTS OF 'EM.

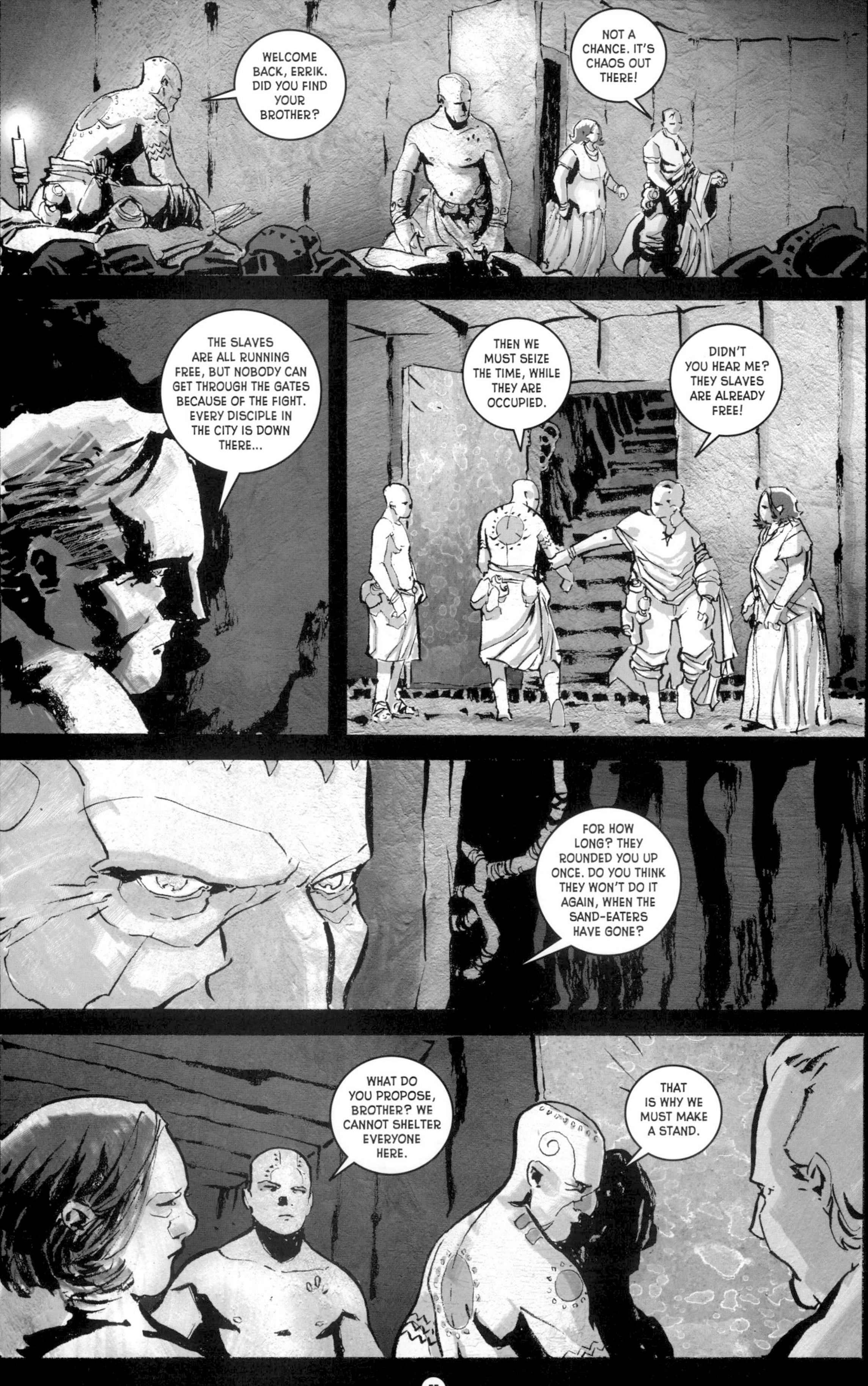
WELCOME BACK, ERRIK. DID YOU FIND YOUR BROTHER?
NOT A CHANCE. IT'S CHAOS OUT THERE!
THE SLAVES ARE ALL RUNNING FREE, BUT NOBODY CAN GET THROUGH THE GATES BECAUSE OF THE FIGHT. EVERY DISCIPLE IN THE CITY IS DOWN THERE...
THEN WE MUST SEIZE THE TIME, WHILE THEY ARE OCCUPIED.
DIDN'T YOU HEAR ME? THEY SLAVES ARE ALREADY FREE!
FOR HOW LONG? THEY ROUNDED YOU UP ONCE. DO YOU THINK THEY WON'T DO IT AGAIN, WHEN THE SAND-EATERS HAVE GONE?
WHAT DO YOU PROPOSE, BROTHER? WE CANNOT SHELTER EVERYONE HERE.
THAT IS WHY WE MUST MAKE A STAND.

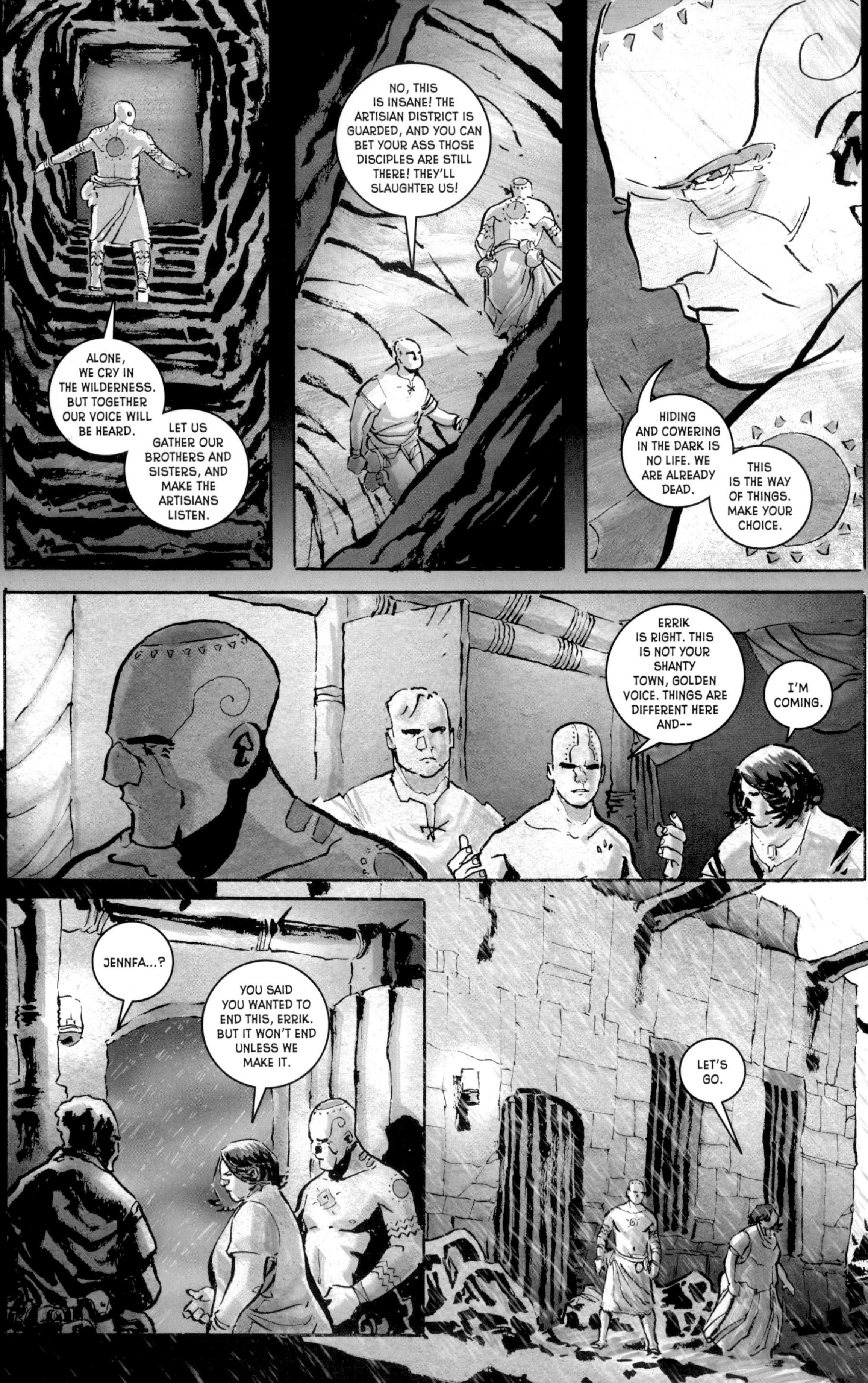
ALONE, WE CRY IN THE WILDERNESS. BUT TOGETHER OUR VOICE WILL BE HEARD.
LET US GATHER OUR BROTHERS AND SISTERS, AND MAKE THE ARTISIANS LISTEN.
NO, THIS IS INSANE! THE ARTISIAN DISTRICT IS GUARDED, AND YOU CAN BET YOUR ASS THOSE DISCIPLES ARE STILL THERE! THEY'LL SLAUGHTER US!
HIDING AND COWERING IN THE DARK IS NO LIFE. WE ARE ALREADY DEAD.
THIS IS THE WAY OF THINGS. MAKE YOUR CHOICE.
ERRIK IS RIGHT. THIS IS NOT YOUR SHANTY TOWN, GOLDEN VOICE. THINGS ARE DIFFERENT HERE AND--
I'M COMING.
JENNFA...?
YOU SAID YOU WANTED TO END THIS, ERRIK. BUT IT WON'T END UNLESS WE MAKE IT.
LET'S GO.

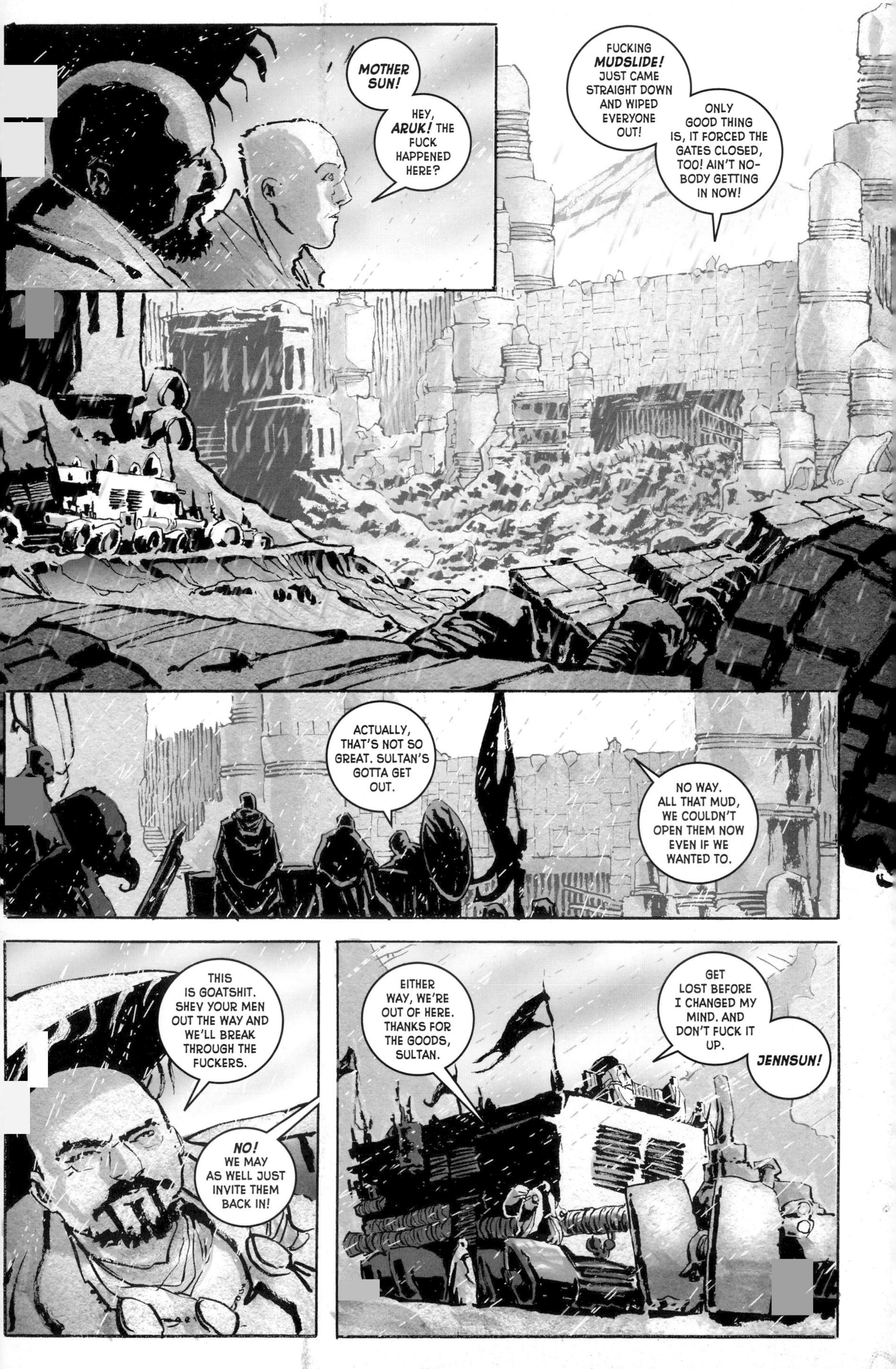
MOTHER SUN!
HEY, ARUK! THE FUCK HAPPENED HERE?
FUCKING MUDSLIDE! JUST CAME STRAIGHT DOWN AND WIPED EVERYONE OUT!
ONLY GOOD THING IS, IT FORCED THE GATES CLOSED, TOO! AIN'T NO-BODY GETTING IN NOW!
ACTUALLY, THAT'S NOT SO GREAT. SULTAN'S GOTTA GET OUT.
NO WAY. ALL THAT MUD, WE COULDN'T OPEN THEM NOW EVEN IF WE WANTED TO.
THIS IS GOATSHIT. SHEV YOUR MEN OUT THE WAY AND WE'LL BREAK THROUGH THE FUCKERS.
NO! WE MAY AS WELL JUST INVITE THEM BACK IN!
EITHER WAY, WE'RE OUT OF HERE. THANKS FOR THE GOODS, SULTAN.
GET LOST BEFORE I CHANGED MY MIND. AND DON'T FUCK IT UP.
JENNSUN!

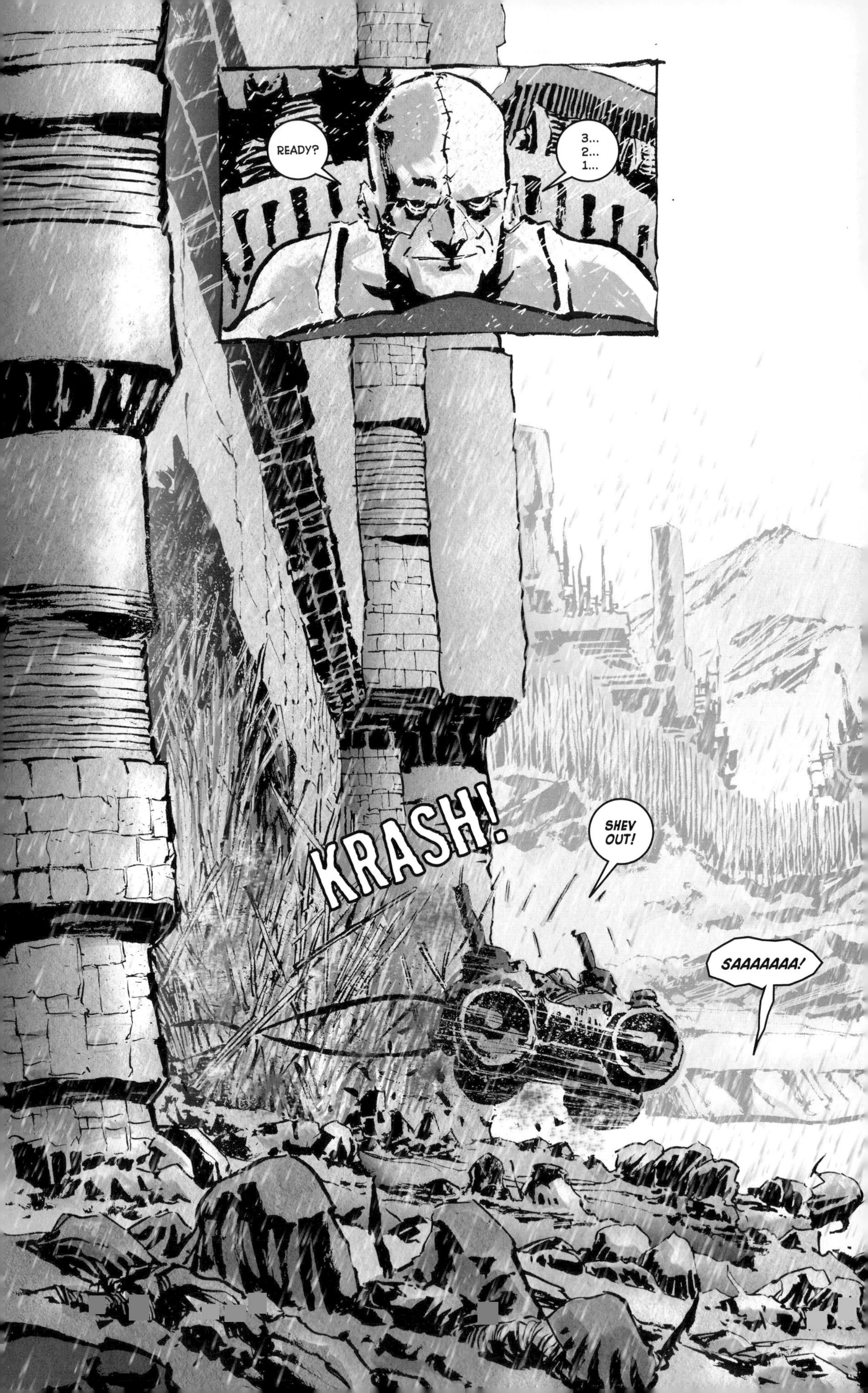
READY?
3...
2...
1...
KRASH!
SHEV OUT!
SAAAAAAA!

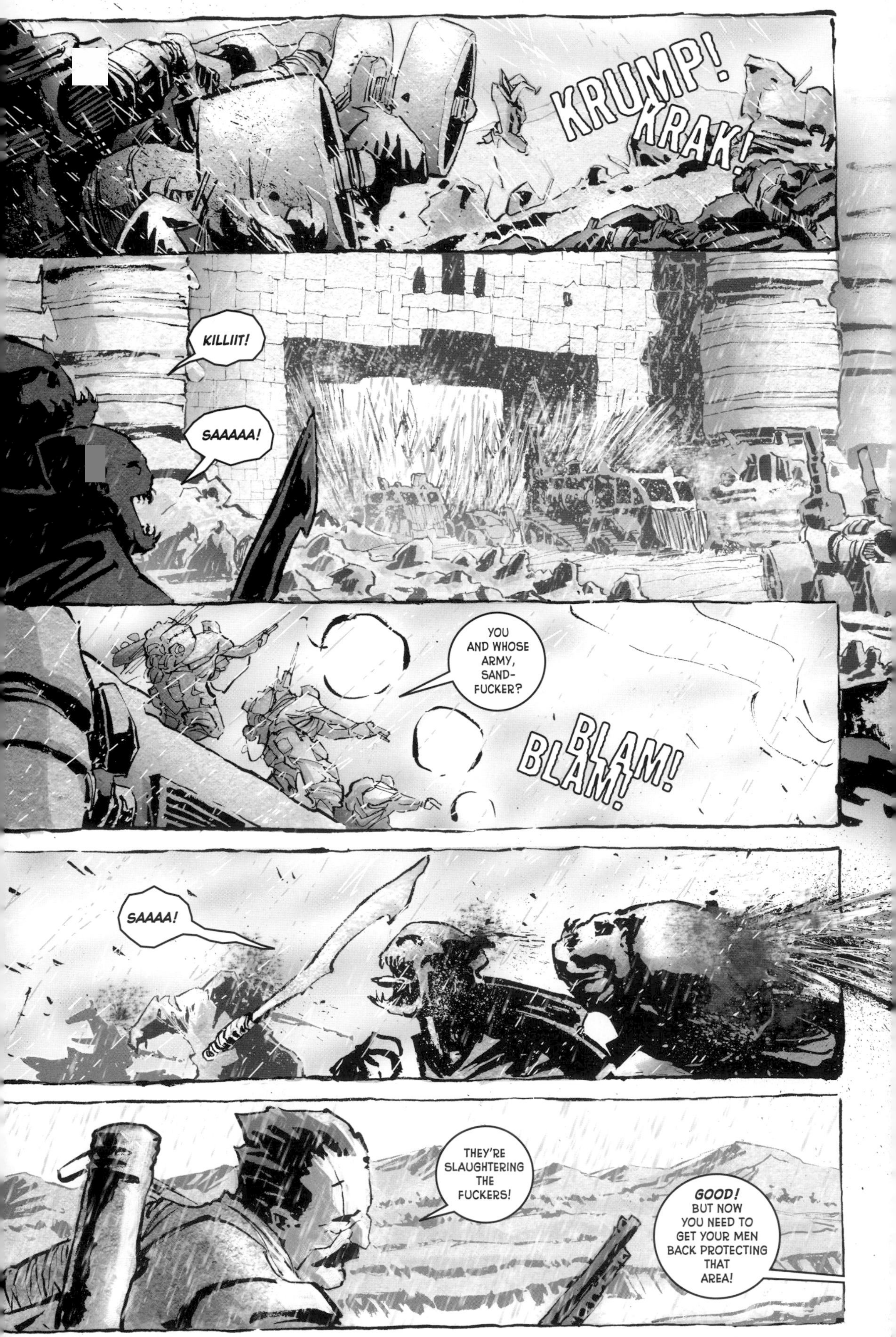
KRUMP!
KRAK!
KILLIIT!
SAAAAA!
YOU AND WHOSE ARMY, SAND-FUCKER?
BLAM!
BLAM!
SAAAA!
THEY'RE SLAUGHTERING THE FUCKERS!
GOOD! BUT NOW YOU NEED TO GET YOUR MEN BACK PROTECTING THAT AREA!

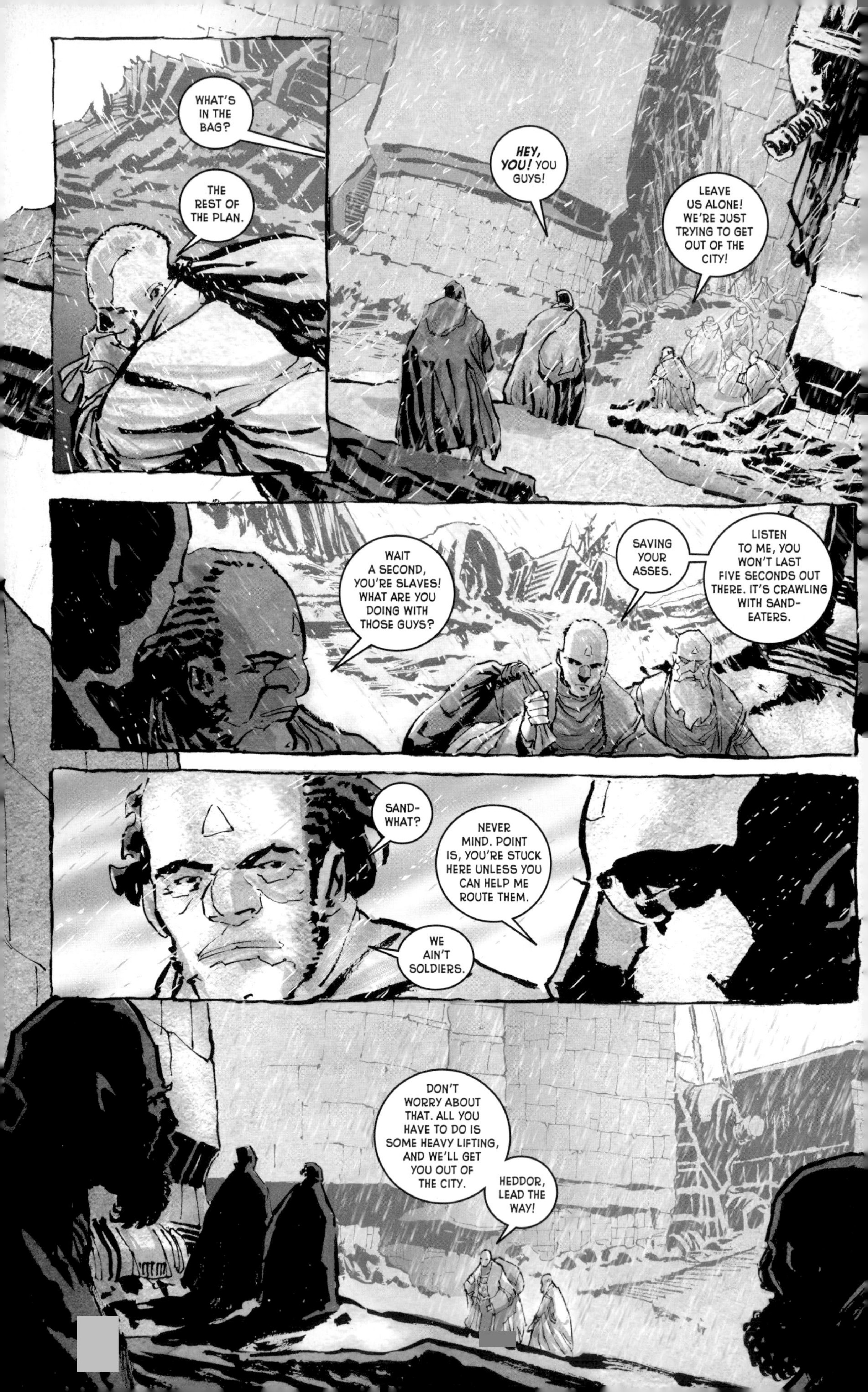
WHAT'S IN THE BAG?
THE REST OF THE PLAN.
HEY, YOU! YOU GUYS!
LEAVE US ALONE! WE'RE JUST TRYING TO GET OUT OF THE CITY!
WAIT A SECOND, YOU'RE SLAVES! WHAT ARE YOU DOING WITH THOSE GUYS?
SAVING YOUR ASSES.
LISTEN TO ME, YOU WON'T LAST FIVE SECONDS OUT THERE. IT'S CRAWLING WITH SAND-EATERS.
SAND-WHAT?
NEVER MIND. POINT IS, YOU'RE STUCK HERE UNLESS YOU CAN HELP ME ROUTE THEM.
WE AIN'T SOLDIERS.
DON'T WORRY ABOUT THAT. ALL YOU HAVE TO DO IS SOME HEAVY LIFTING, AND WE'LL GET YOU OUT OF THE CITY.
HEDDOR, LEAD THE WAY!

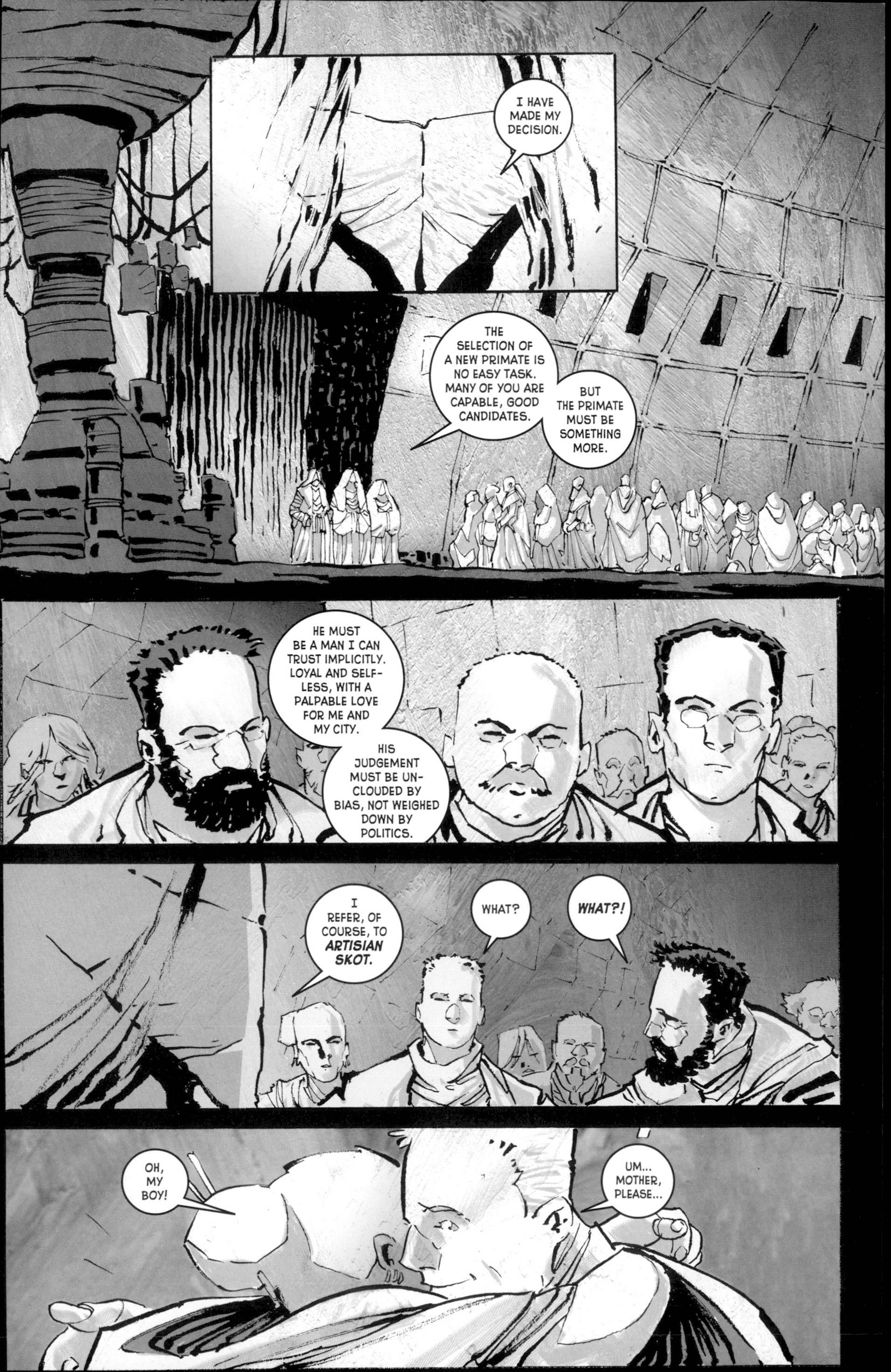
I HAVE MADE MY DECISION.
THE SELECTION OF A NEW PRIMATE IS NO EASY TASK. MANY OF YOU ARE CAPABLE, GOOD CANDIDATES.
BUT THE PRIMATE MUST BE SOMETHING MORE.
HE MUST BE A MAN I CAN TRUST IMPLICITLY. LOYAL AND SELF-LESS, WITH A PALPABLE LOVE FOR ME AND MY CITY.
HIS JUDGEMENT MUST BE UN-CLOUDED BY BIAS, NOT WEIGHED DOWN BY POLITICS.
I REFER, OF COURSE, TO ***ARTISIAN SKOT.***
WHAT?
WHAT?!
OH, MY BOY!
UM... MOTHER, PLEASE...

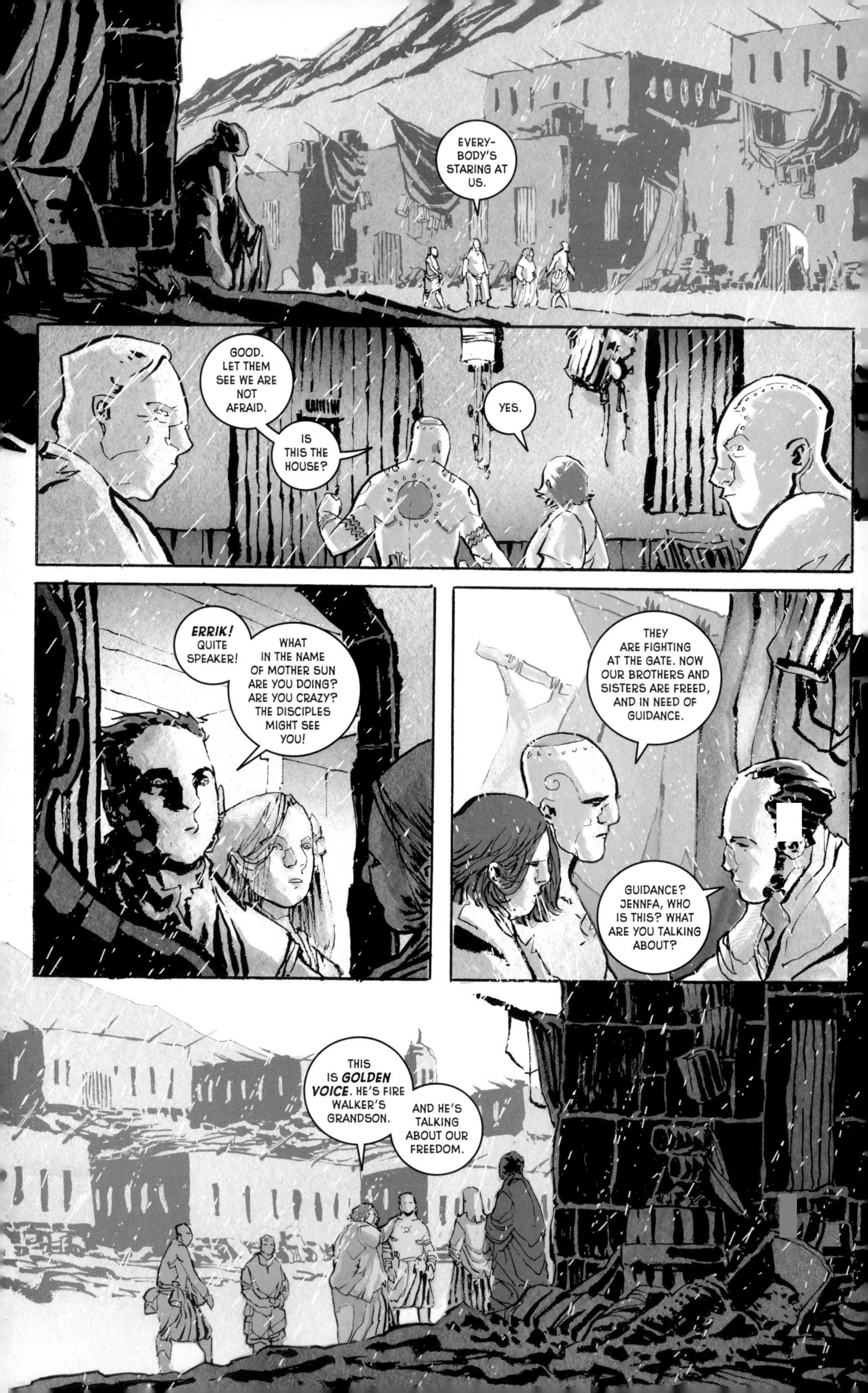
EVERY-BODY'S STARING AT US.
GOOD. LET THEM SEE WE ARE NOT AFRAID.
YES.
IS THIS THE HOUSE?
ERRIK! QUITE SPEAKER!
WHAT IN THE NAME OF MOTHER SUN ARE YOU DOING? ARE YOU CRAZY? THE DISCIPLES MIGHT SEE YOU!
THEY ARE FIGHTING AT THE GATE. NOW OUR BROTHERS AND SISTERS ARE FREED, AND IN NEED OF GUIDANCE.
GUIDANCE? JENNFA, WHO IS THIS? WHAT ARE YOU TALKING ABOUT?
THIS IS GOLDEN VOICE. HE'S FIRE WALKER'S GRANDSON.
AND HE'S TALKING ABOUT OUR FREEDOM.

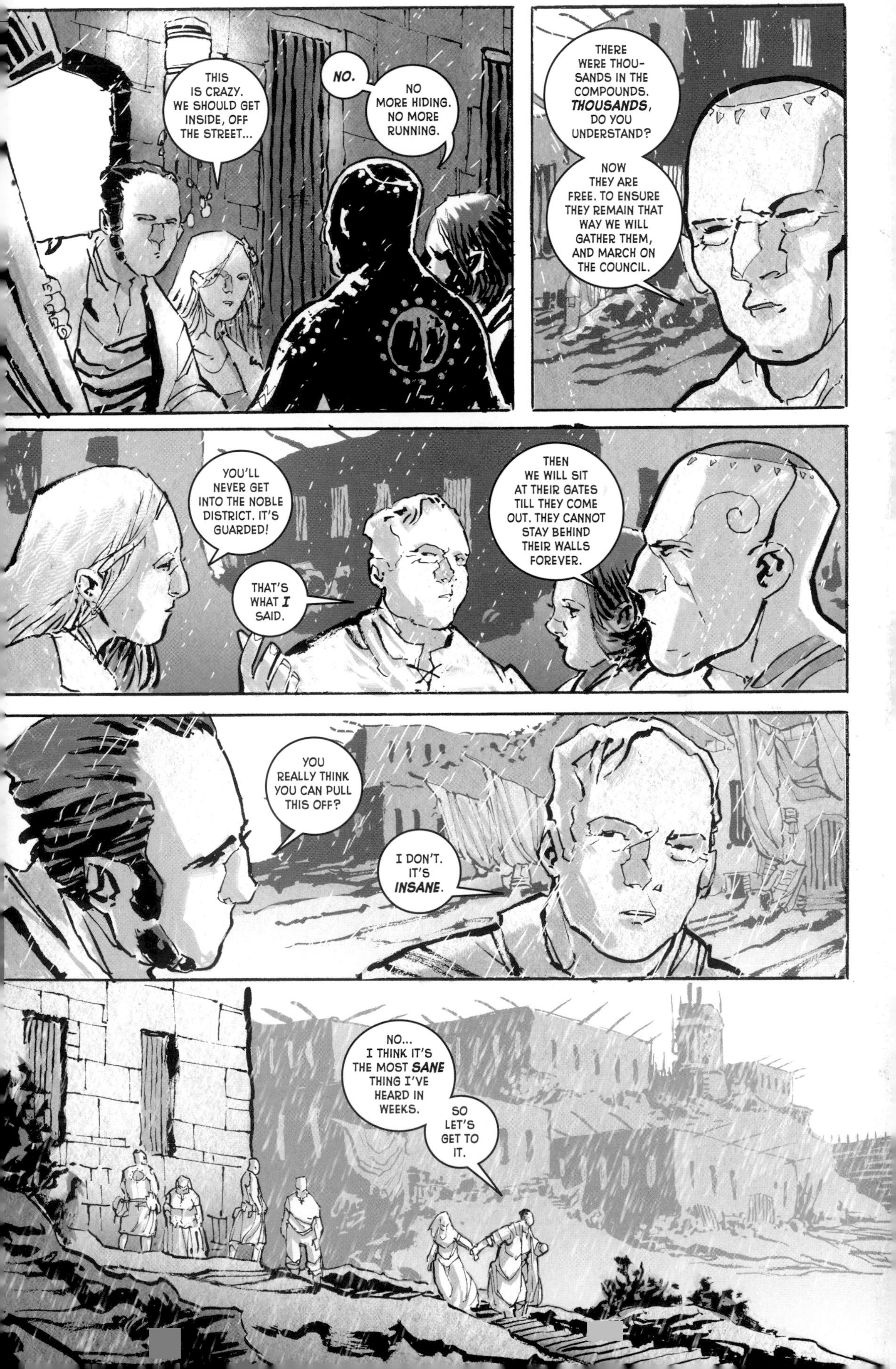
THIS IS CRAZY. WE SHOULD GET INSIDE, OFF THE STREET...
NO.
NO MORE HIDING. NO MORE RUNNING.
THERE WERE THOUSANDS IN THE COMPOUNDS. THOUSANDS, DO YOU UNDERSTAND?
NOW THEY ARE FREE. TO ENSURE THEY REMAIN THAT WAY WE WILL GATHER THEM, AND MARCH ON THE COUNCIL.
YOU'LL NEVER GET INTO THE NOBLE DISTRICT. IT'S GUARDED!
THAT'S WHAT I SAID.
THEN WE WILL SIT AT THEIR GATES TILL THEY COME OUT. THEY CANNOT STAY BEHIND THEIR WALLS FOREVER.
YOU REALLY THINK YOU CAN PULL THIS OFF?
I DON'T. IT'S INSANE.
NO... I THINK IT'S THE MOST SANE THING I'VE HEARD IN WEEKS.
SO LET'S GET TO IT.

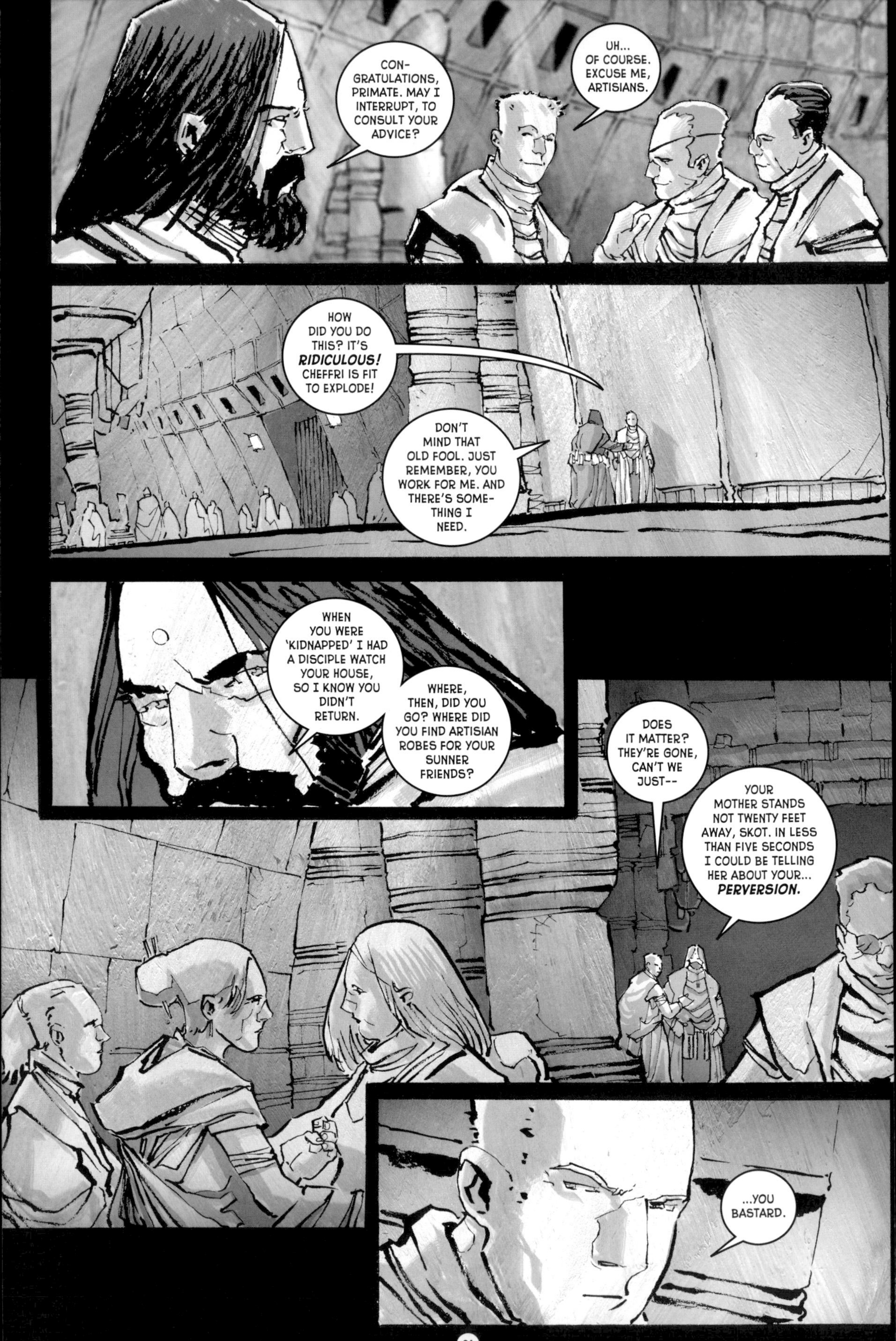
CON-
GRATULATIONS, PRIMATE. MAY I INTERRUPT, TO CONSULT YOUR ADVICE?
UH... OF COURSE. EXCUSE ME, ARTISIANS.
HOW DID YOU DO THIS? IT'S *RIDICULOUS!* CHEFFRI IS FIT TO EXPLODE!
DON'T MIND THAT OLD FOOL. JUST REMEMBER, YOU WORK FOR ME. AND THERE'S SOME-
THING I NEED.
WHEN YOU WERE 'KIDNAPPED' I HAD A DISCIPLE WATCH YOUR HOUSE, SO I KNOW YOU DIDN'T RETURN.
WHERE, THEN, DID YOU GO? WHERE DID YOU FIND ARTISIAN ROBES FOR YOUR SUNNER FRIENDS?
DOES IT MATTER? THEY'RE GONE, CAN'T WE JUST--
YOUR MOTHER STANDS NOT TWENTY FEET AWAY, SKOT. IN LESS THAN FIVE SECONDS I COULD BE TELLING HER ABOUT YOUR... **PERVERSION.**
...YOU BASTARD.

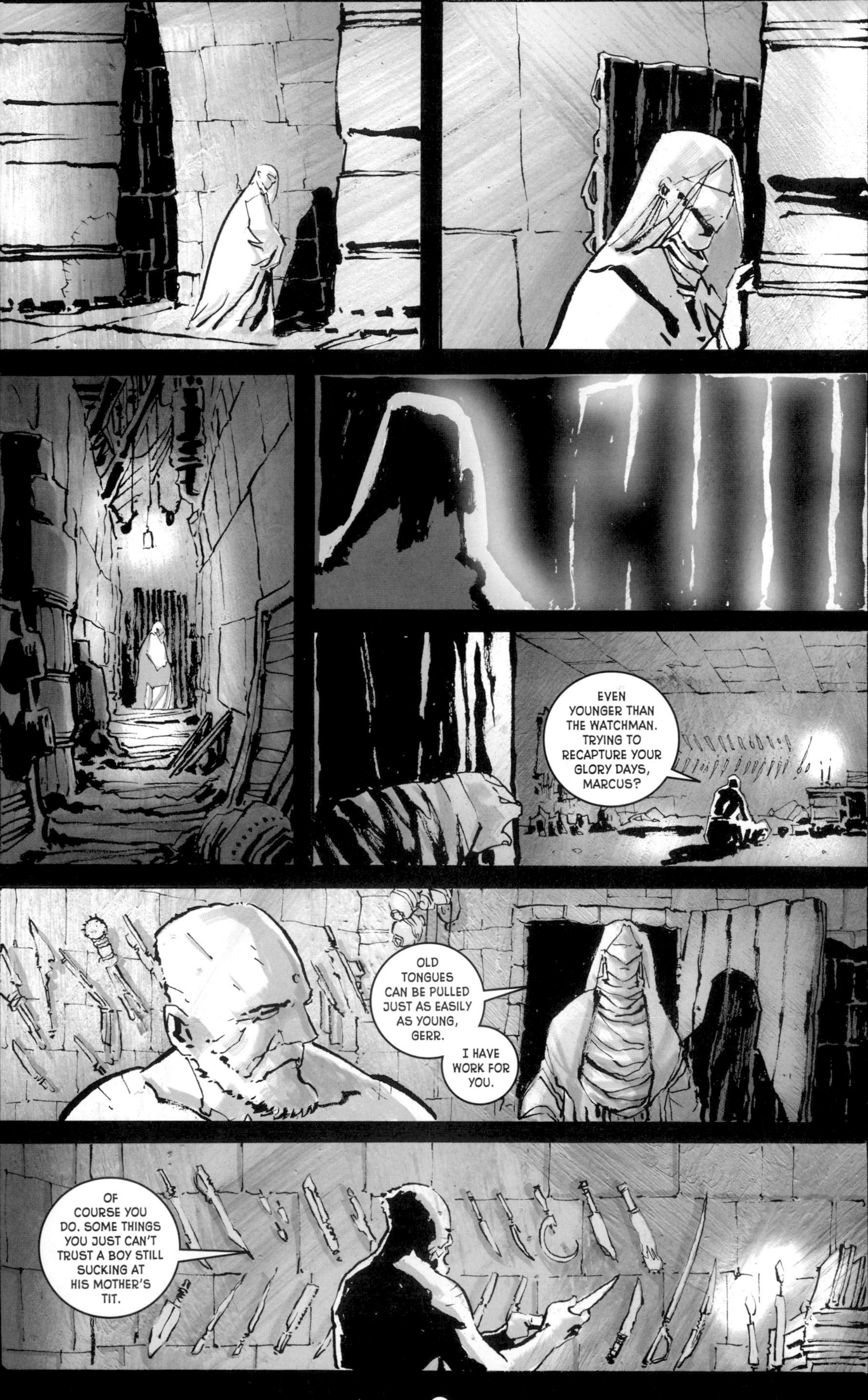
EVEN YOUNGER THAN THE WATCHMAN. TRYING TO RECAPTURE YOUR GLORY DAYS, MARCUS?
OLD TONGUES CAN BE PULLED JUST AS EASILY AS YOUNG, GERR.
I HAVE WORK FOR YOU.
OF COURSE YOU DO. SOME THINGS YOU JUST CAN'T TRUST A BOY STILL SUCKING AT HIS MOTHER'S TIT.

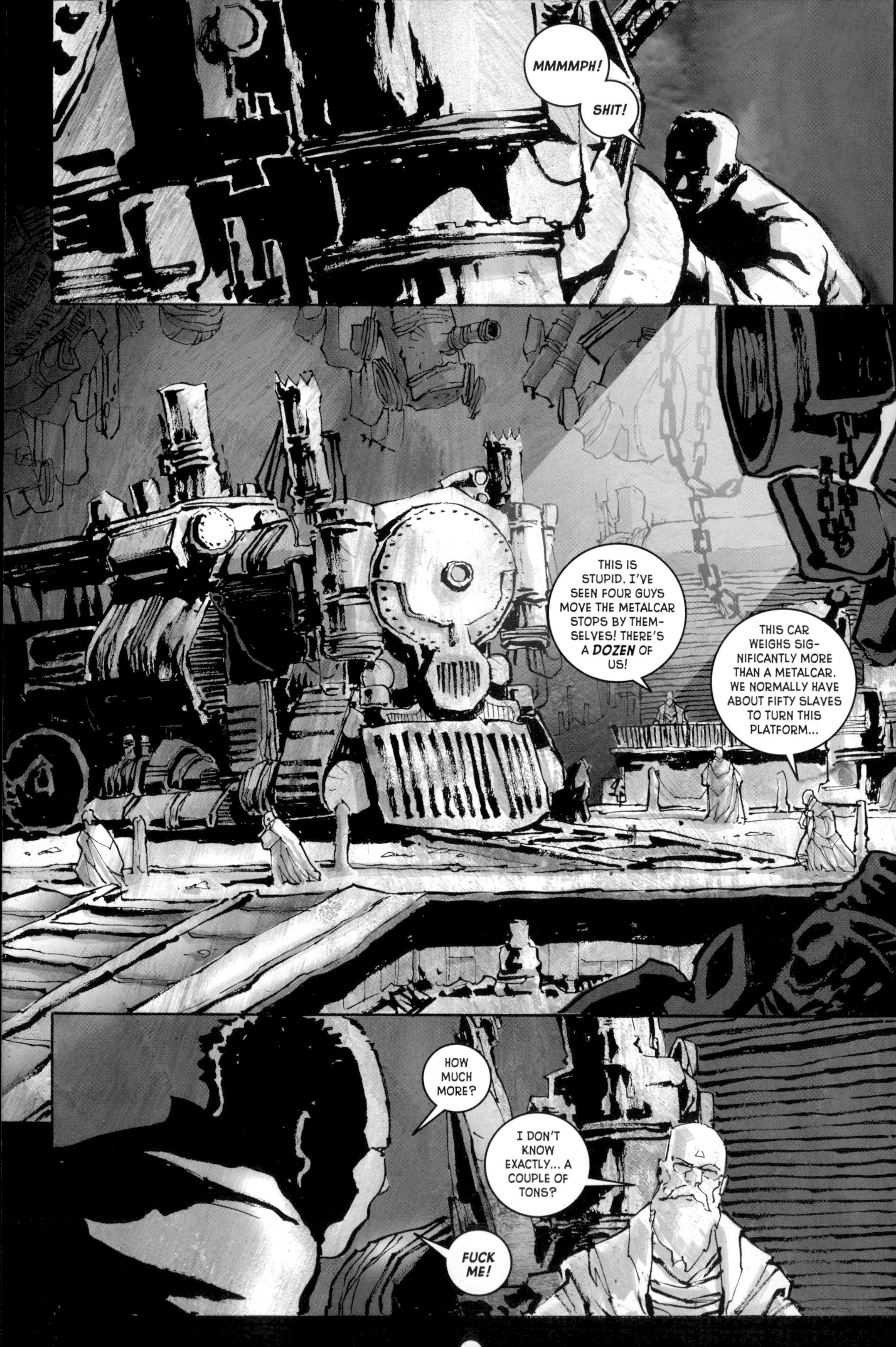
MMMMPH!
SHIT!
THIS IS STUPID. I'VE SEEN FOUR GUYS MOVE THE METALCAR STOPS BY THEM-SELVES! THERE'S A *DOZEN* OF US!
THIS CAR WEIGHS SIG-NIFICANTLY MORE THAN A METALCAR. WE NORMALLY HAVE ABOUT FIFTY SLAVES TO TURN THIS PLATFORM...
HOW MUCH MORE?
I DON'T KNOW EXACTLY... A COUPLE OF TONS?
FUCK ME!

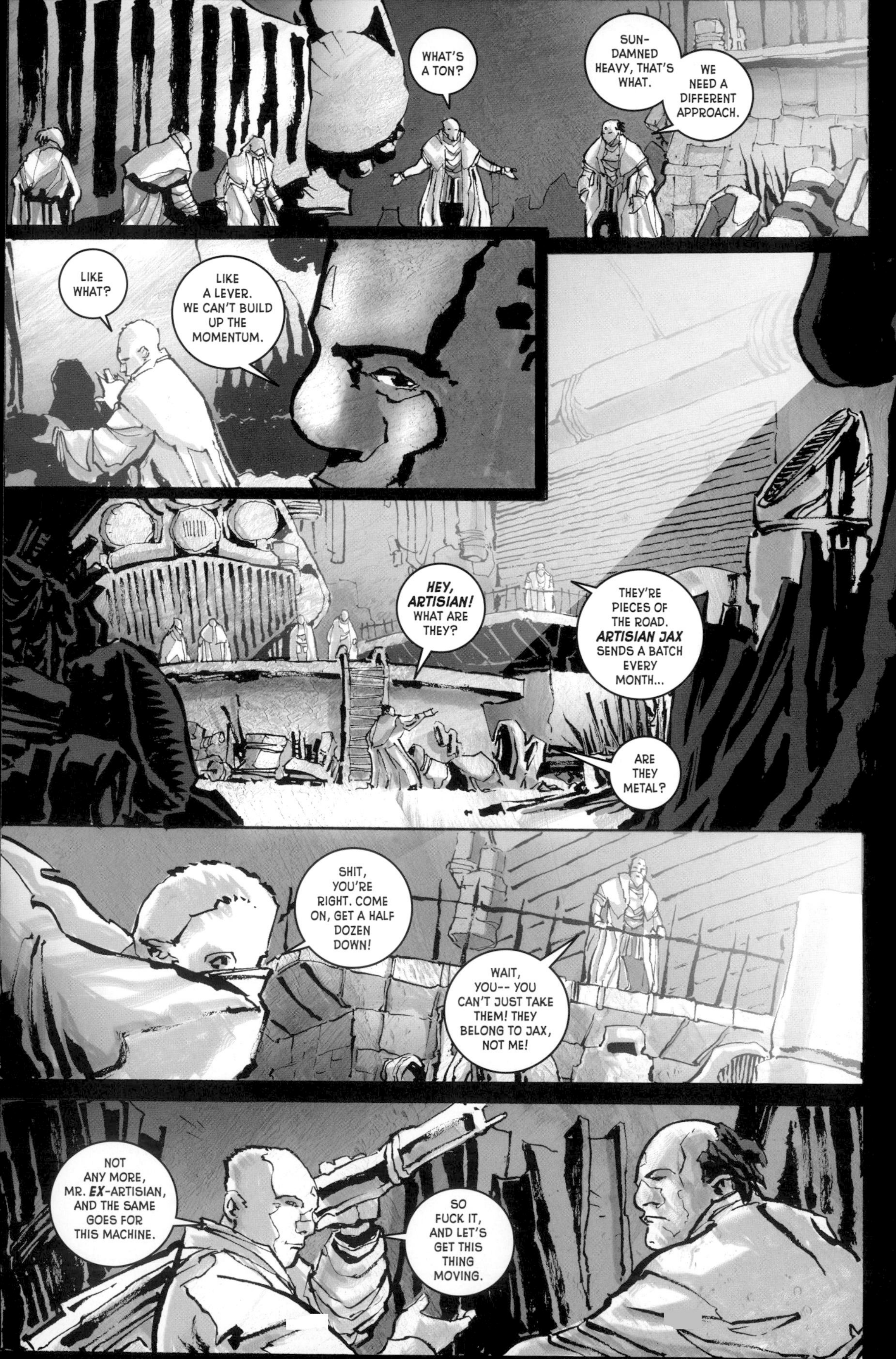
WHAT'S A TON?
SUN-DAMNED HEAVY, THAT'S WHAT.
WE NEED A DIFFERENT APPROACH.
LIKE WHAT?
LIKE A LEVER. WE CAN'T BUILD UP THE MOMENTUM.
HEY, ARTISIAN! WHAT ARE THEY?
THEY'RE PIECES OF THE ROAD. ARTISIAN JAX SENDS A BATCH EVERY MONTH...
ARE THEY METAL?
SHIT, YOU'RE RIGHT. COME ON, GET A HALF DOZEN DOWN!
WAIT, YOU-- YOU CAN'T JUST TAKE THEM! THEY BELONG TO JAX, NOT ME!
NOT ANY MORE, MR. EX-ARTISIAN, AND THE SAME GOES FOR THIS MACHINE.
SO FUCK IT, AND LET'S GET THIS THING MOVING.

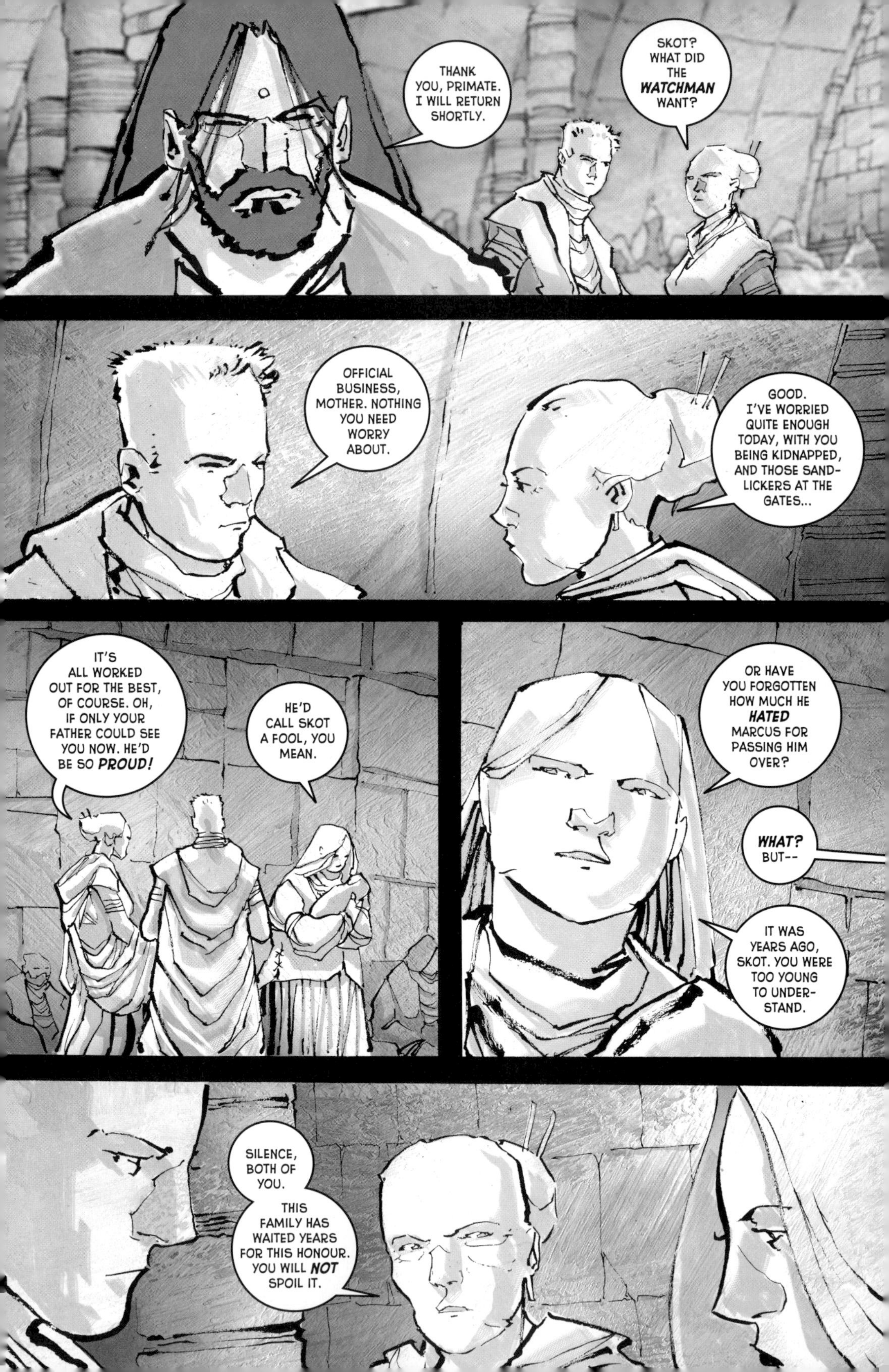

THANK YOU, PRIMATE. I WILL RETURN SHORTLY.
SKOT? WHAT DID THE WATCHMAN WANT?
OFFICIAL BUSINESS, MOTHER. NOTHING YOU NEED WORRY ABOUT.
GOOD. I'VE WORRIED QUITE ENOUGH TODAY, WITH YOU BEING KIDNAPPED, AND THOSE SAND-LICKERS AT THE GATES...
IT'S ALL WORKED OUT FOR THE BEST, OF COURSE. OH, IF ONLY YOUR FATHER COULD SEE YOU NOW. HE'D BE SO PROUD!
HE'D CALL SKOT A FOOL, YOU MEAN.
OR HAVE YOU FORGOTTEN HOW MUCH HE HATED MARCUS FOR PASSING HIM OVER?
WHAT? BUT--
IT WAS YEARS AGO, SKOT. YOU WERE TOO YOUNG TO UNDER-STAND.
SILENCE, BOTH OF YOU.
THIS FAMILY HAS WAITED YEARS FOR THIS HONOUR. YOU WILL NOT SPOIL IT.

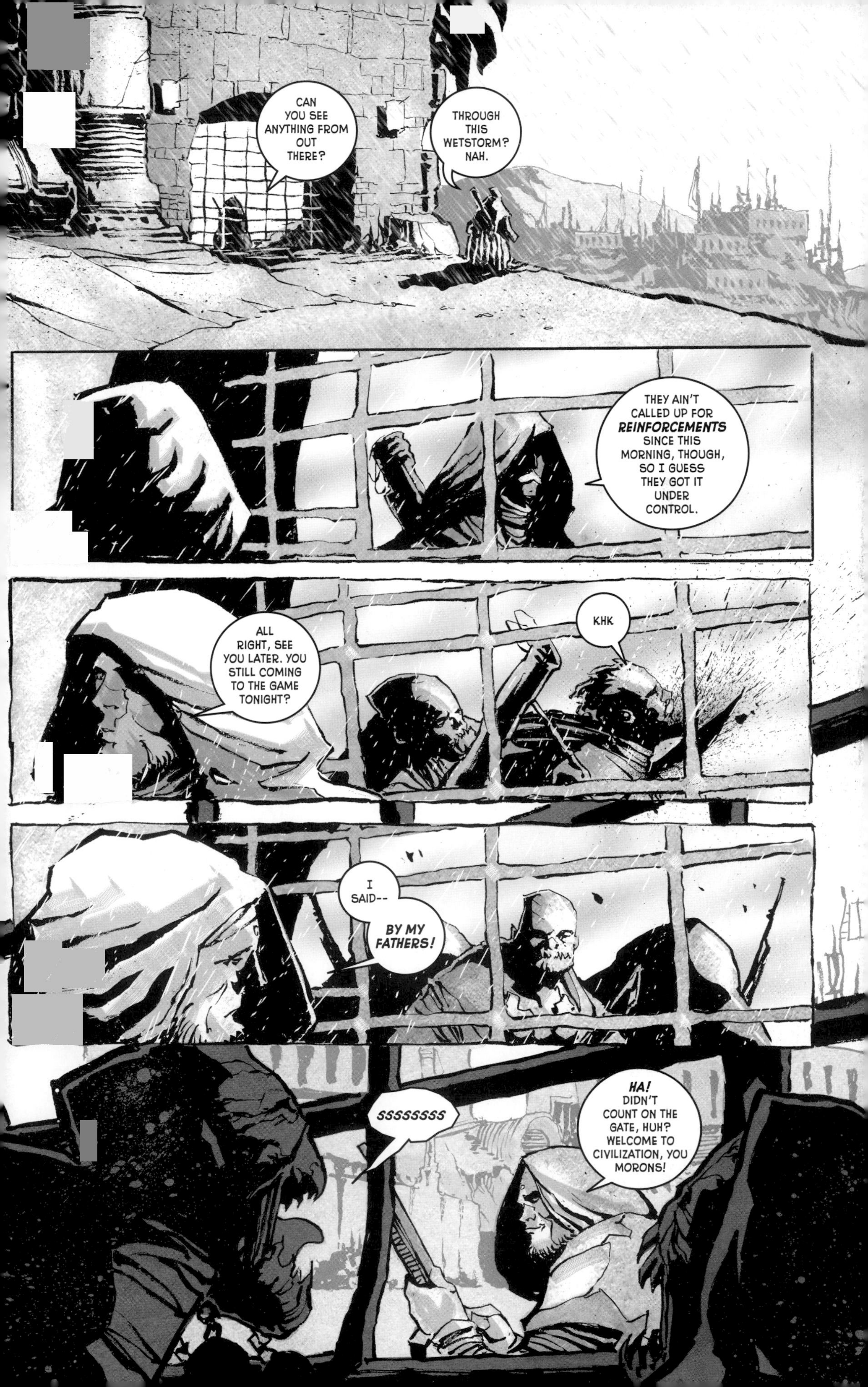
CAN YOU SEE ANYTHING FROM OUT THERE?
THROUGH THIS WETSTORM? NAH.
THEY AIN'T CALLED UP FOR REINFORCEMENTS SINCE THIS MORNING, THOUGH, SO I GUESS THEY GOT IT UNDER CONTROL.
ALL RIGHT, SEE YOU LATER. YOU STILL COMING TO THE GAME TONIGHT?
KHK
I SAID--
BY MY FATHERS!
SSSSSSSS
HA! DIDN'T COUNT ON THE GATE, HUH? WELCOME TO CIVILIZATION, YOU MORONS!

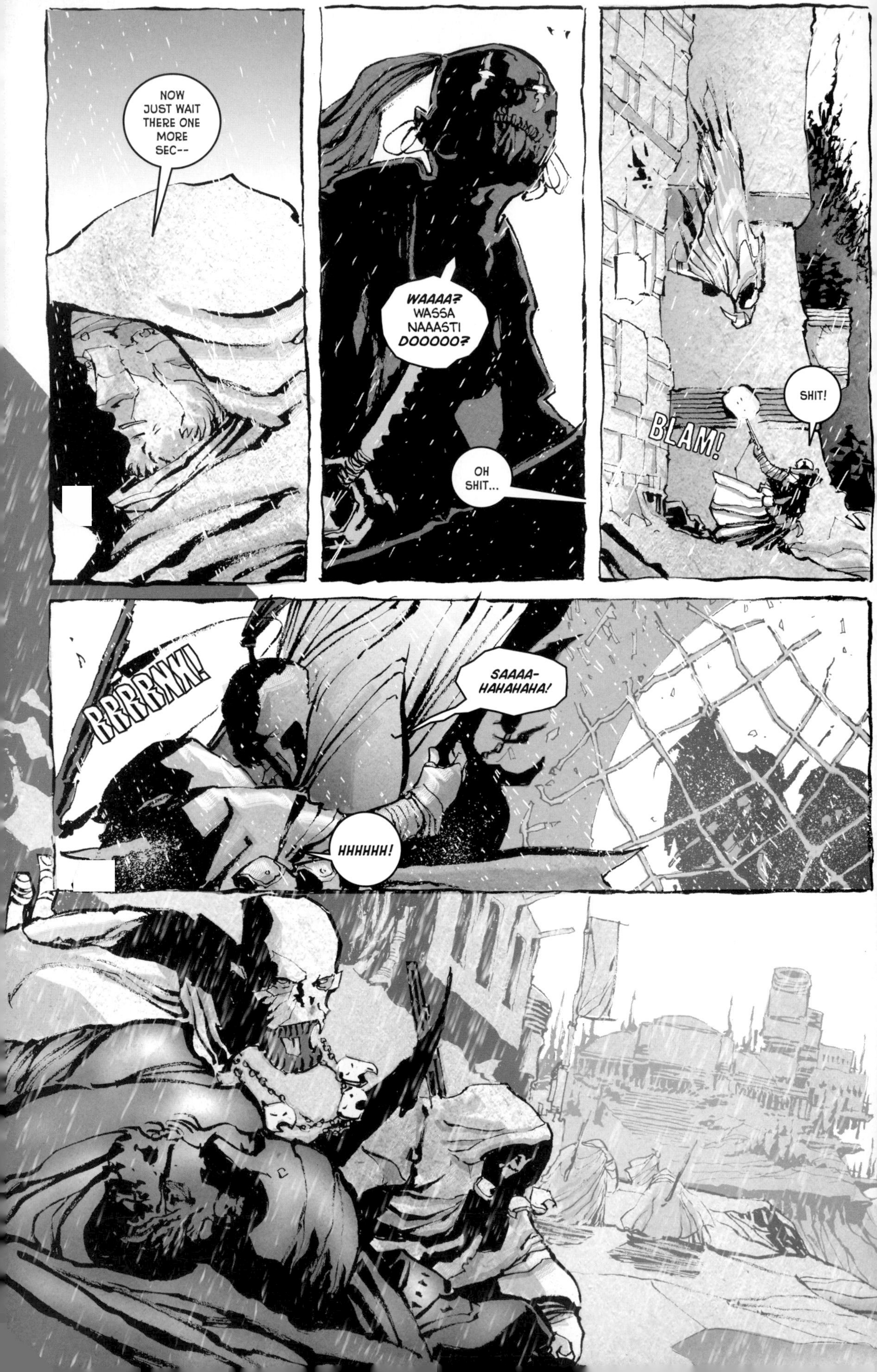
NOW JUST WAIT THERE ONE MORE SEC--
WAAAA? WASSA NAAASTI DOOOOO?
OH SHIT...
BLAM!
SHIT!
RRRRNX!
SAAAA-HAHAHAHA!
HHHHHH!

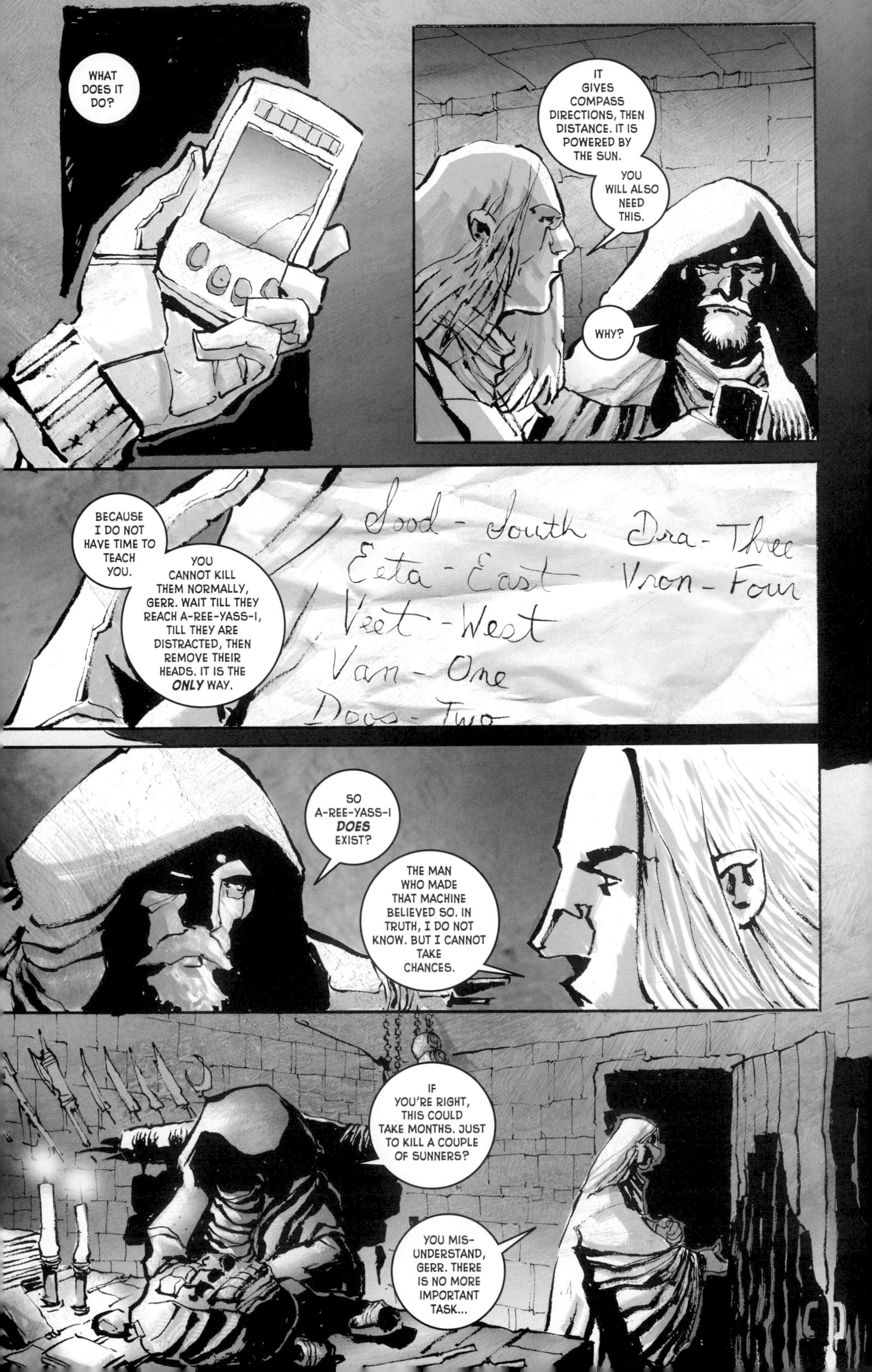
WHAT DOES IT DO?
IT GIVES COMPASS DIRECTIONS, THEN DISTANCE. IT IS POWERED BY THE SUN.
YOU WILL ALSO NEED THIS.
WHY?
BECAUSE I DO NOT HAVE TIME TO TEACH YOU.
Sood - South Dra - Three
Eeta - East Vron - Four
Veet - West
Van - One
Doos - Two
YOU CANNOT KILL THEM NORMALLY, GERR. WAIT TILL THEY REACH A-REE-YASS-I, TILL THEY ARE DISTRACTED, THEN REMOVE THEIR HEADS. IT IS THE ***ONLY*** WAY.
SO A-REE-YASS-I ***DOES*** EXIST?
THE MAN WHO MADE THAT MACHINE BELIEVED SO. IN TRUTH, I DO NOT KNOW. BUT I CANNOT TAKE CHANCES.
IF YOU'RE RIGHT, THIS COULD TAKE MONTHS. JUST TO KILL A COUPLE OF SUNNERS?
YOU MIS-UNDERSTAND, GERR. THERE IS NO MORE IMPORTANT TASK...

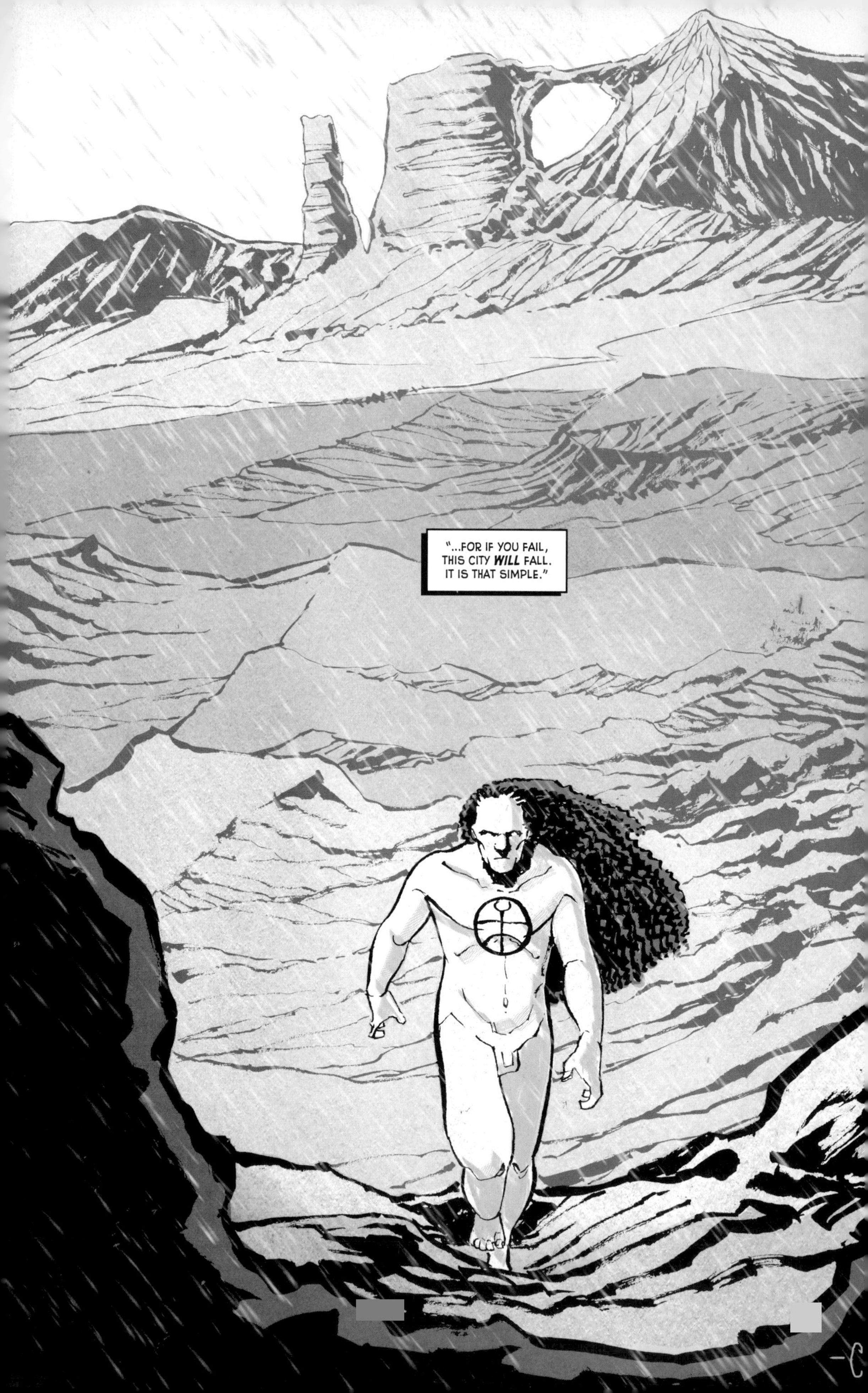
"...FOR IF YOU FAIL, THIS CITY WILL FALL. IT IS THAT SIMPLE."

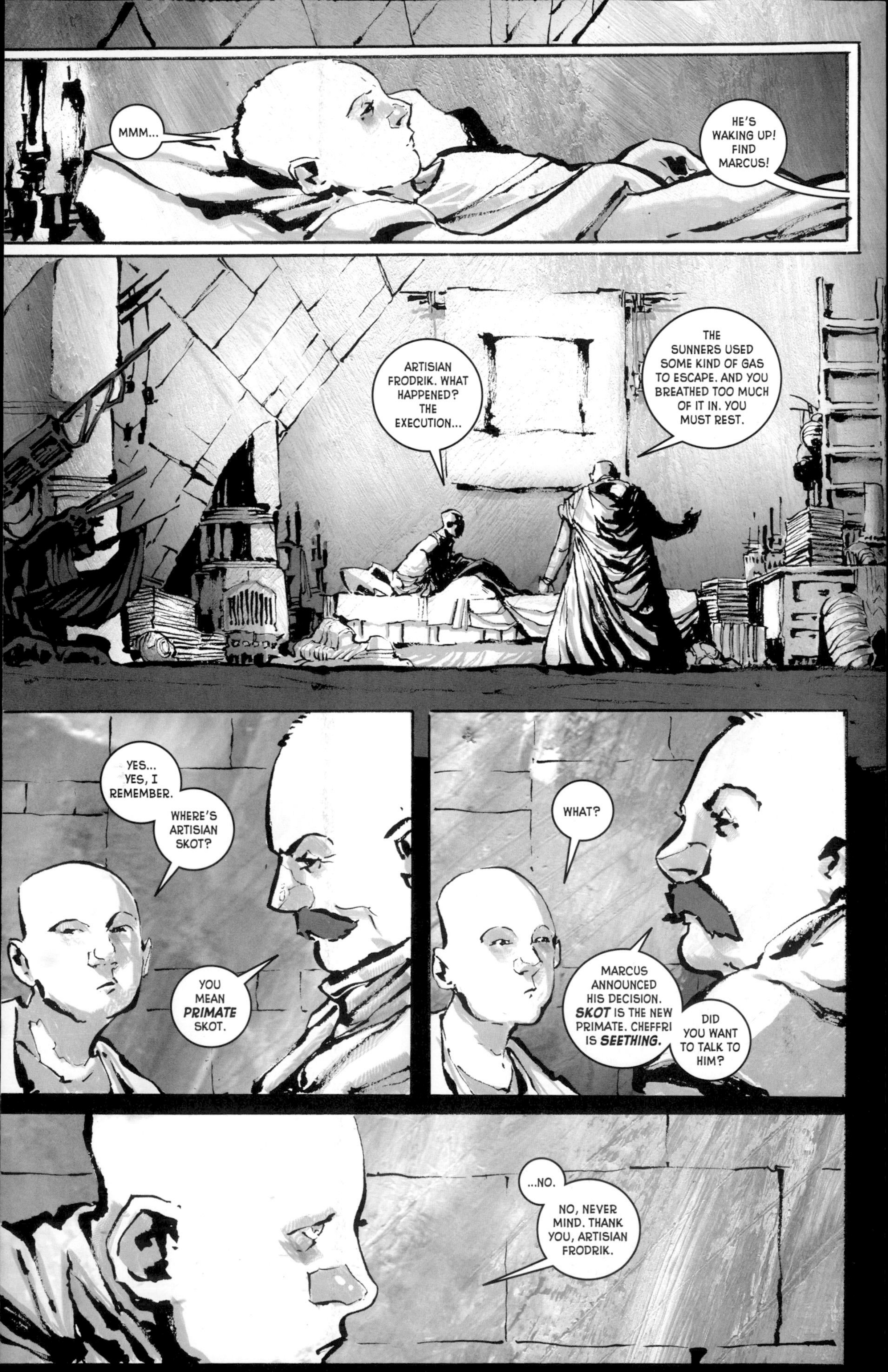
MMM...
HE'S WAKING UP! FIND MARCUS!
ARTISIAN FRODRIK. WHAT HAPPENED? THE EXECUTION...
THE SUNNERS USED SOME KIND OF GAS TO ESCAPE. AND YOU BREATHED TOO MUCH OF IT IN. YOU MUST REST.
YES... YES, I REMEMBER.
WHERE'S ARTISIAN SKOT?
YOU MEAN *PRIMATE* SKOT.
WHAT?
MARCUS ANNOUNCED HIS DECISION. *SKOT* IS THE NEW PRIMATE. CHEFFRI IS *SEETHING.*
DID YOU WANT TO TALK TO HIM?
...NO.
NO, NEVER MIND. THANK YOU, ARTISIAN FRODRIK.

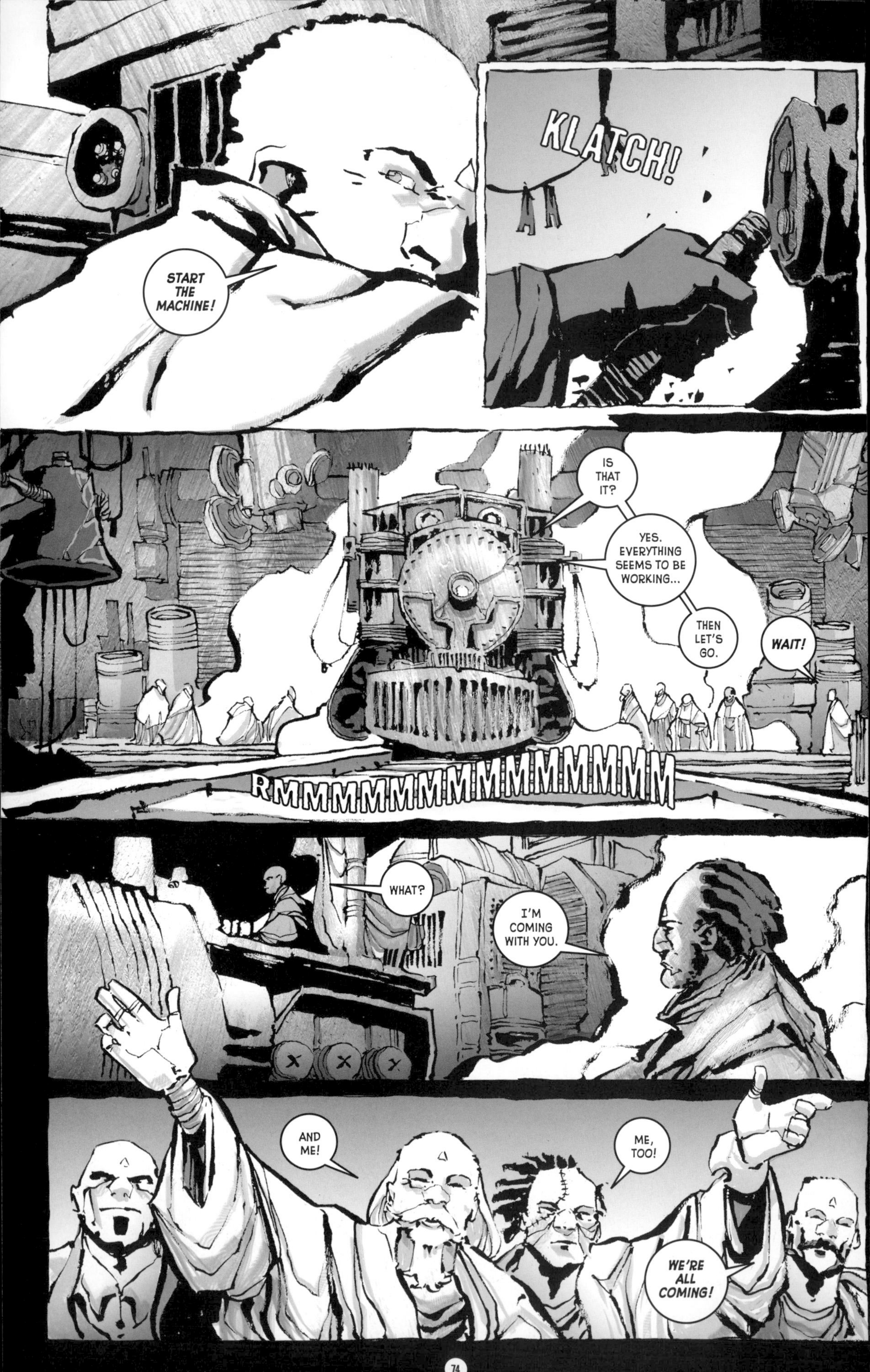
START THE MACHINE!
KLATCH!
IS THAT IT?
YES. EVERYTHING SEEMS TO BE WORKING...
THEN LET'S GO.
WAIT!
RMMMMMMMMMMMMMMMMMMM
WHAT?
I'M COMING WITH YOU.
AND ME!
ME, TOO!
WE'RE ALL COMING!

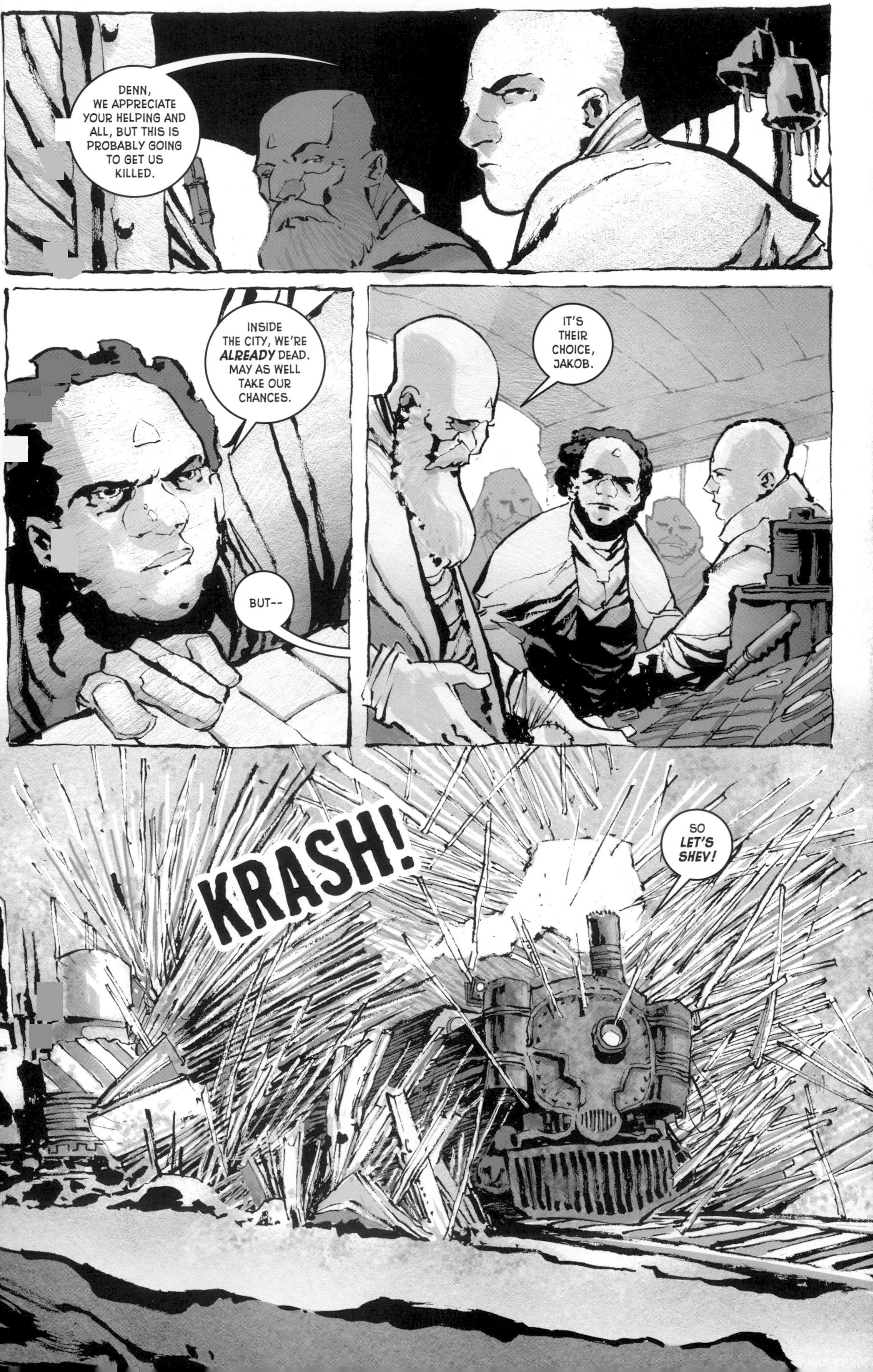
DENN, WE APPRECIATE YOUR HELPING AND ALL, BUT THIS IS PROBABLY GOING TO GET US KILLED.
INSIDE THE CITY, WE'RE *ALREADY* DEAD. MAY AS WELL TAKE OUR CHANCES.
BUT--
IT'S THEIR CHOICE, JAKOB.
KRASH!
SO *LET'S SHEV!*

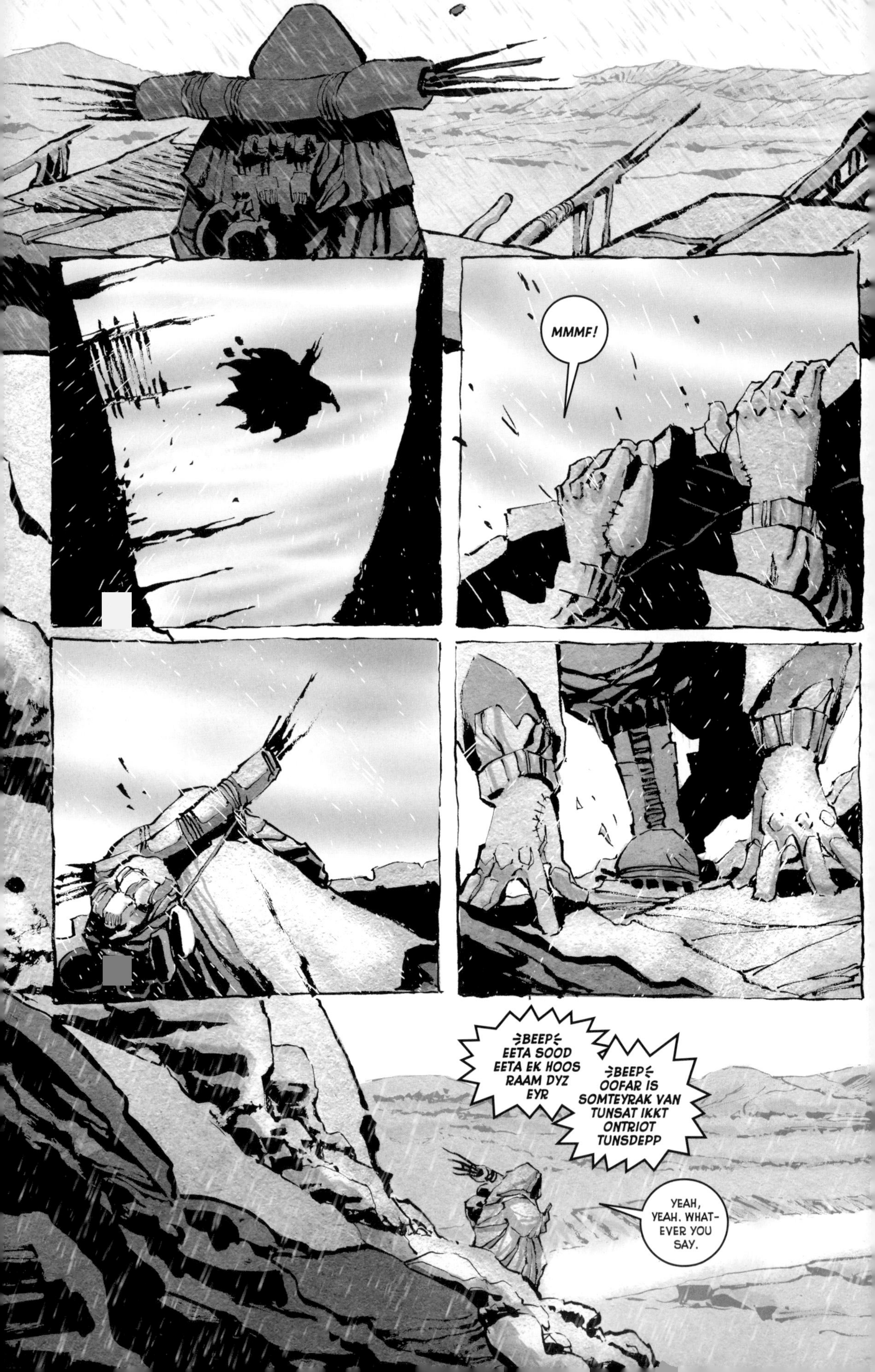
MMMF!
≶BEEP≶ EETA SOOD EETA EK HOOS RAAM DYZ EYR
≶BEEP≶ OOFAR IS SOMTEYRAK VAN TUNSAT IKKT ONTRIOT TUNSDEPP
YEAH, YEAH. WHAT-EVER YOU SAY.

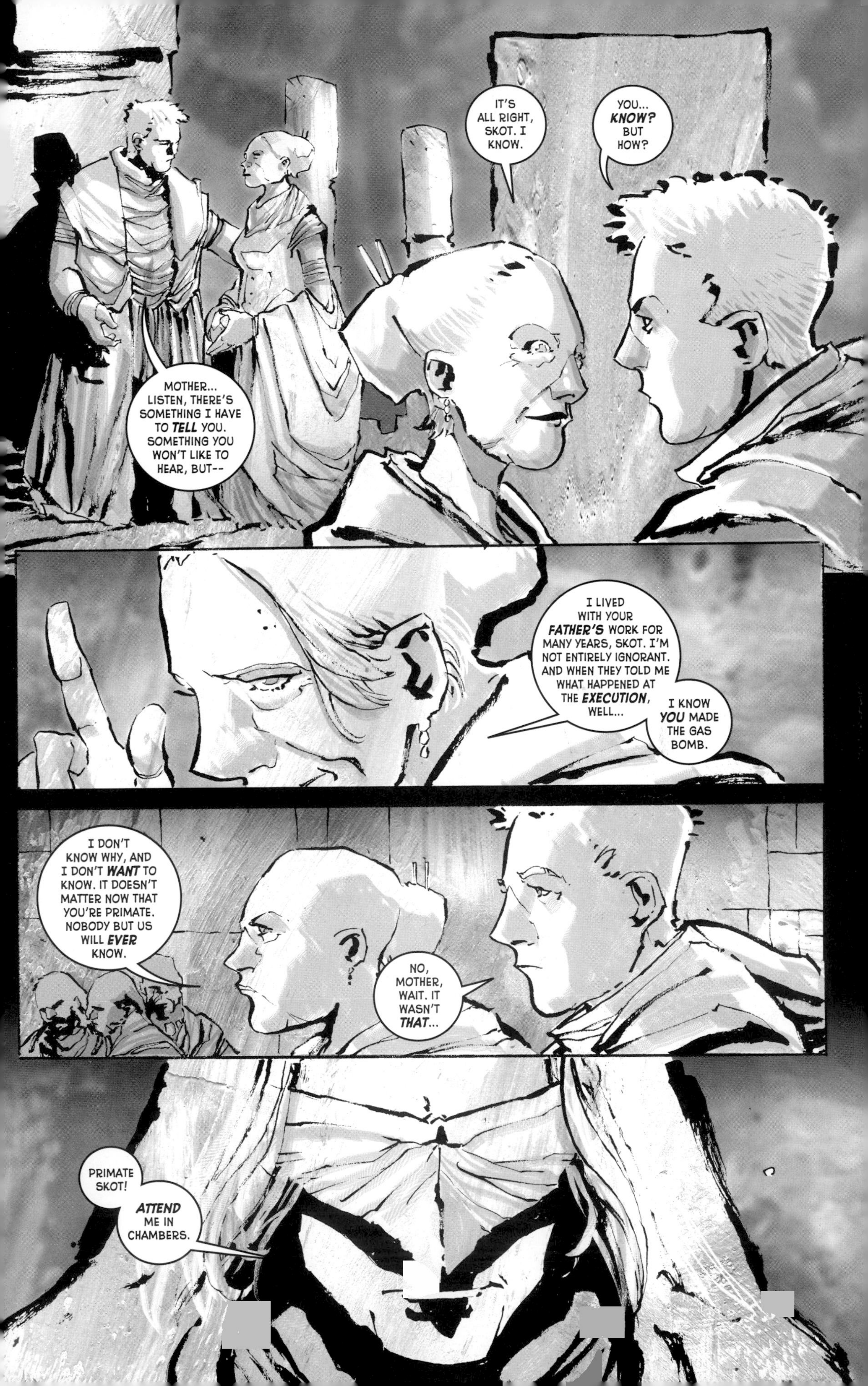
MOTHER... LISTEN, THERE'S SOMETHING I HAVE TO TELL YOU. SOMETHING YOU WON'T LIKE TO HEAR, BUT--
IT'S ALL RIGHT, SKOT. I KNOW.
YOU... KNOW? BUT HOW?
I LIVED WITH YOUR FATHER'S WORK FOR MANY YEARS, SKOT. I'M NOT ENTIRELY IGNORANT. AND WHEN THEY TOLD ME WHAT HAPPENED AT THE EXECUTION, WELL...
I KNOW YOU MADE THE GAS BOMB.
I DON'T KNOW WHY, AND I DON'T WANT TO KNOW. IT DOESN'T MATTER NOW THAT YOU'RE PRIMATE. NOBODY BUT US WILL EVER KNOW.
NO, MOTHER, WAIT. IT WASN'T THAT...
PRIMATE SKOT!
ATTEND ME IN CHAMBERS.

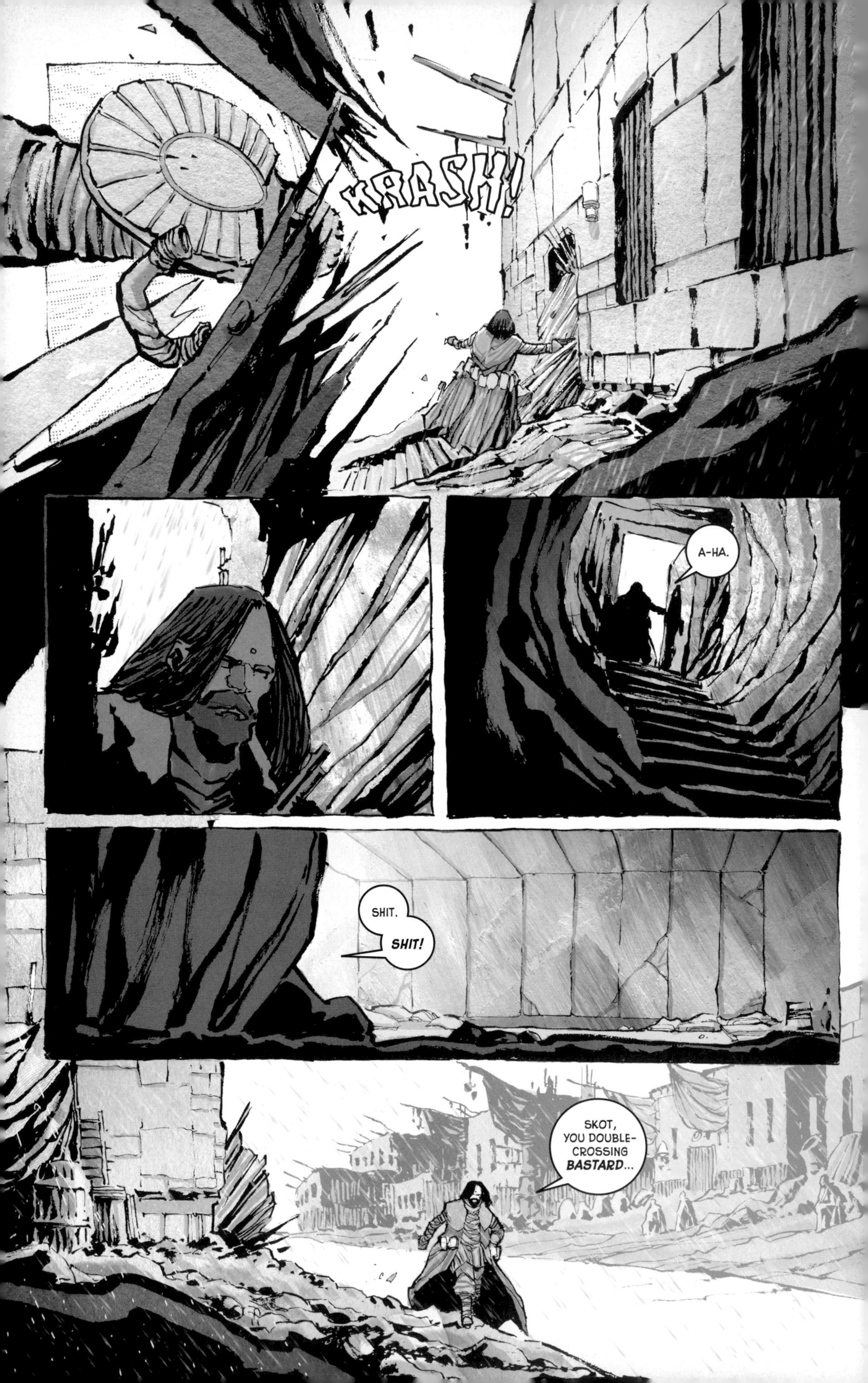
KRASH!
A-HA.
SHIT.
SHIT!
SKOT, YOU DOUBLE-CROSSING BASTARD...

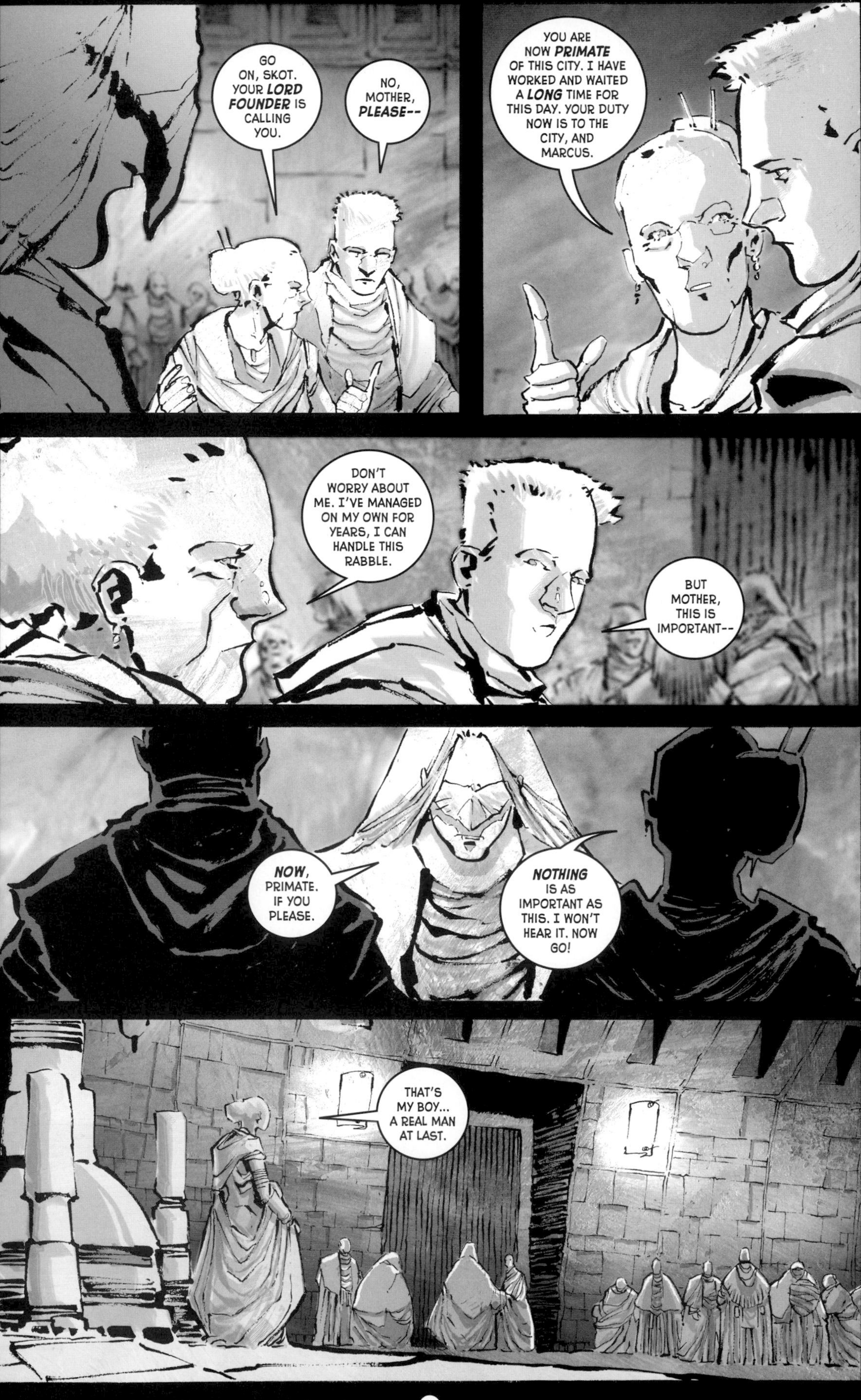
GO ON, SKOT. YOUR LORD FOUNDER IS CALLING YOU.
NO, MOTHER, PLEASE--
YOU ARE NOW PRIMATE OF THIS CITY. I HAVE WORKED AND WAITED A LONG TIME FOR THIS DAY. YOUR DUTY NOW IS TO THE CITY, AND MARCUS.
DON'T WORRY ABOUT ME. I'VE MANAGED ON MY OWN FOR YEARS, I CAN HANDLE THIS RABBLE.
BUT MOTHER, THIS IS IMPORTANT--
NOW, PRIMATE. IF YOU PLEASE.
NOTHING IS AS IMPORTANT AS THIS. I WON'T HEAR IT. NOW GO!
THAT'S MY BOY... A REAL MAN AT LAST.

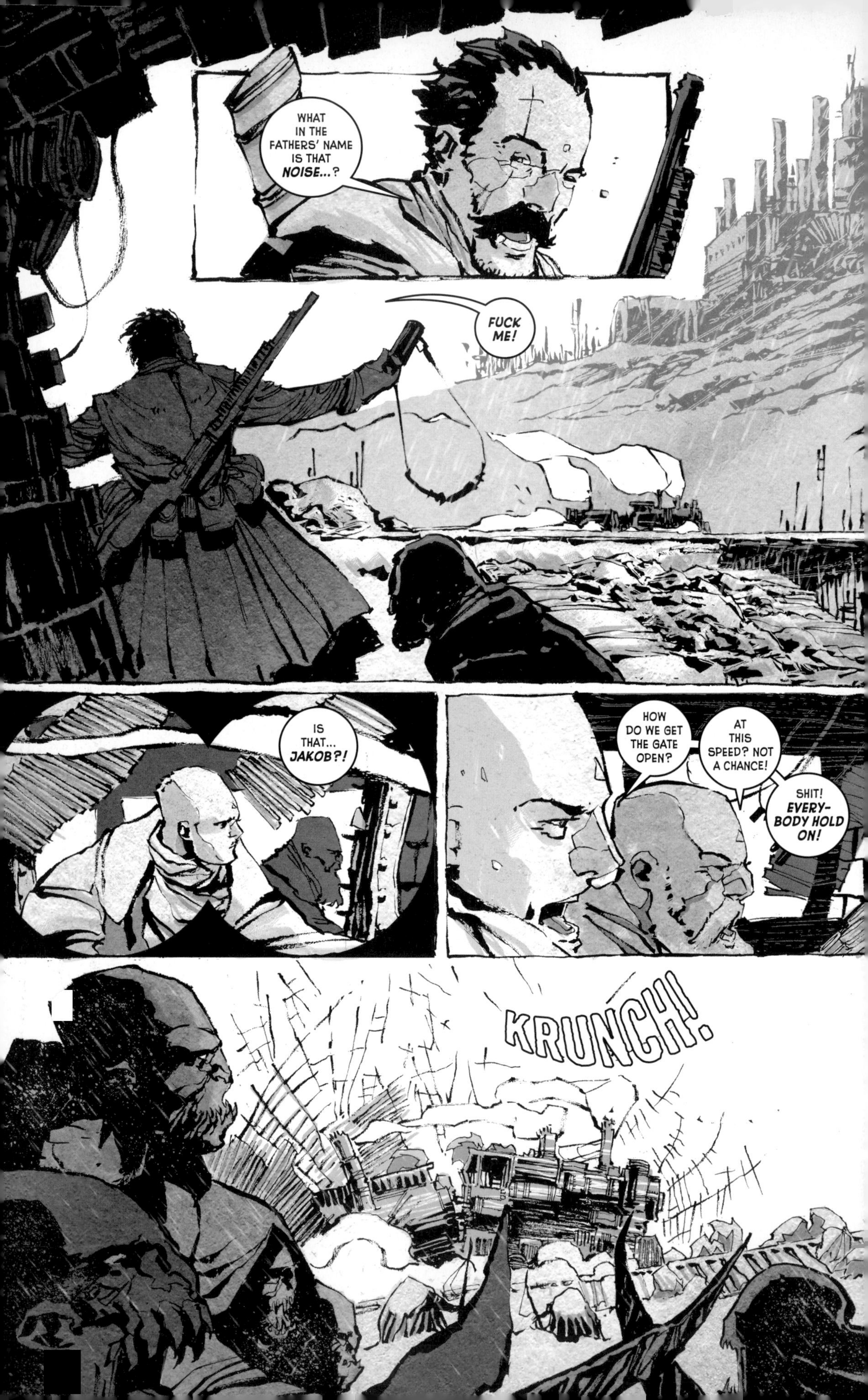
WHAT IN THE FATHERS' NAME IS THAT NOISE...?
FUCK ME!
IS THAT... JAKOB?!
HOW DO WE GET THE GATE OPEN?
AT THIS SPEED? NOT A CHANCE!
SHIT! EVERY-BODY HOLD ON!
KRUNCH!

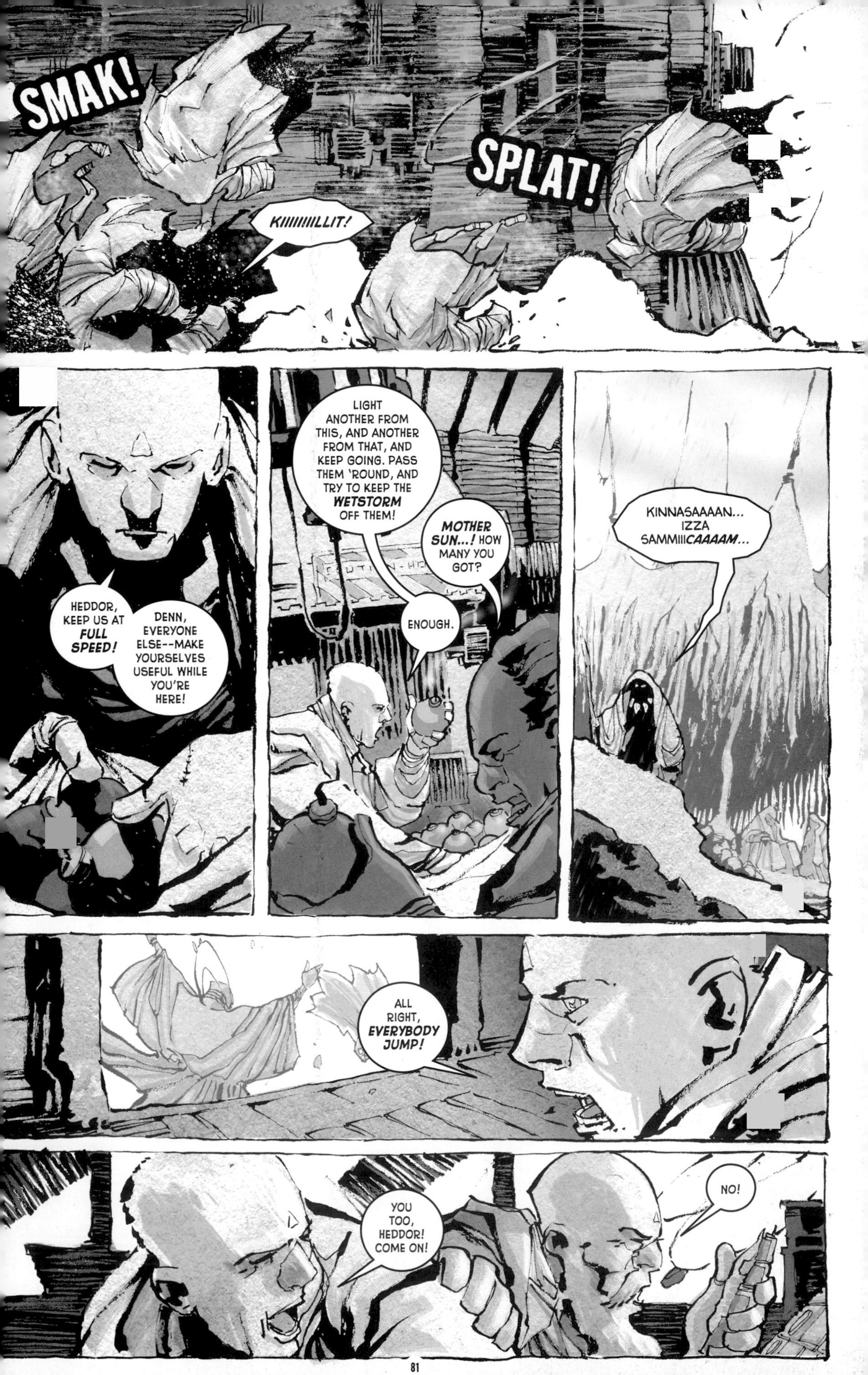
SMAK!
KIIIIIIIILLIT!
SPLAT!
HEDDOR, KEEP US AT FULL SPEED!
DENN, EVERYONE ELSE--MAKE YOURSELVES USEFUL WHILE YOU'RE HERE!
LIGHT ANOTHER FROM THIS, AND ANOTHER FROM THAT, AND KEEP GOING. PASS THEM 'ROUND, AND TRY TO KEEP THE WETSTORM OFF THEM!
MOTHER SUN...! HOW MANY YOU GOT?
ENOUGH.
KINNASAAAAN... IZZA SAMMIIICAAAAM...
ALL RIGHT, EVERYBODY JUMP!
YOU TOO, HEDDOR! COME ON!
NO!

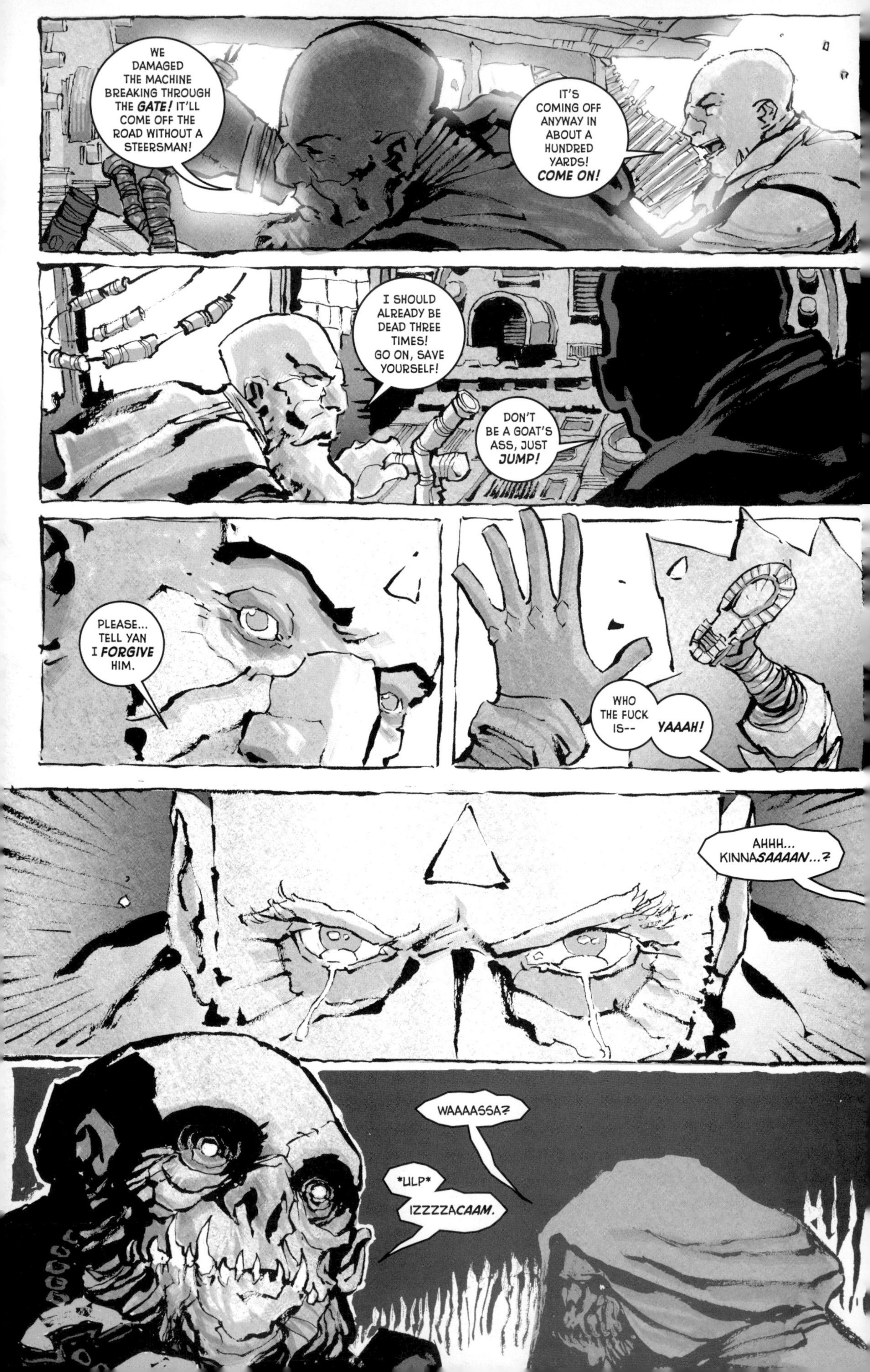
WE DAMAGED THE MACHINE BREAKING THROUGH THE GATE! IT'LL COME OFF THE ROAD WITHOUT A STEERSMAN!
IT'S COMING OFF ANYWAY IN ABOUT A HUNDRED YARDS! COME ON!
I SHOULD ALREADY BE DEAD THREE TIMES! GO ON, SAVE YOURSELF!
DON'T BE A GOAT'S ASS, JUST JUMP!
PLEASE... TELL YAN I FORGIVE HIM.
WHO THE FUCK IS--
YAAAH!
AHHH... KINNASAAAAN...?
WAAAASSA?
ULP
IZZZZACAAM.

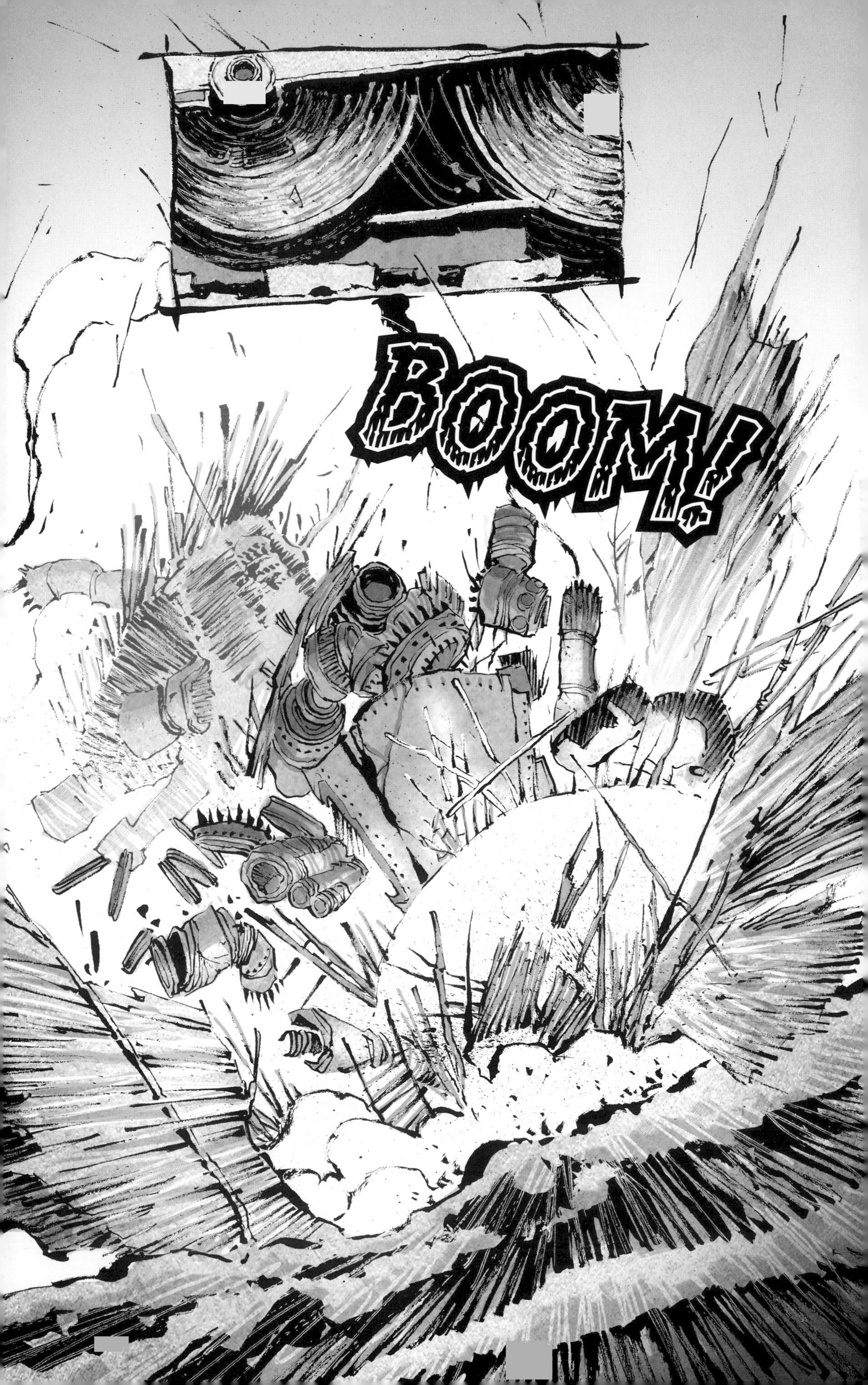
BOOM!

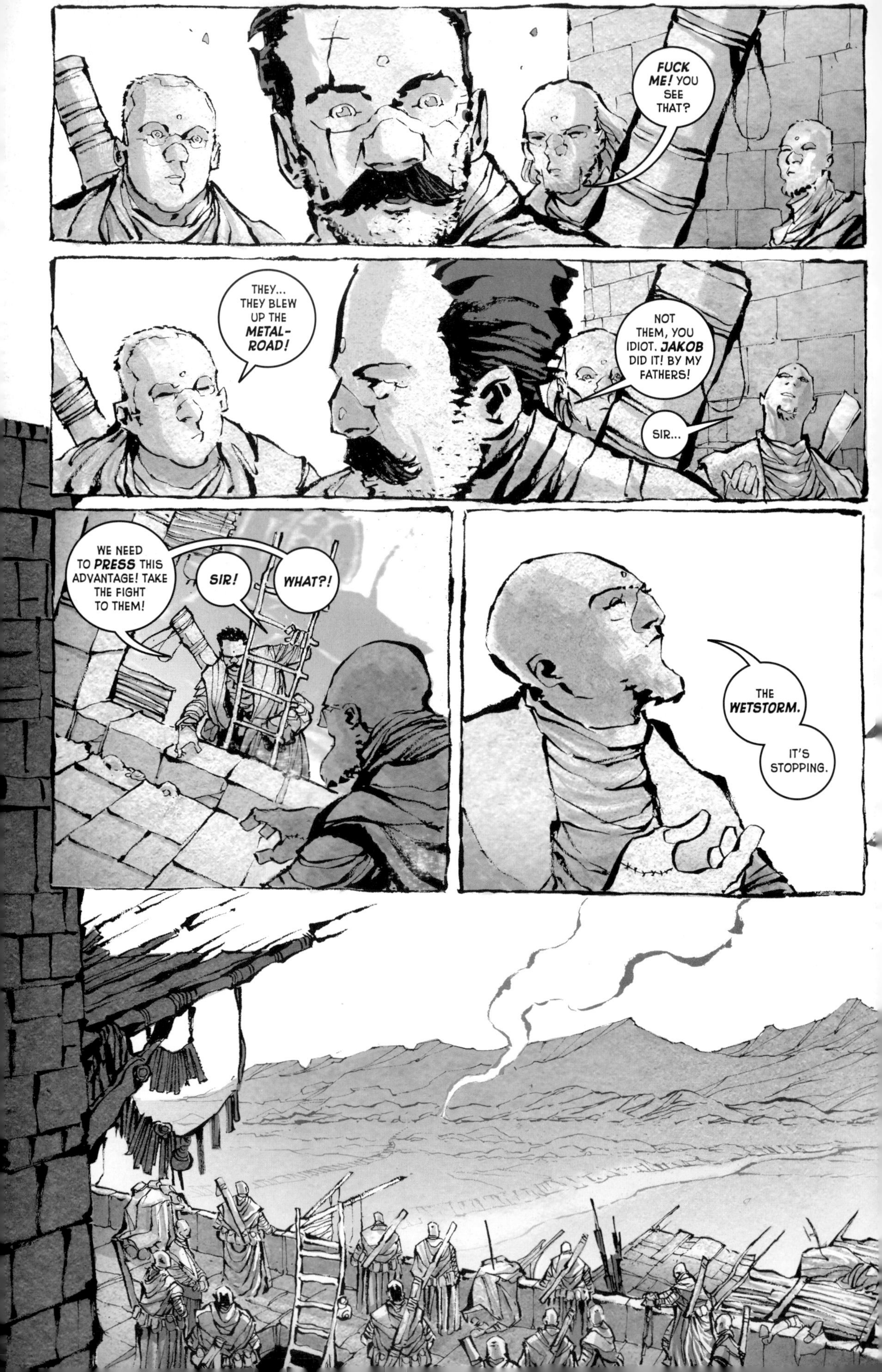
FUCK ME! YOU SEE THAT?
THEY... THEY BLEW UP THE METAL-ROAD!
NOT THEM, YOU IDIOT. JAKOB DID IT! BY MY FATHERS!
SIR...
WE NEED TO PRESS THIS ADVANTAGE! TAKE THE FIGHT TO THEM!
SIR!
WHAT?!
THE WETSTORM.
IT'S STOPPING.

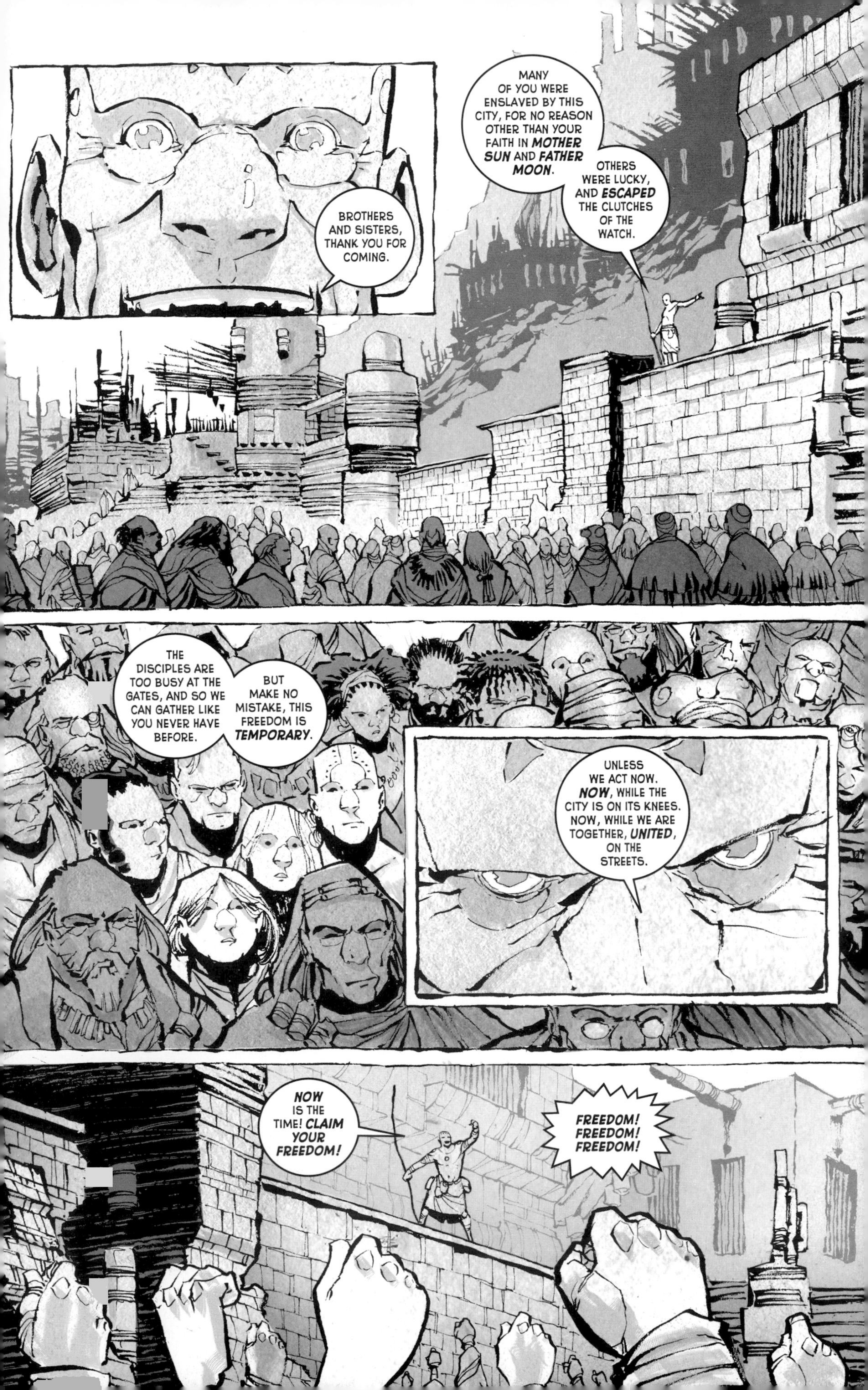
BROTHERS AND SISTERS, THANK YOU FOR COMING.
MANY OF YOU WERE ENSLAVED BY THIS CITY, FOR NO REASON OTHER THAN YOUR FAITH IN MOTHER SUN AND FATHER MOON.
OTHERS WERE LUCKY, AND ESCAPED THE CLUTCHES OF THE WATCH.
THE DISCIPLES ARE TOO BUSY AT THE GATES, AND SO WE CAN GATHER LIKE YOU NEVER HAVE BEFORE.
BUT MAKE NO MISTAKE, THIS FREEDOM IS TEMPORARY.
UNLESS WE ACT NOW. NOW, WHILE THE CITY IS ON ITS KNEES. NOW, WHILE WE ARE TOGETHER, UNITED, ON THE STREETS.
NOW IS THE TIME! CLAIM YOUR FREEDOM!
FREEDOM! FREEDOM! FREEDOM!

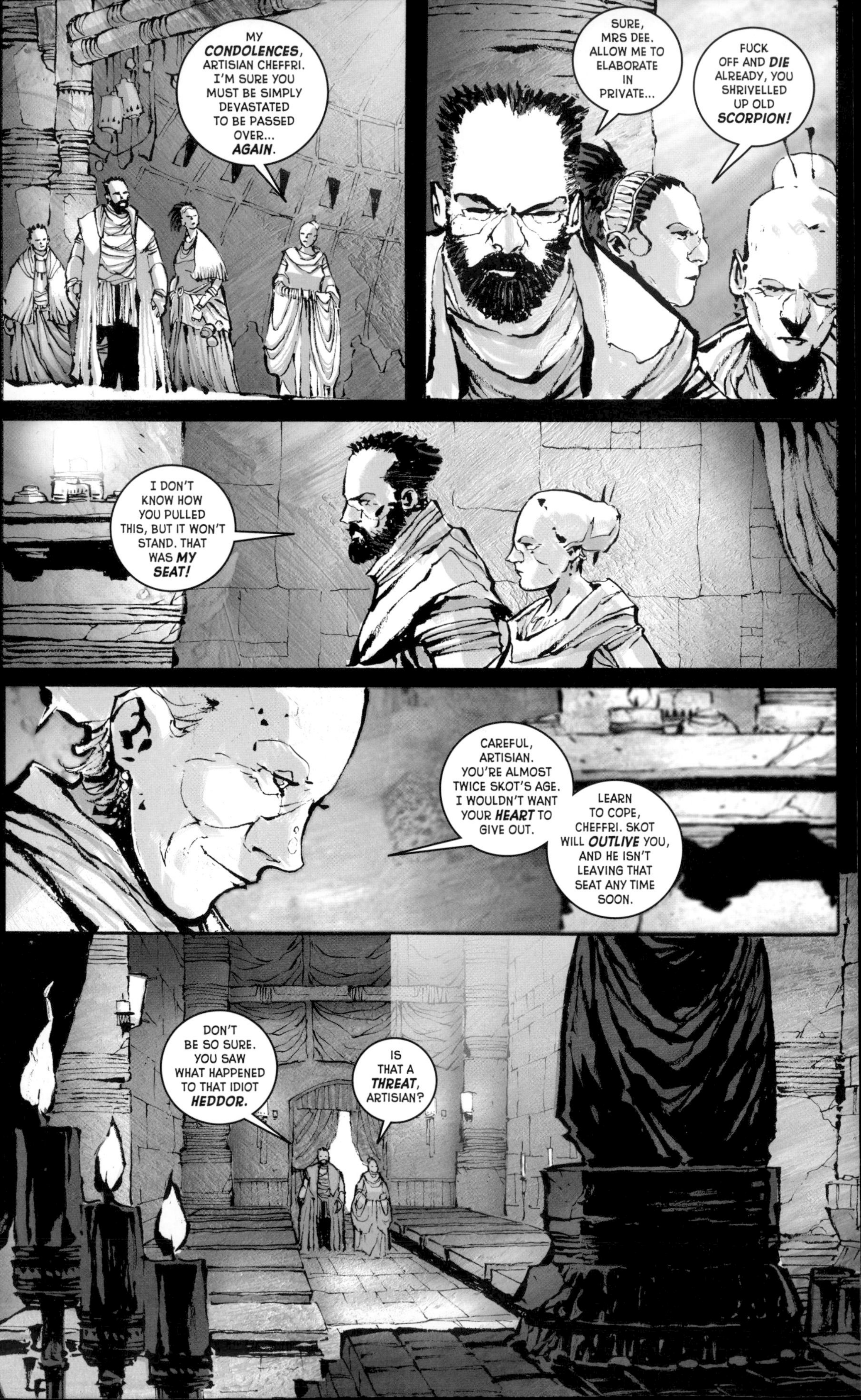
MY CONDOLENCES, ARTISIAN CHEFFRI. I'M SURE YOU MUST BE SIMPLY DEVASTATED TO BE PASSED OVER... AGAIN.
SURE, MRS DEE. ALLOW ME TO ELABORATE IN PRIVATE...
FUCK OFF AND DIE ALREADY, YOU SHRIVELLED UP OLD SCORPION!
I DON'T KNOW HOW YOU PULLED THIS, BUT IT WON'T STAND. THAT WAS MY SEAT!
CAREFUL, ARTISIAN. YOU'RE ALMOST TWICE SKOT'S AGE. I WOULDN'T WANT YOUR HEART TO GIVE OUT.
LEARN TO COPE, CHEFFRI. SKOT WILL OUTLIVE YOU, AND HE ISN'T LEAVING THAT SEAT ANY TIME SOON.
DON'T BE SO SURE. YOU SAW WHAT HAPPENED TO THAT IDIOT HEDDOR.
IS THAT A THREAT, ARTISIAN?

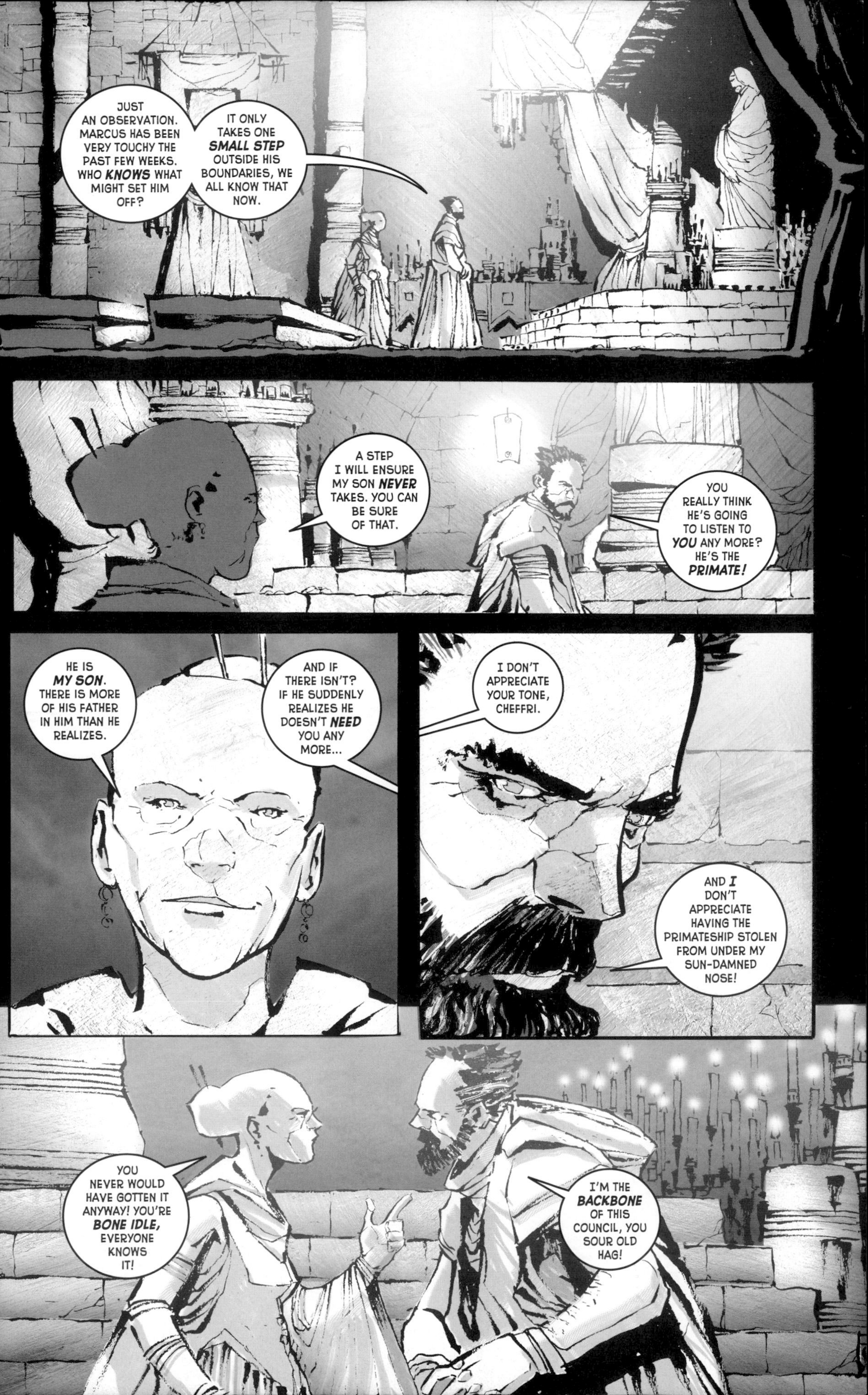
JUST AN OBSERVATION. MARCUS HAS BEEN VERY TOUCHY THE PAST FEW WEEKS. WHO KNOWS WHAT MIGHT SET HIM OFF?
IT ONLY TAKES ONE SMALL STEP OUTSIDE HIS BOUNDARIES, WE ALL KNOW THAT NOW.
A STEP I WILL ENSURE MY SON NEVER TAKES. YOU CAN BE SURE OF THAT.
YOU REALLY THINK HE'S GOING TO LISTEN TO YOU ANY MORE? HE'S THE PRIMATE!
HE IS MY SON. THERE IS MORE OF HIS FATHER IN HIM THAN HE REALIZES.
AND IF THERE ISN'T? IF HE SUDDENLY REALIZES HE DOESN'T NEED YOU ANY MORE...
I DON'T APPRECIATE YOUR TONE, CHEFFRI.
AND I DON'T APPRECIATE HAVING THE PRIMATESHIP STOLEN FROM UNDER MY SUN-DAMNED NOSE!
YOU NEVER WOULD HAVE GOTTEN IT ANYWAY! YOU'RE BONE IDLE, EVERYONE KNOWS IT!
I'M THE BACKBONE OF THIS COUNCIL, YOU SOUR OLD HAG!

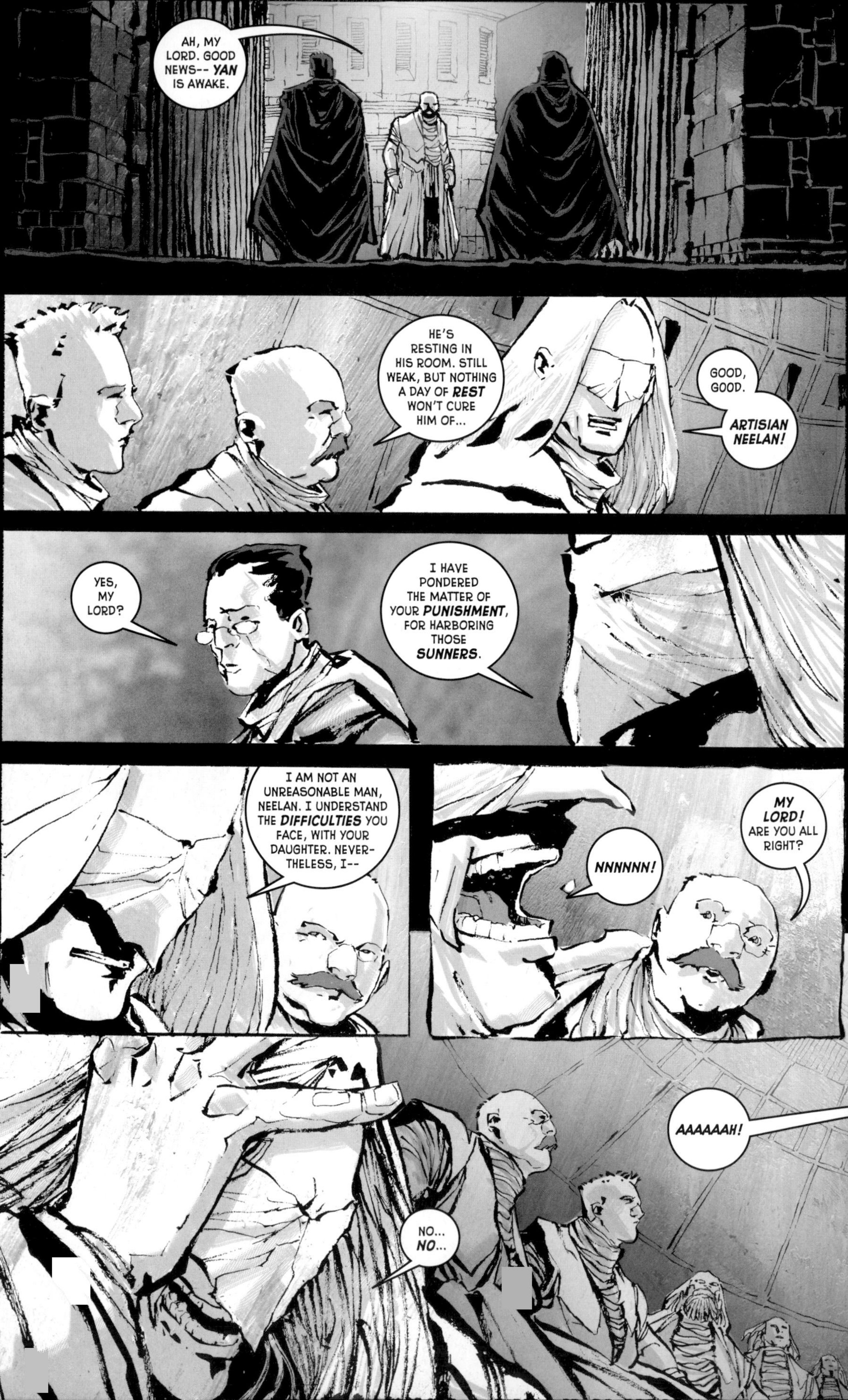

AH, MY LORD. GOOD NEWS-- YAN IS AWAKE.
HE'S RESTING IN HIS ROOM. STILL WEAK, BUT NOTHING A DAY OF REST WON'T CURE HIM OF...
GOOD, GOOD.
ARTISIAN NEELAN!
YES, MY LORD?
I HAVE PONDERED THE MATTER OF YOUR PUNISHMENT, FOR HARBORING THOSE SUNNERS.
I AM NOT AN UNREASONABLE MAN, NEELAN. I UNDERSTAND THE DIFFICULTIES YOU FACE, WITH YOUR DAUGHTER. NEVER-THELESS, I--
NNNNNN!
MY LORD! ARE YOU ALL RIGHT?
AAAAAAH!
NO... NO...

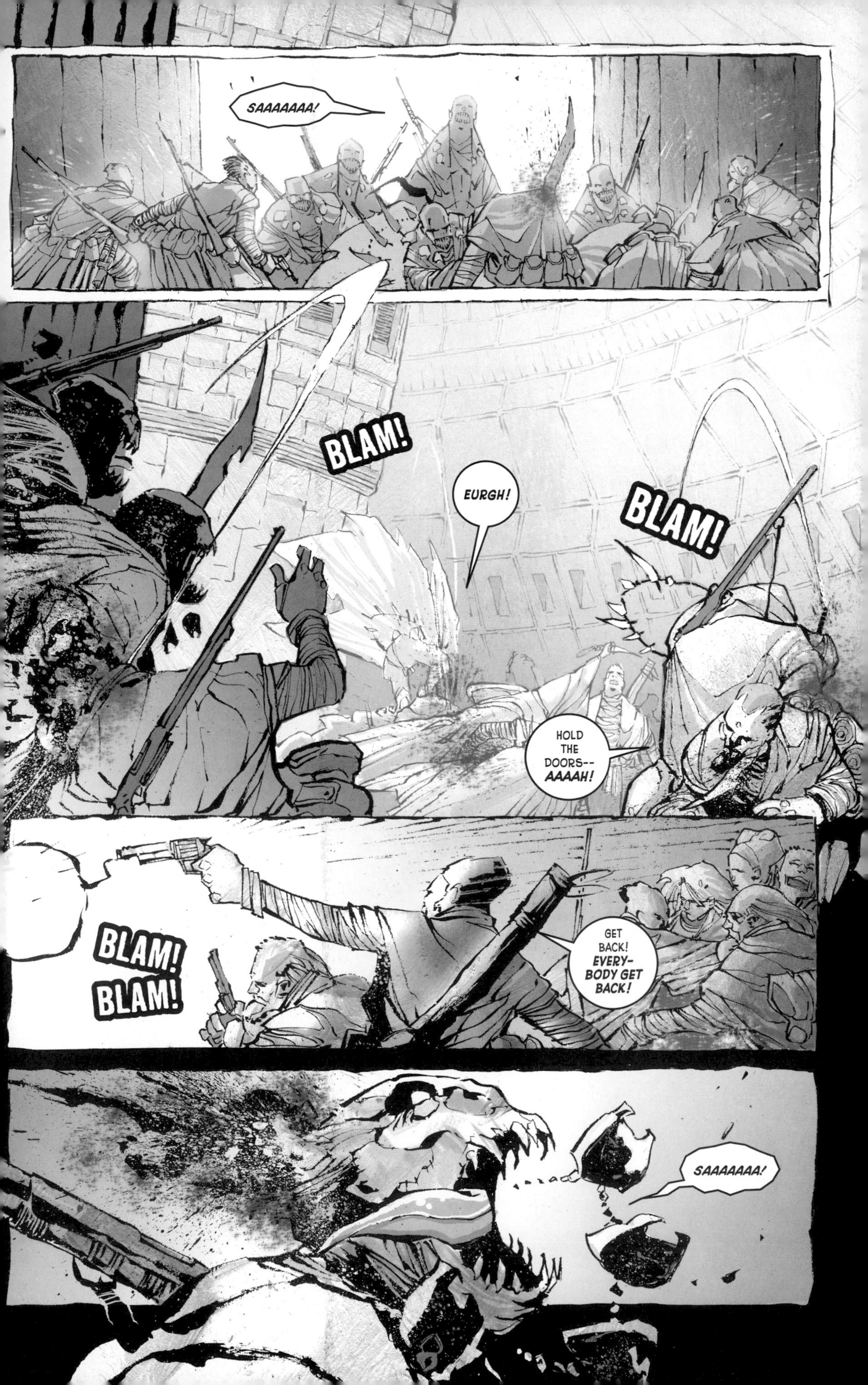
SAAAAAAA!
BLAM!
EURGH!
BLAM!
HOLD THE DOORS-- AAAAH!
BLAM! BLAM!
GET BACK! EVERY-BODY GET BACK!
SAAAAAAA!

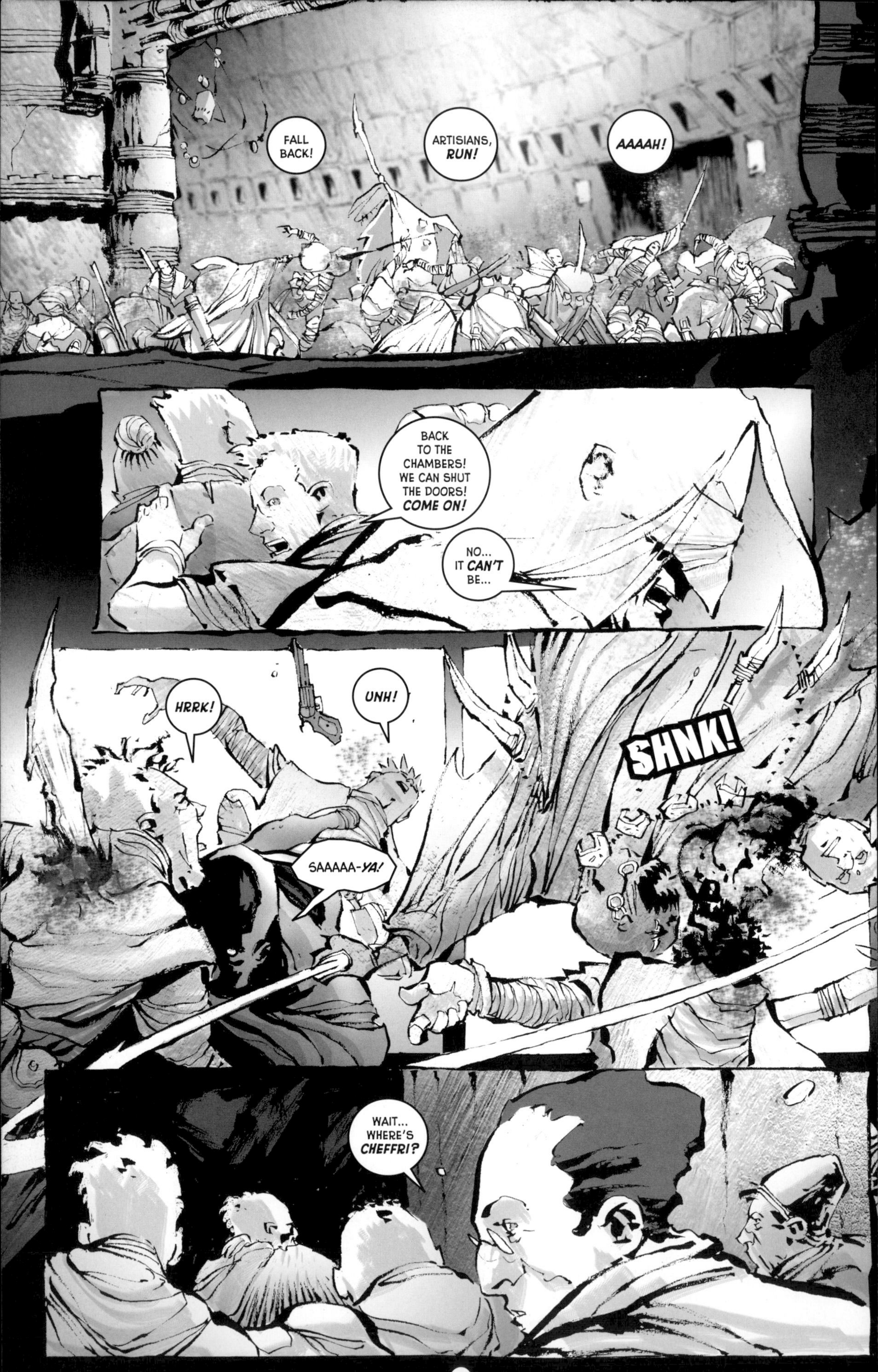
FALL BACK!
ARTISIANS, RUN!
AAAAH!
BACK TO THE CHAMBERS! WE CAN SHUT THE DOORS! COME ON!
NO... IT CAN'T BE...
HRRK!
UNH!
SHNK!
SAAAAA-YA!
WAIT... WHERE'S CHEFFRI?

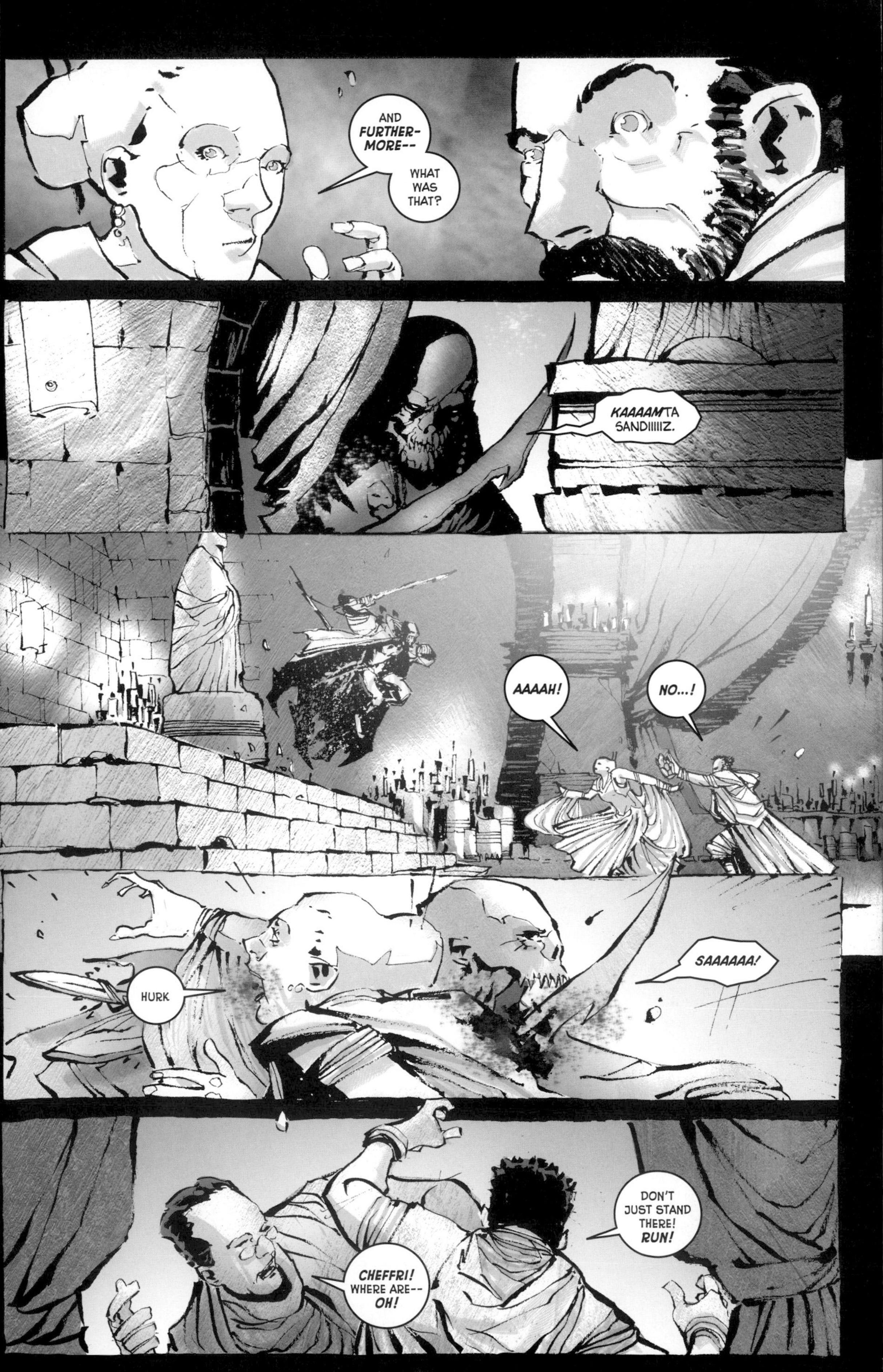
AND FURTHER-MORE--
WHAT WAS THAT?
KAAAAMTA SANDIIIIIZ.
AAAAH!
NO...!
HURK
SAAAAAA!
DON'T JUST STAND THERE! RUN!
CHEFFRI! WHERE ARE-- OH!

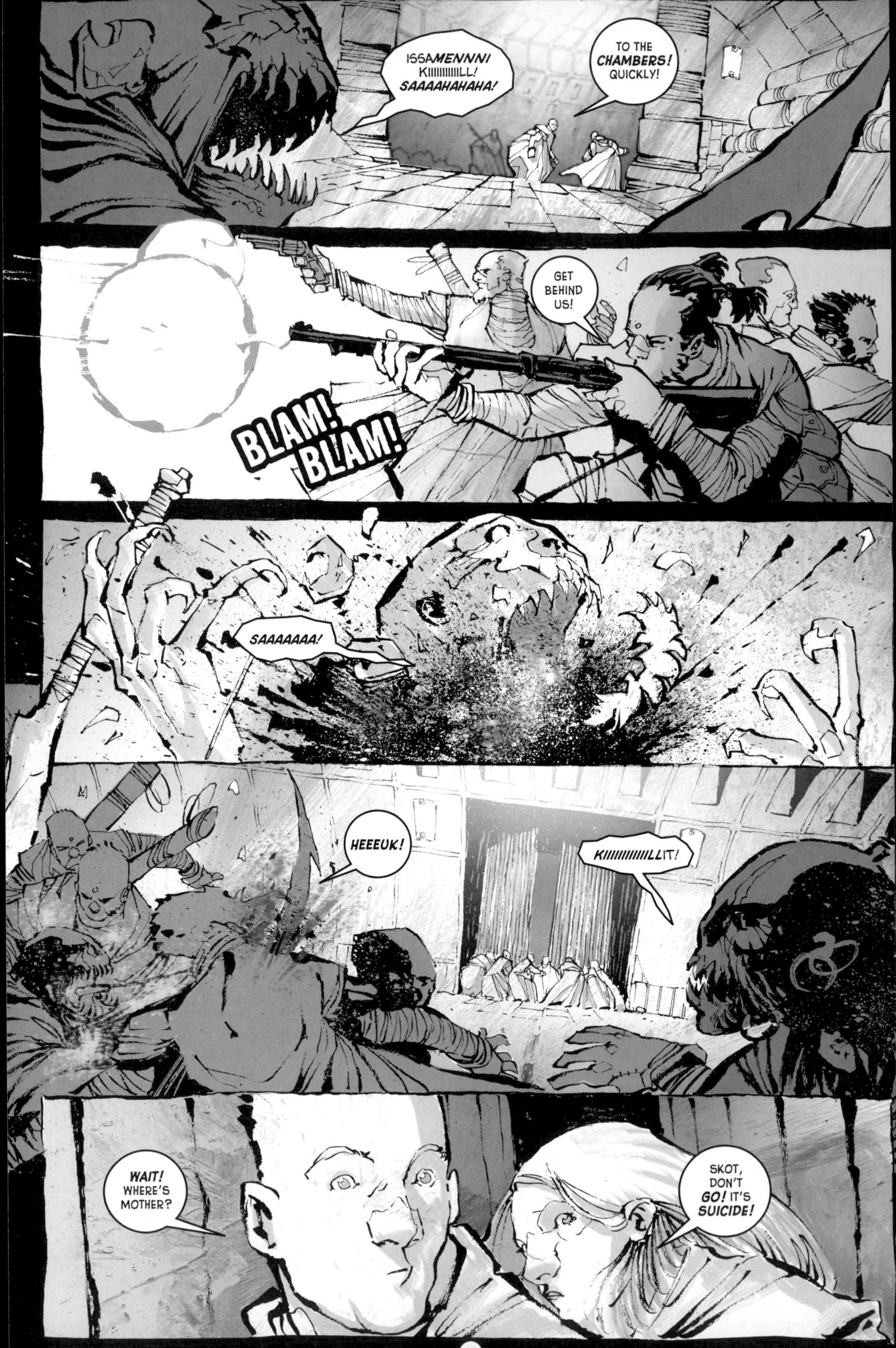
ISSA*MENNNI* KIIIIIIIIIIILL! *SAAAAHAHAHA!*
TO THE *CHAMBERS!* QUICKLY!
GET BEHIND US!
BLAM! BLAM!
SAAAAAAA!
HEEEUK!
*KIIIIIIIIIIIILL*IT!
WAIT! WHERE'S MOTHER?
SKOT, DON'T *GO!* IT'S *SUICIDE!*

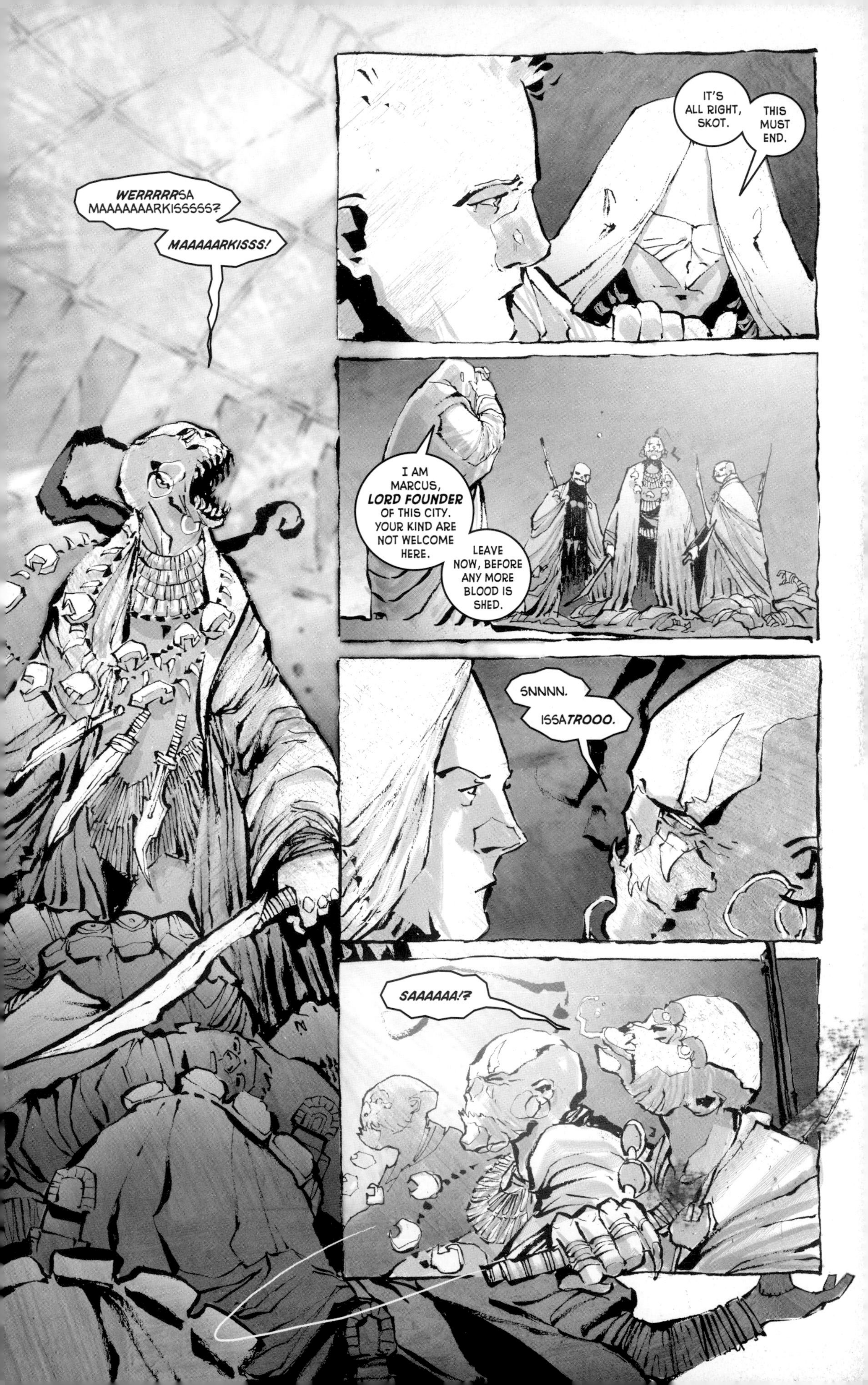

IT'S ALL RIGHT, SKOT.
THIS MUST END.
WERRRRRSA MAAAAAAAARKISSSSS?
MAAAAARKISSS!
I AM MARCUS, LORD FOUNDER OF THIS CITY. YOUR KIND ARE NOT WELCOME HERE.
LEAVE NOW, BEFORE ANY MORE BLOOD IS SHED.
SNNNN.
ISSATROOO.
SAAAAAA!?

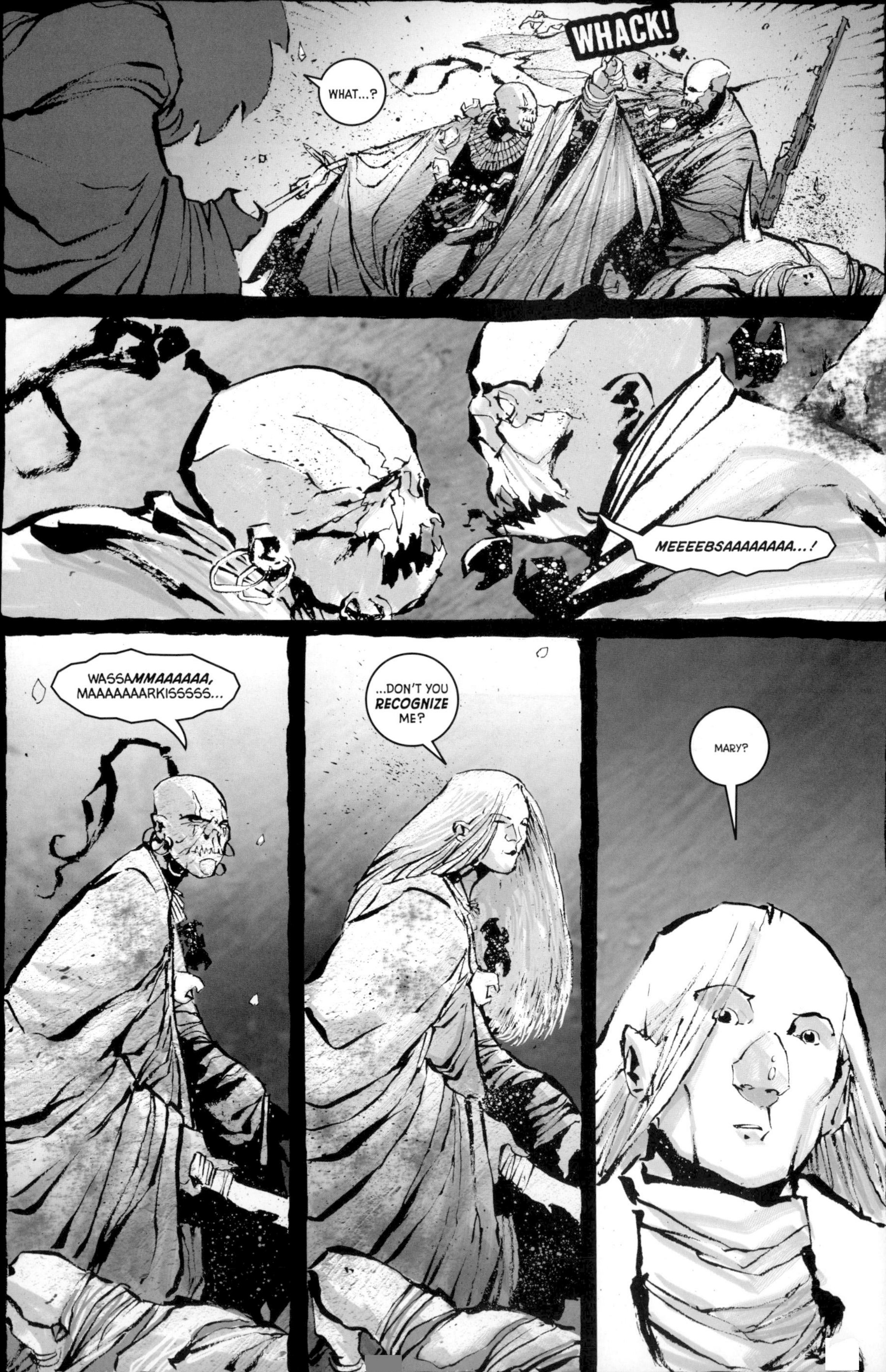
WHACK!
WHAT...?
MEEEEBSAAAAAAAA...!
WASSAMMAAAAAA, MAAAAAAARKISSSSS...
...DON'T YOU RECOGNIZE ME?
MARY?

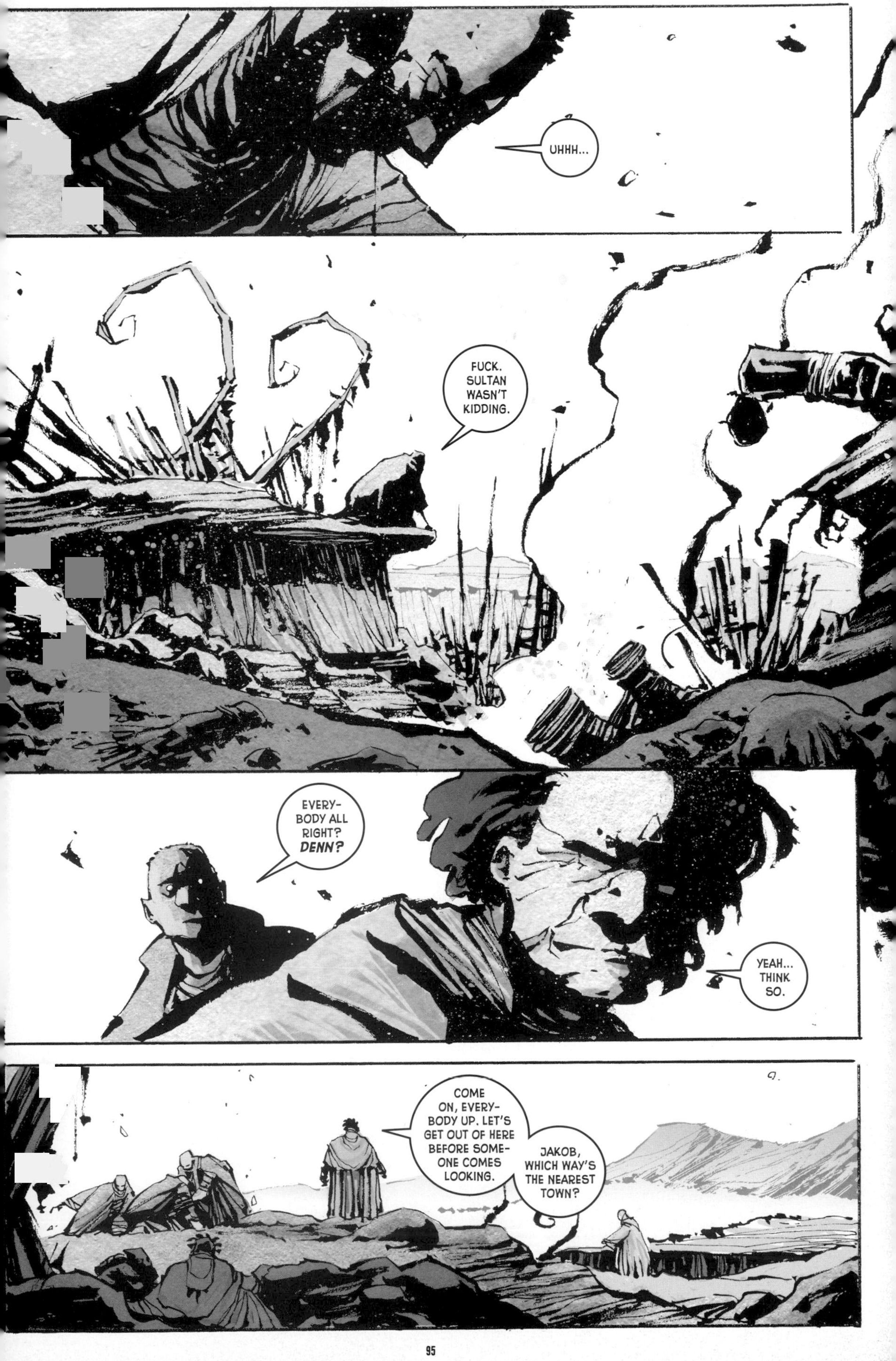
UHHH...
FUCK. SULTAN WASN'T KIDDING.
EVERY-BODY ALL RIGHT? DENN?
YEAH... THINK SO.
COME ON, EVERY-BODY UP. LET'S GET OUT OF HERE BEFORE SOME-ONE COMES LOOKING.
JAKOB, WHICH WAY'S THE NEAREST TOWN?

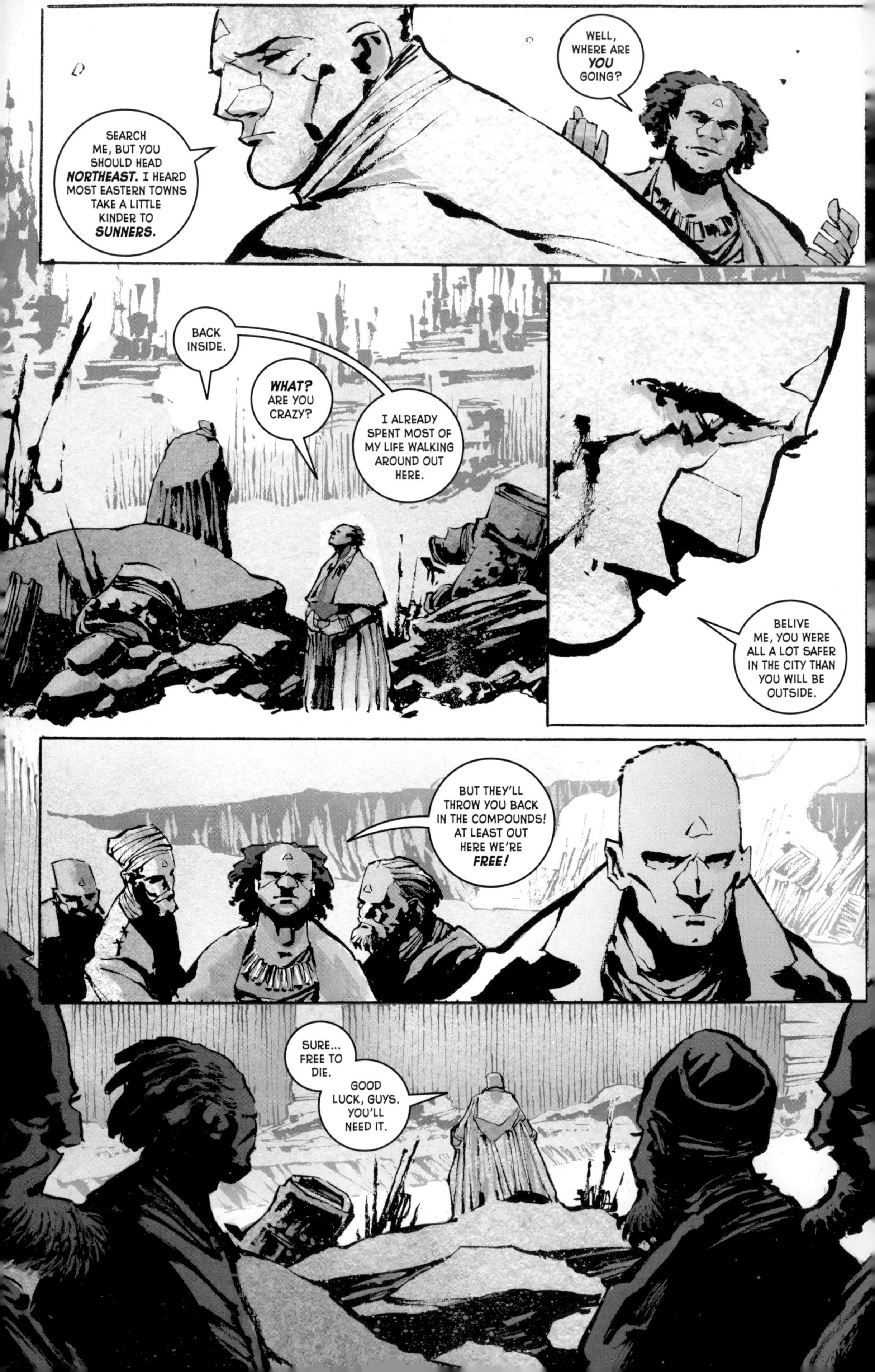
SEARCH ME, BUT YOU SHOULD HEAD NORTHEAST. I HEARD MOST EASTERN TOWNS TAKE A LITTLE KINDER TO SUNNERS.
WELL, WHERE ARE YOU GOING?
BACK INSIDE.
WHAT? ARE YOU CRAZY?
I ALREADY SPENT MOST OF MY LIFE WALKING AROUND OUT HERE.
BELIVE ME, YOU WERE ALL A LOT SAFER IN THE CITY THAN YOU WILL BE OUTSIDE.
BUT THEY'LL THROW YOU BACK IN THE COMPOUNDS! AT LEAST OUT HERE WE'RE FREE!
SURE... FREE TO DIE.
GOOD LUCK, GUYS. YOU'LL NEED IT.

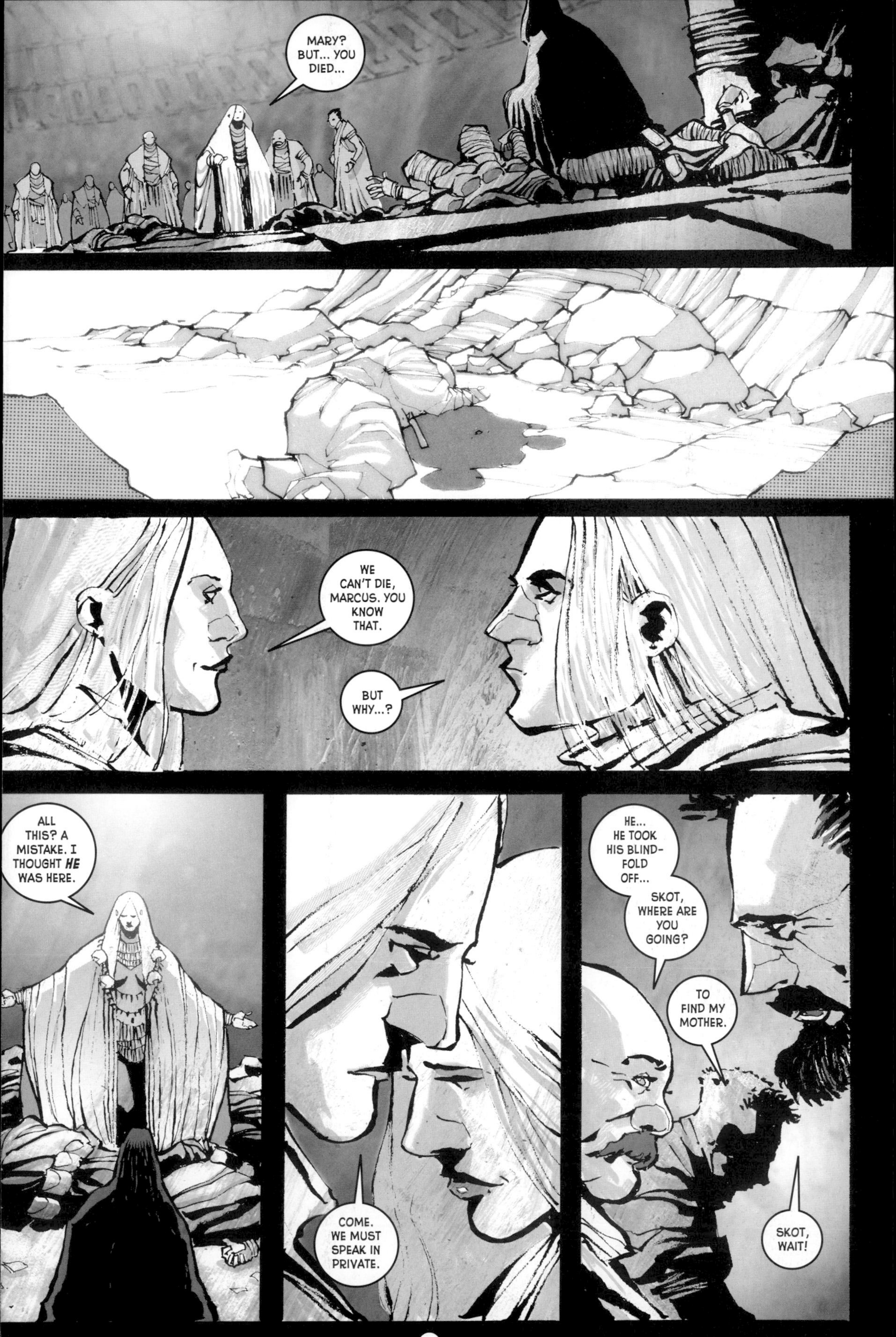
MARY? BUT... YOU DIED...
WE CAN'T DIE, MARCUS. YOU KNOW THAT.
BUT WHY...?
ALL THIS? A MISTAKE. I THOUGHT *HE* WAS HERE.
COME. WE MUST SPEAK IN PRIVATE.
HE... HE TOOK HIS BLIND-FOLD OFF...
SKOT, WHERE ARE YOU GOING?
TO FIND MY MOTHER.
SKOT, WAIT!

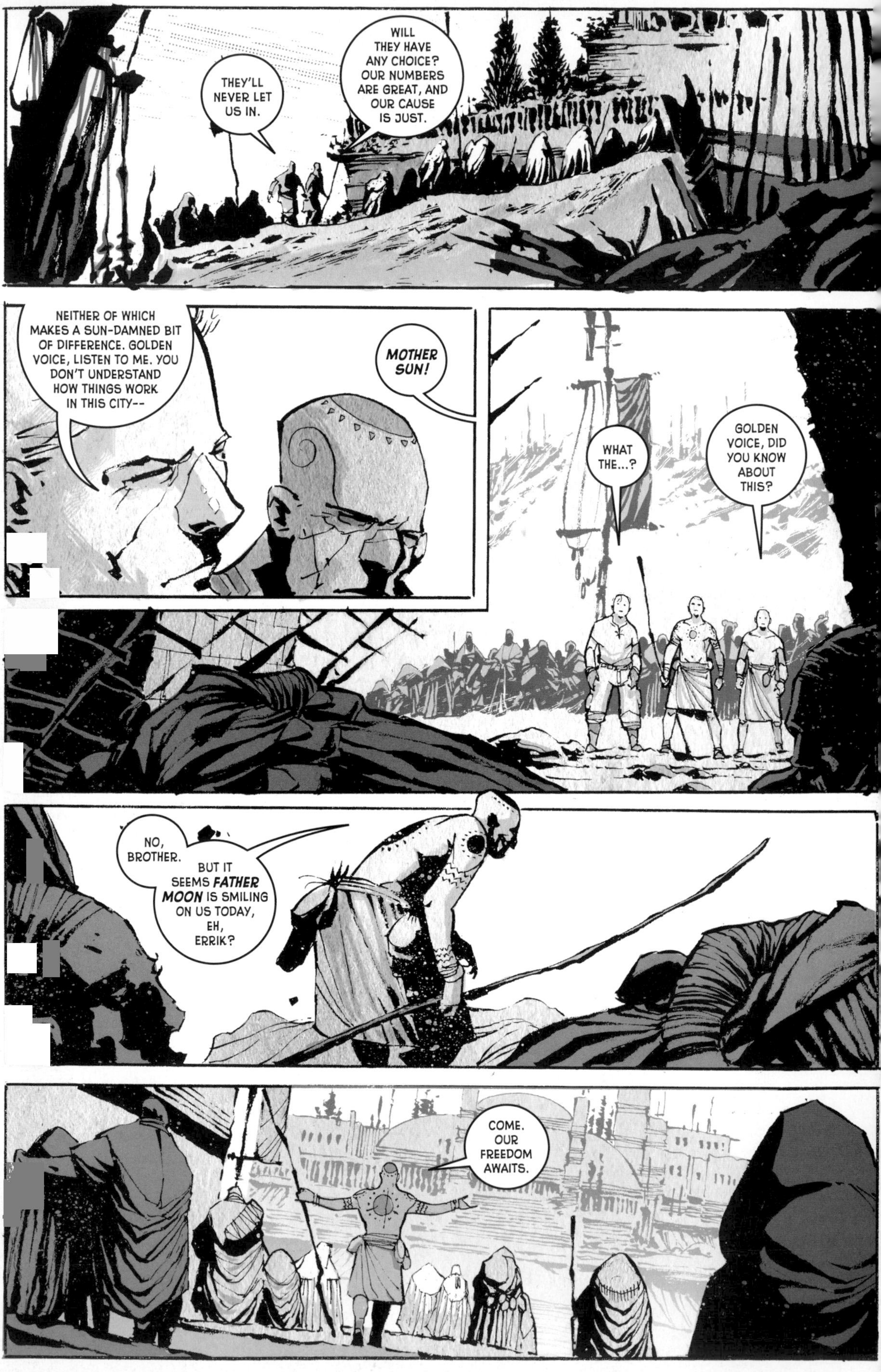
THEY'LL NEVER LET US IN.
WILL THEY HAVE ANY CHOICE? OUR NUMBERS ARE GREAT, AND OUR CAUSE IS JUST.
NEITHER OF WHICH MAKES A SUN-DAMNED BIT OF DIFFERENCE. GOLDEN VOICE, LISTEN TO ME. YOU DON'T UNDERSTAND HOW THINGS WORK IN THIS CITY--
MOTHER SUN!
WHAT THE...?
GOLDEN VOICE, DID YOU KNOW ABOUT THIS?
NO, BROTHER.
BUT IT SEEMS FATHER MOON IS SMILING ON US TODAY, EH, ERRIK?
COME. OUR FREEDOM AWAITS.

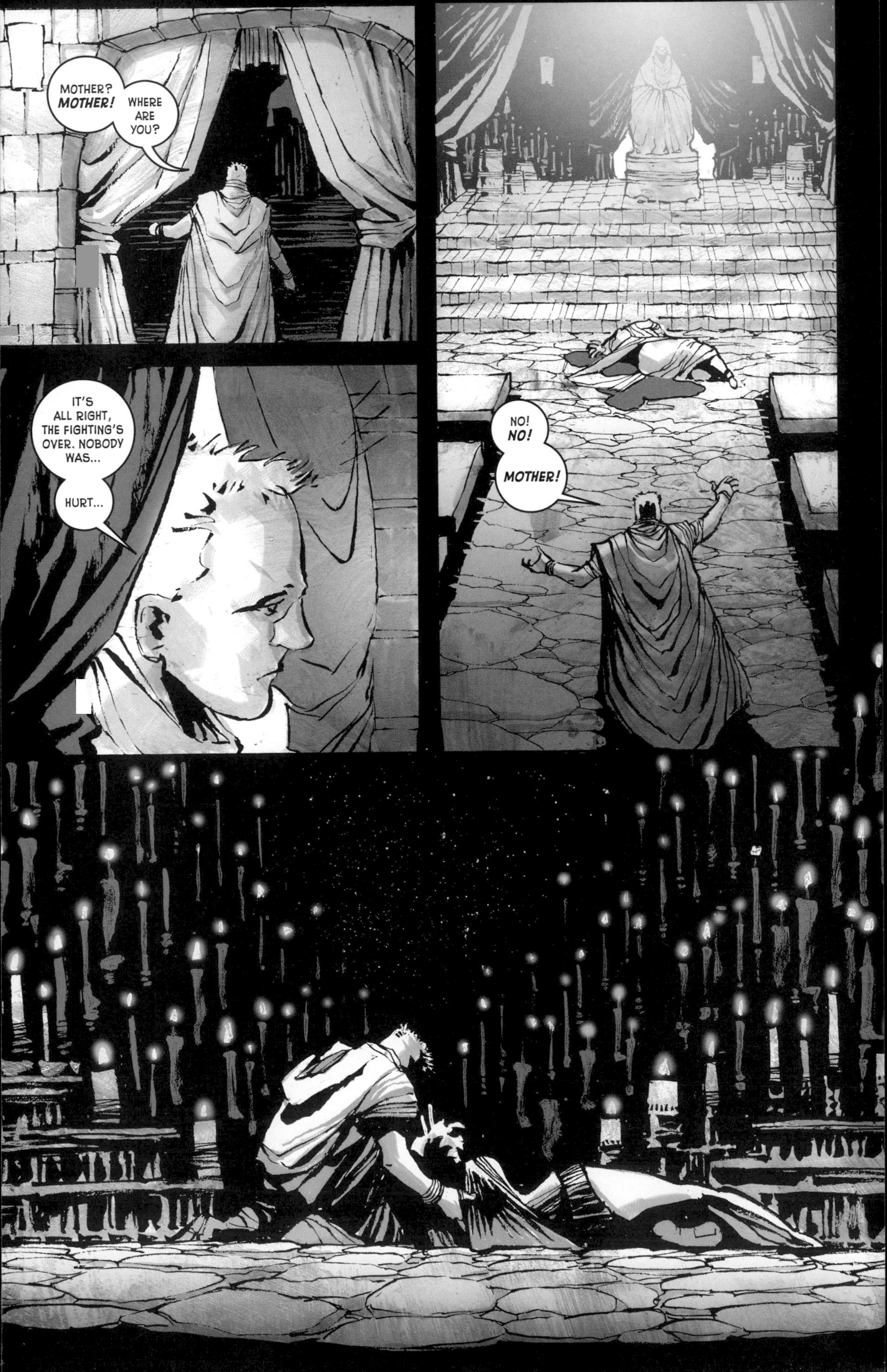
MOTHER? MOTHER!
WHERE ARE YOU?
IT'S ALL RIGHT, THE FIGHTING'S OVER. NOBODY WAS...
HURT...
NO! NO!
MOTHER!

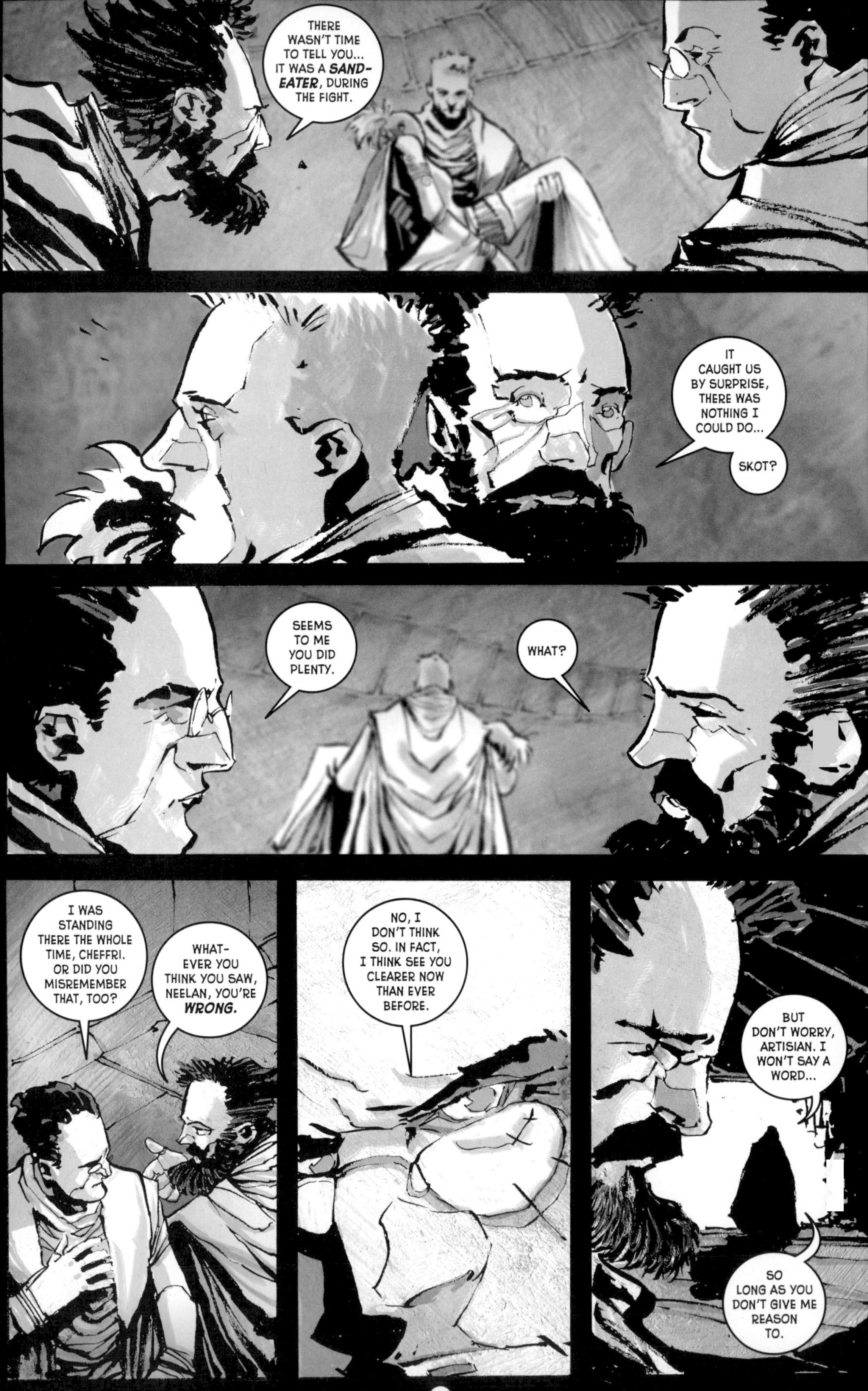
THERE WASN'T TIME TO TELL YOU... IT WAS A **SAND-EATER**, DURING THE FIGHT.
IT CAUGHT US BY SURPRISE, THERE WAS NOTHING I COULD DO...
SKOT?
SEEMS TO ME YOU DID PLENTY.
WHAT?
I WAS STANDING THERE THE WHOLE TIME, CHEFFRI. OR DID YOU MISREMEMBER THAT, TOO?
WHATEVER YOU THINK YOU SAW, NEELAN, YOU'RE ***WRONG.***
NO, I DON'T THINK SO. IN FACT, I THINK SEE YOU CLEARER NOW THAN EVER BEFORE.
BUT DON'T WORRY, ARTISIAN. I WON'T SAY A WORD...
SO LONG AS YOU DON'T GIVE ME REASON TO.

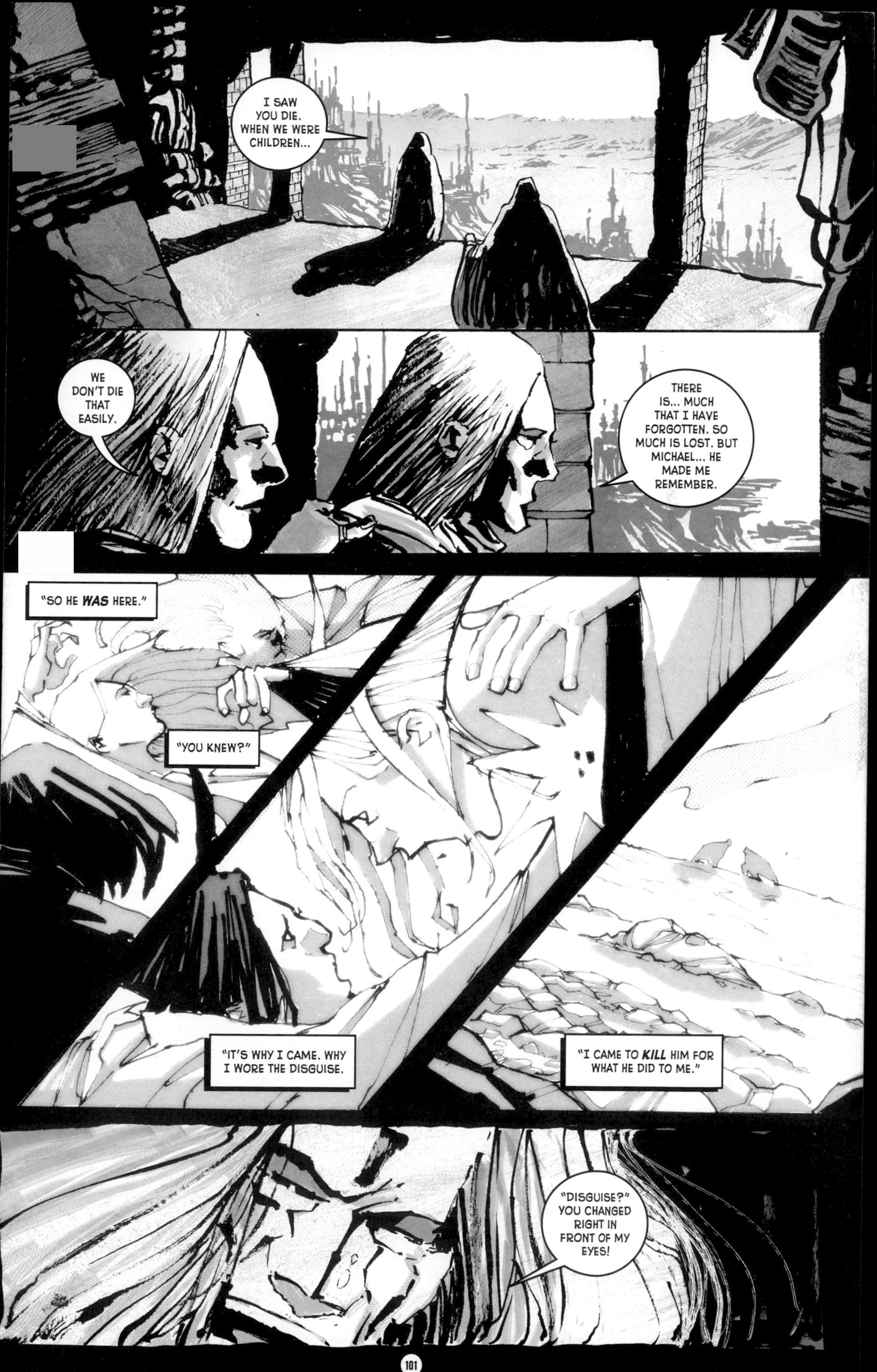
I SAW YOU DIE. WHEN WE WERE CHILDREN...
WE DON'T DIE THAT EASILY.
THERE IS... MUCH THAT I HAVE FORGOTTEN. SO MUCH IS LOST. BUT MICHAEL... HE MADE ME REMEMBER.
"SO HE WAS HERE."
"YOU KNEW?"
"IT'S WHY I CAME. WHY I WORE THE DISGUISE.
"I CAME TO KILL HIM FOR WHAT HE DID TO ME."
"DISGUISE?" YOU CHANGED RIGHT IN FRONT OF MY EYES!

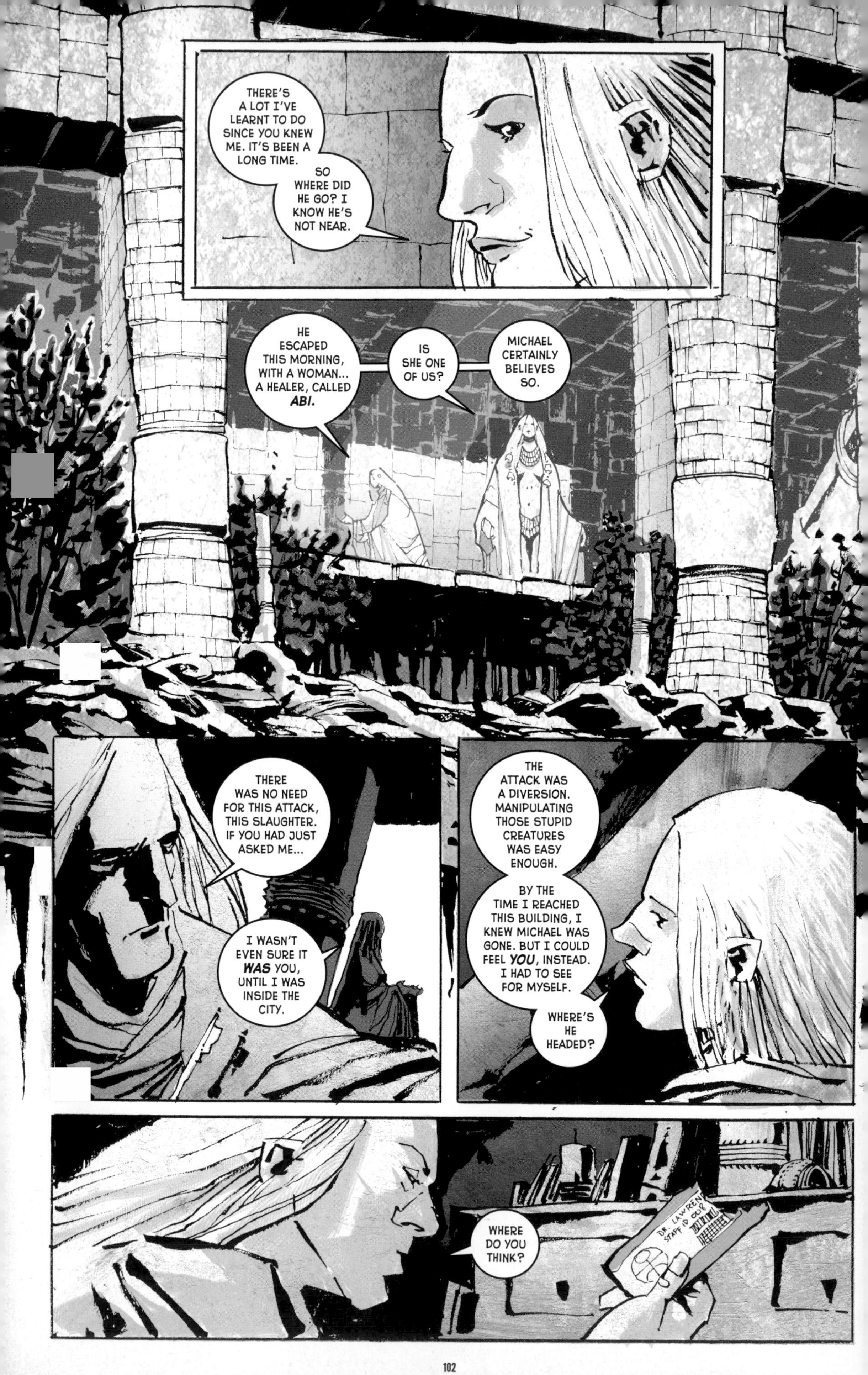
THERE'S A LOT I'VE LEARNT TO DO SINCE YOU KNEW ME. IT'S BEEN A LONG TIME.
SO WHERE DID HE GO? I KNOW HE'S NOT NEAR.
HE ESCAPED THIS MORNING, WITH A WOMAN... A HEALER, CALLED *ABI.*
IS SHE ONE OF US?
MICHAEL CERTAINLY BELIEVES SO.
THERE WAS NO NEED FOR THIS ATTACK, THIS SLAUGHTER. IF YOU HAD JUST ASKED ME...
I WASN'T EVEN SURE IT *WAS* YOU, UNTIL I WAS INSIDE THE CITY.
THE ATTACK WAS A DIVERSION. MANIPULATING THOSE STUPID CREATURES WAS EASY ENOUGH.
BY THE TIME I REACHED THIS BUILDING, I KNEW MICHAEL WAS GONE. BUT I COULD FEEL *YOU*, INSTEAD. I HAD TO SEE FOR MYSELF.
WHERE'S HE HEADED?
WHERE DO YOU THINK?
DR. LAWREN
STAFF ID 008

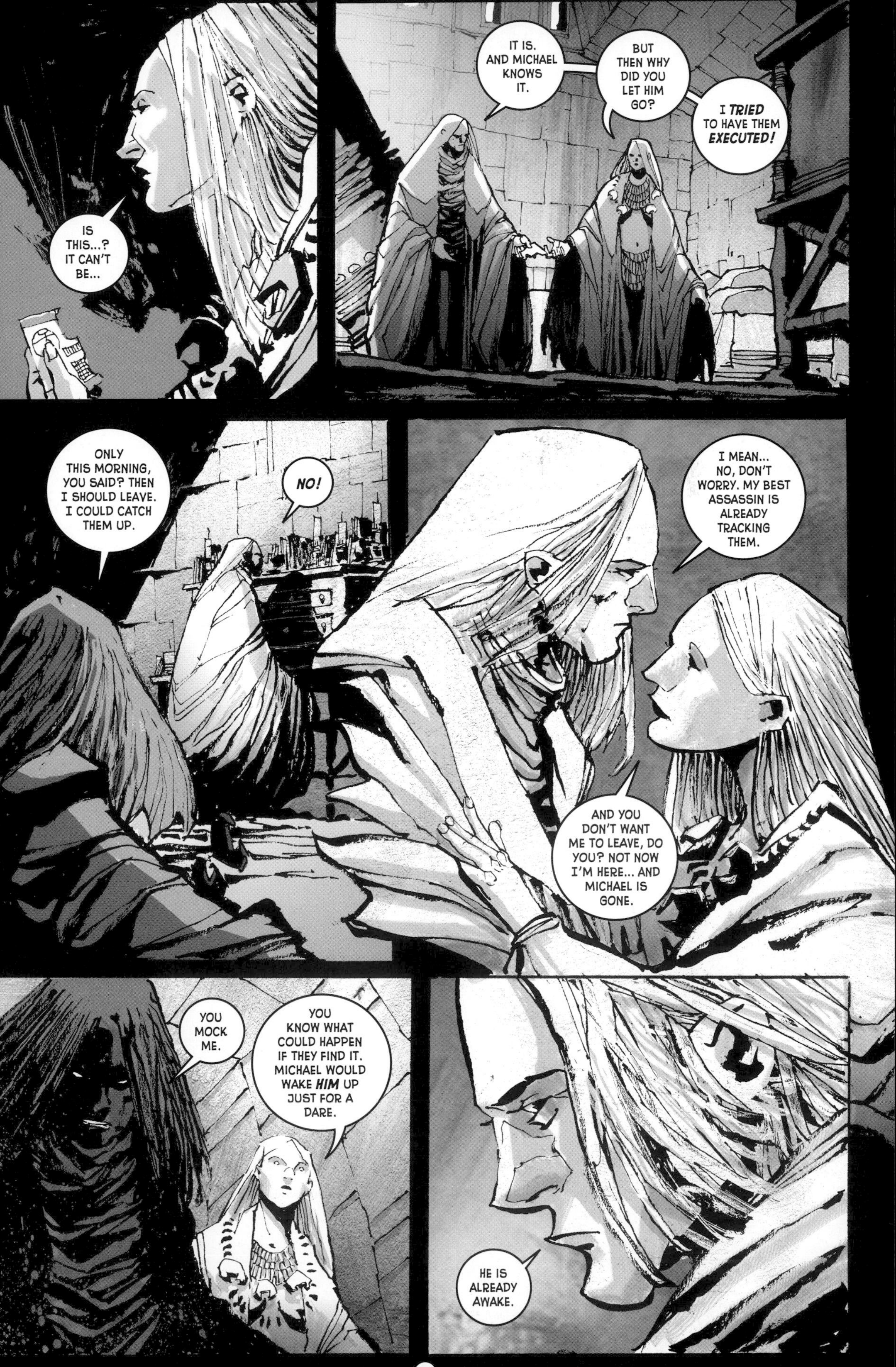

IS THIS...? IT CAN'T BE...
IT IS. AND MICHAEL KNOWS IT.
BUT THEN WHY DID YOU LET HIM GO?
I TRIED TO HAVE THEM EXECUTED!
ONLY THIS MORNING, YOU SAID? THEN I SHOULD LEAVE. I COULD CATCH THEM UP.
NO!
I MEAN... NO, DON'T WORRY. MY BEST ASSASSIN IS ALREADY TRACKING THEM.
AND YOU DON'T WANT ME TO LEAVE, DO YOU? NOT NOW I'M HERE... AND MICHAEL IS GONE.
YOU MOCK ME.
YOU KNOW WHAT COULD HAPPEN IF THEY FIND IT. MICHAEL WOULD WAKE HIM UP JUST FOR A DARE.
HE IS ALREADY AWAKE.

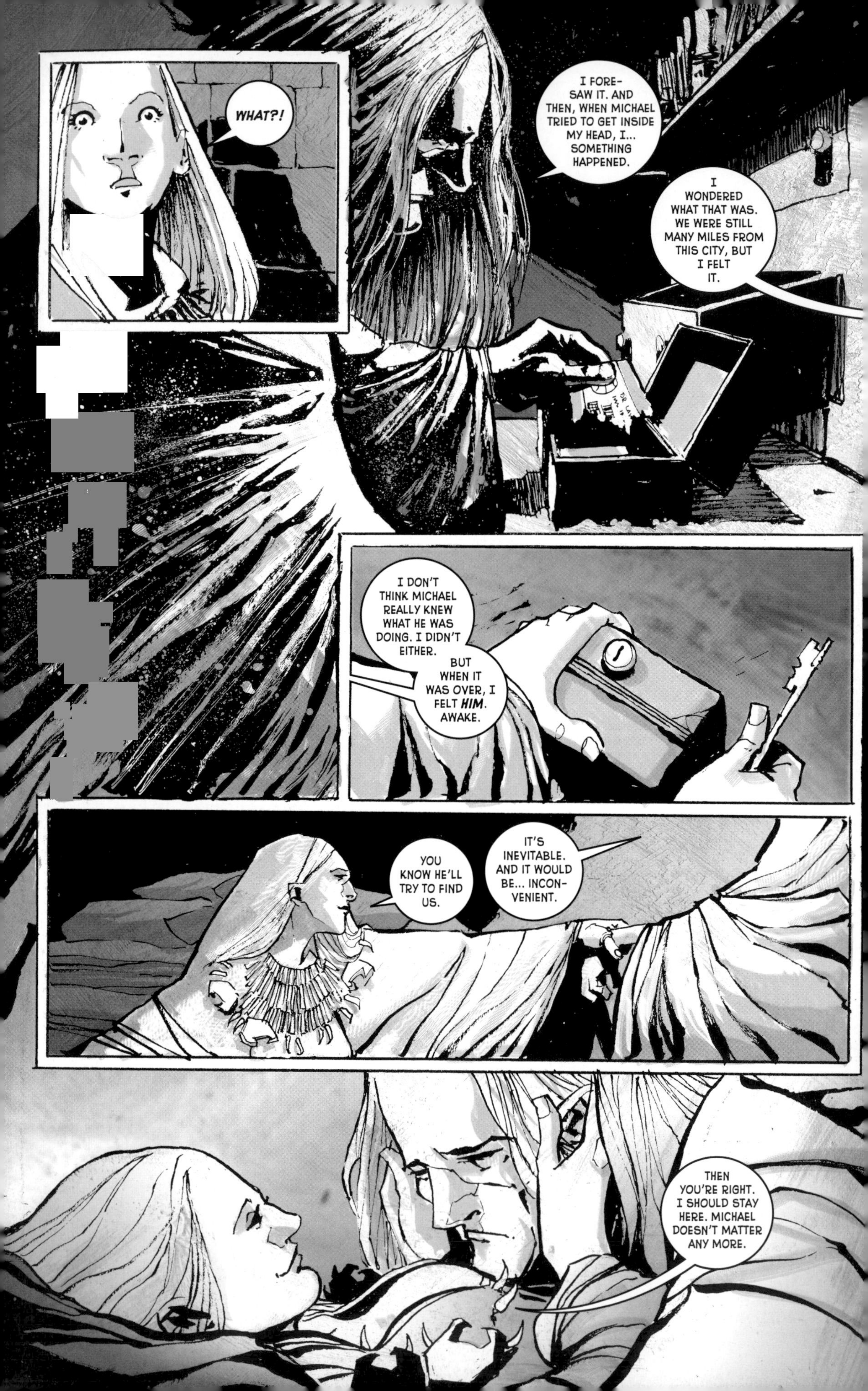
WHAT?!
I FORE-SAW IT. AND THEN, WHEN MICHAEL TRIED TO GET INSIDE MY HEAD, I... SOMETHING HAPPENED.
I WONDERED WHAT THAT WAS. WE WERE STILL MANY MILES FROM THIS CITY, BUT I FELT IT.
I DON'T THINK MICHAEL REALLY KNEW WHAT HE WAS DOING. I DIDN'T EITHER.
BUT WHEN IT WAS OVER, I FELT *HIM*. AWAKE.
YOU KNOW HE'LL TRY TO FIND US.
IT'S INEVITABLE. AND IT WOULD BE... INCON-VENIENT.
THEN YOU'RE RIGHT. I SHOULD STAY HERE. MICHAEL DOESN'T MATTER ANY MORE.

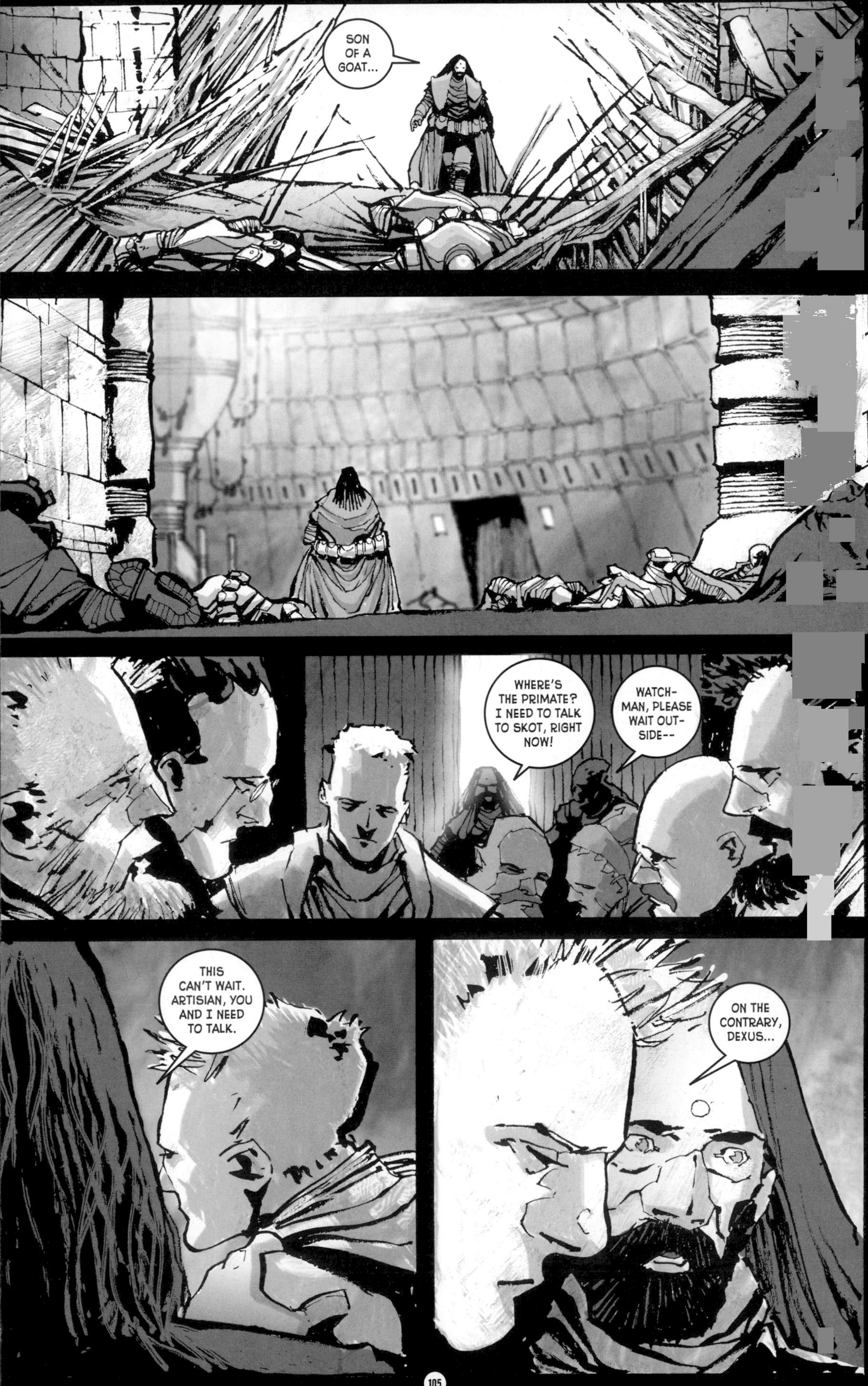
SON OF A GOAT...
WHERE'S THE PRIMATE? I NEED TO TALK TO SKOT, RIGHT NOW!
WATCH-MAN, PLEASE WAIT OUT-SIDE--
THIS CAN'T WAIT. ARTISIAN, YOU AND I NEED TO TALK.
ON THE CONTRARY, DEXUS...

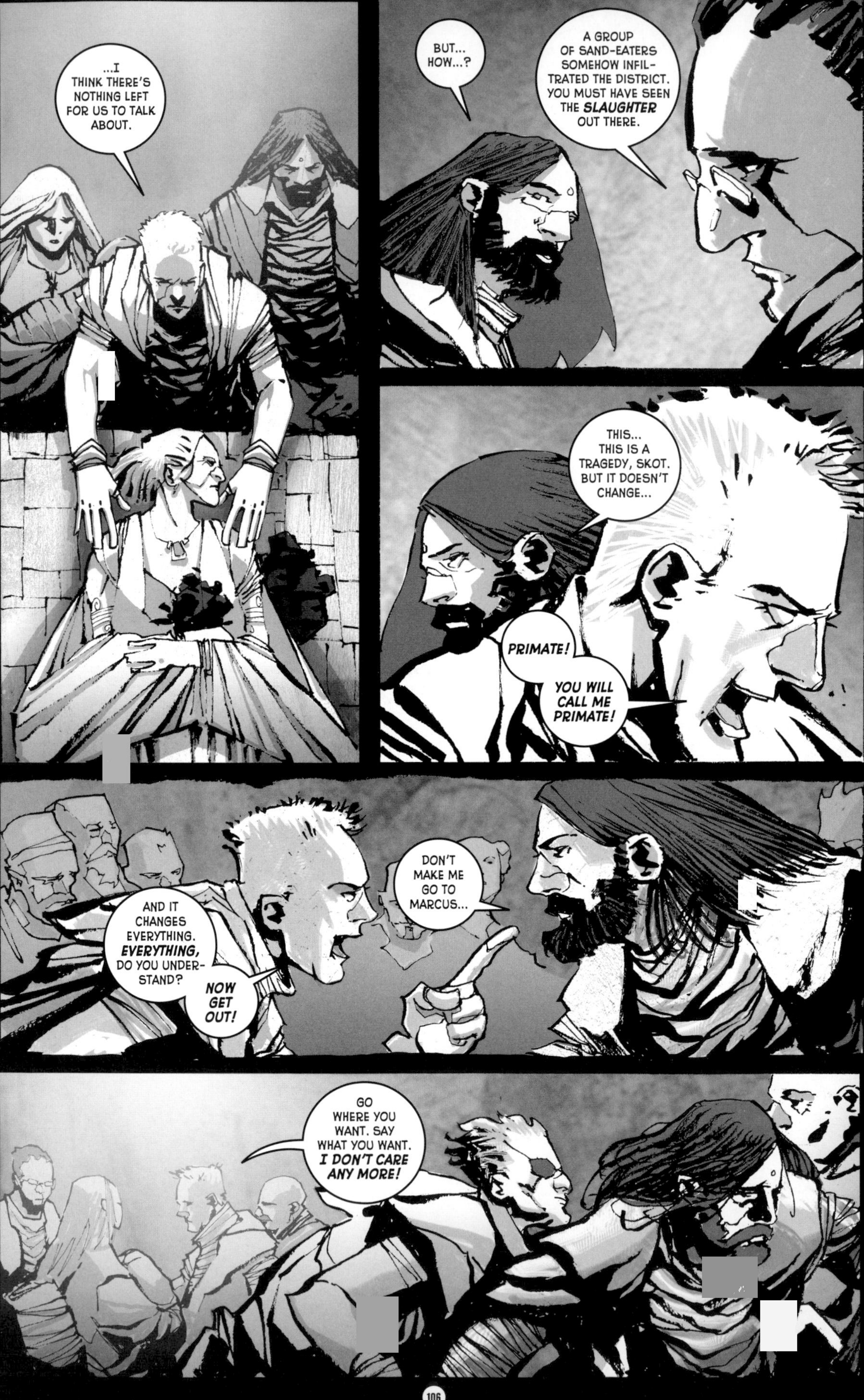
...I THINK THERE'S NOTHING LEFT FOR US TO TALK ABOUT.
BUT... HOW...?
A GROUP OF SAND-EATERS SOMEHOW INFIL-TRATED THE DISTRICT. YOU MUST HAVE SEEN THE SLAUGHTER OUT THERE.
THIS... THIS IS A TRAGEDY, SKOT. BUT IT DOESN'T CHANGE...
PRIMATE!
YOU WILL CALL ME PRIMATE!
AND IT CHANGES EVERYTHING. EVERYTHING, DO YOU UNDER-STAND?
NOW GET OUT!
DON'T MAKE ME GO TO MARCUS...
GO WHERE YOU WANT. SAY WHAT YOU WANT. I DON'T CARE ANY MORE!

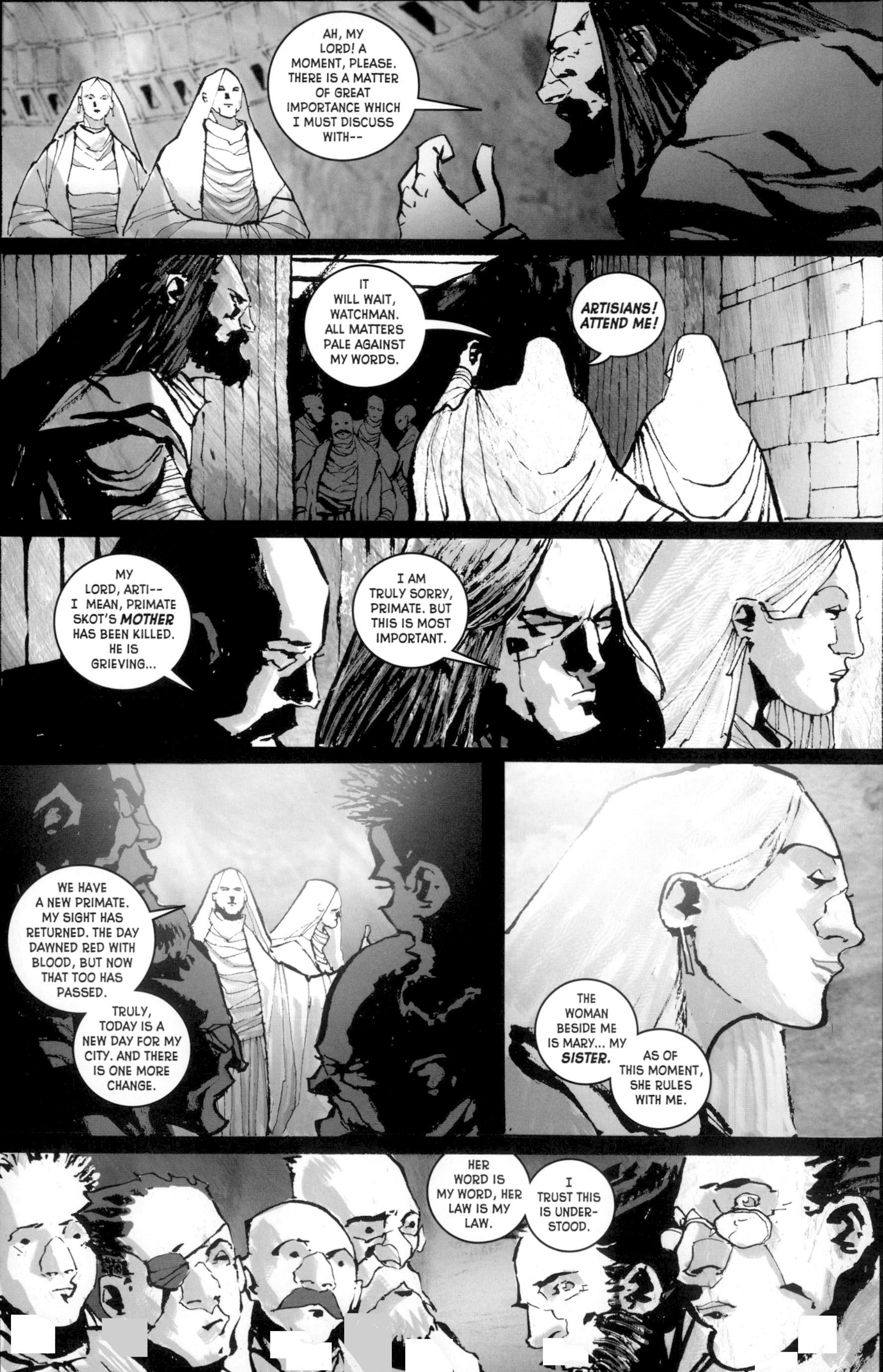
AH, MY LORD! A MOMENT, PLEASE. THERE IS A MATTER OF GREAT IMPORTANCE WHICH I MUST DISCUSS WITH--
IT WILL WAIT, WATCHMAN. ALL MATTERS PALE AGAINST MY WORDS.
ARTISIANS! ATTEND ME!
MY LORD, ARTI-- I MEAN, PRIMATE SKOT'S MOTHER HAS BEEN KILLED. HE IS GRIEVING...
I AM TRULY SORRY, PRIMATE. BUT THIS IS MOST IMPORTANT.
WE HAVE A NEW PRIMATE. MY SIGHT HAS RETURNED. THE DAY DAWNED RED WITH BLOOD, BUT NOW THAT TOO HAS PASSED.
TRULY, TODAY IS A NEW DAY FOR MY CITY. AND THERE IS ONE MORE CHANGE.
THE WOMAN BESIDE ME IS MARY... MY SISTER.
AS OF THIS MOMENT, SHE RULES WITH ME.
HER WORD IS MY WORD, HER LAW IS MY LAW.
I TRUST THIS IS UNDERSTOOD.

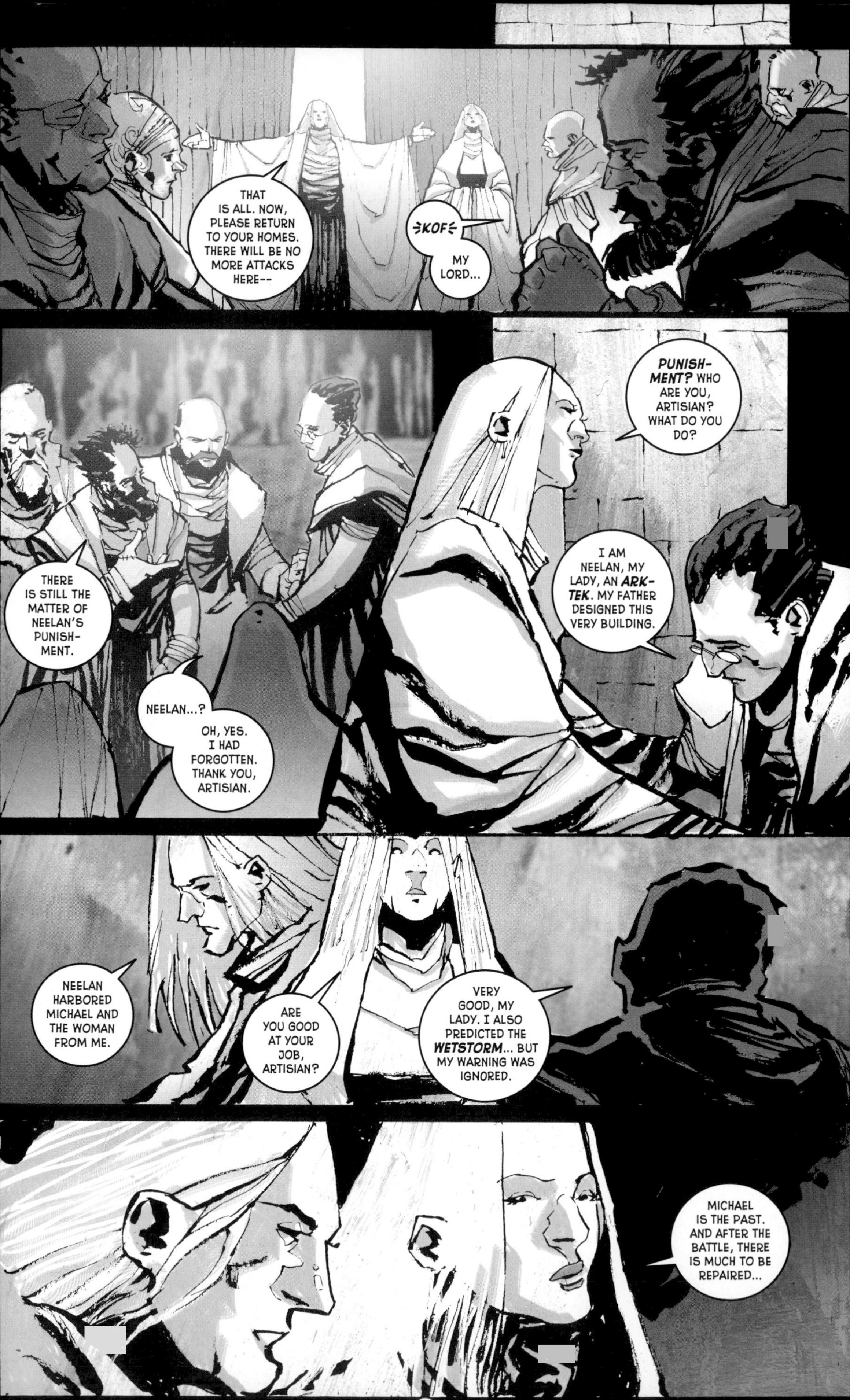
THAT IS ALL. NOW, PLEASE RETURN TO YOUR HOMES. THERE WILL BE NO MORE ATTACKS HERE--
KOF
MY LORD...
THERE IS STILL THE MATTER OF NEELAN'S PUNISH-MENT.
NEELAN...?
OH, YES. I HAD FORGOTTEN. THANK YOU, ARTISIAN.
PUNISH-MENT? WHO ARE YOU, ARTISIAN? WHAT DO YOU DO?
I AM NEELAN, MY LADY, AN ARK-TEK. MY FATHER DESIGNED THIS VERY BUILDING.
NEELAN HARBORED MICHAEL AND THE WOMAN FROM ME.
ARE YOU GOOD AT YOUR JOB, ARTISIAN?
VERY GOOD, MY LADY. I ALSO PREDICTED THE WETSTORM... BUT MY WARNING WAS IGNORED.
MICHAEL IS THE PAST. AND AFTER THE BATTLE, THERE IS MUCH TO BE REPAIRED...

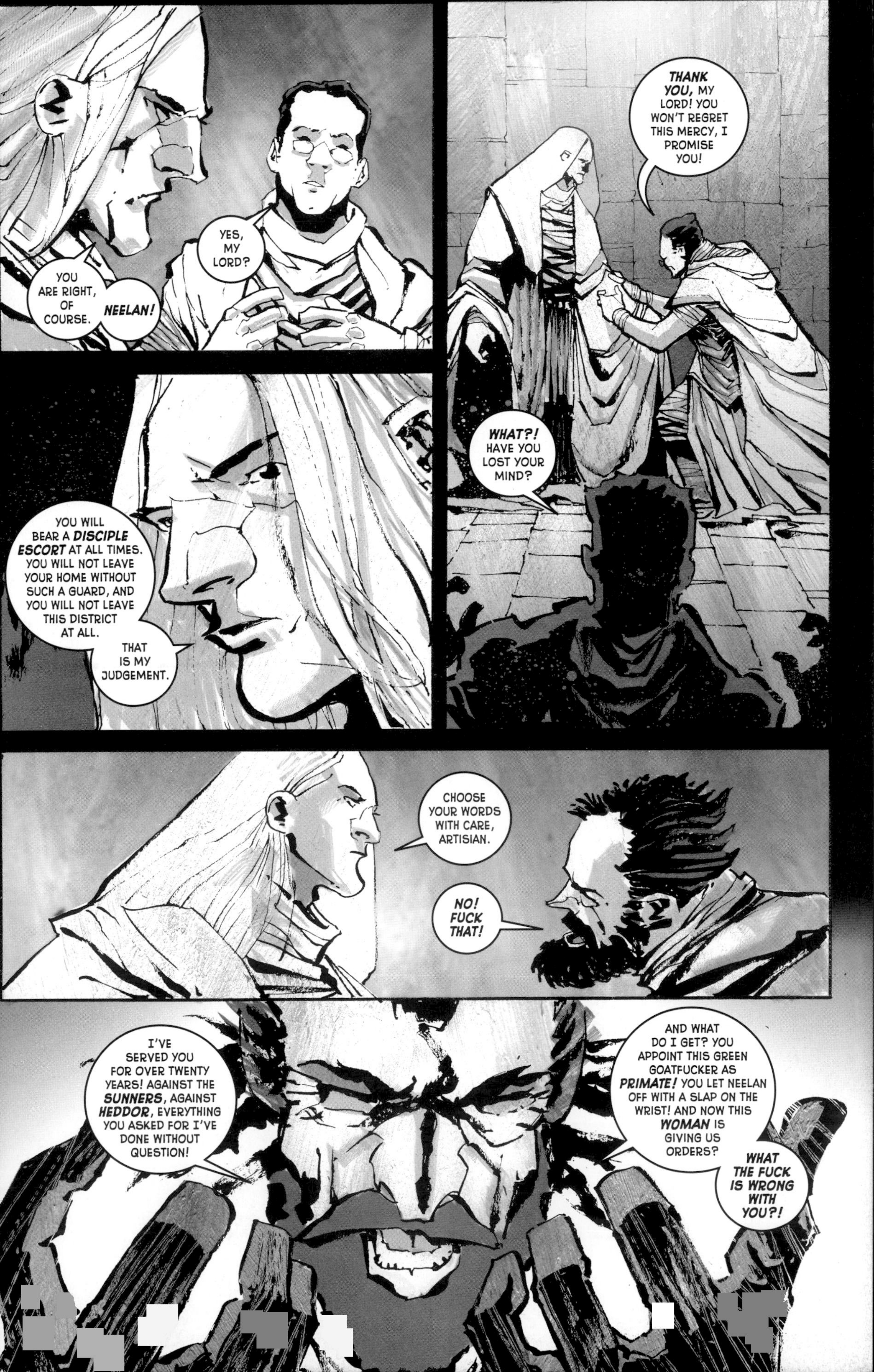

YES, MY LORD?
YOU ARE RIGHT, OF COURSE.
NEELAN!
THANK YOU, MY LORD! YOU WON'T REGRET THIS MERCY, I PROMISE YOU!
YOU WILL BEAR A DISCIPLE ESCORT AT ALL TIMES. YOU WILL NOT LEAVE YOUR HOME WITHOUT SUCH A GUARD, AND YOU WILL NOT LEAVE THIS DISTRICT AT ALL.
THAT IS MY JUDGEMENT.
WHAT?! HAVE YOU LOST YOUR MIND?
CHOOSE YOUR WORDS WITH CARE, ARTISIAN.
NO! FUCK THAT!
I'VE SERVED YOU FOR OVER TWENTY YEARS! AGAINST THE SUNNERS, AGAINST HEDDOR, EVERYTHING YOU ASKED FOR I'VE DONE WITHOUT QUESTION!
AND WHAT DO I GET? YOU APPOINT THIS GREEN GOATFUCKER AS PRIMATE! YOU LET NEELAN OFF WITH A SLAP ON THE WRIST! AND NOW THIS WOMAN IS GIVING US ORDERS?
WHAT THE FUCK IS WRONG WITH YOU?!

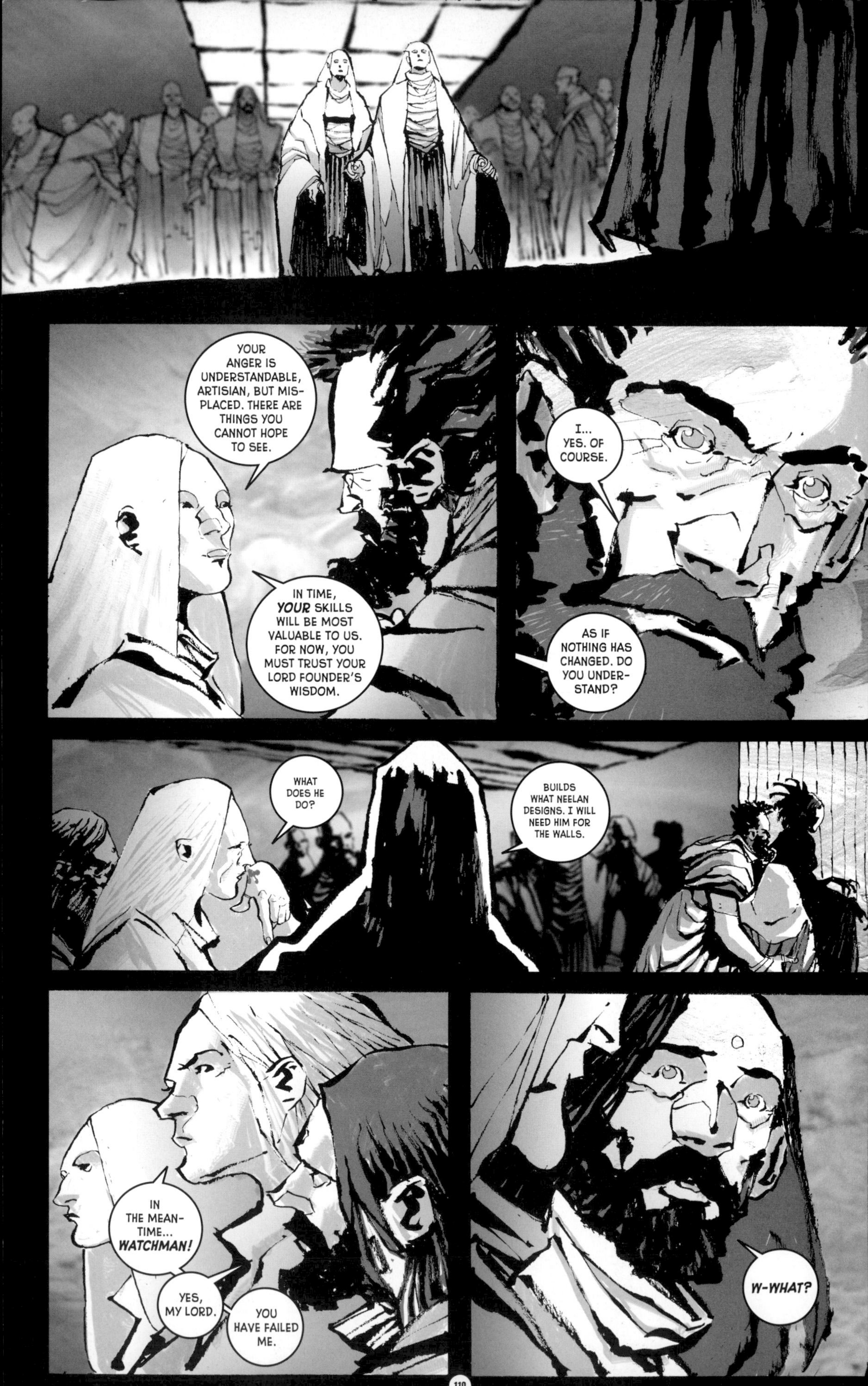

YOUR ANGER IS UNDERSTANDABLE, ARTISIAN, BUT MIS-PLACED. THERE ARE THINGS YOU CANNOT HOPE TO SEE.
IN TIME, *YOUR* SKILLS WILL BE MOST VALUABLE TO US. FOR NOW, YOU MUST TRUST YOUR LORD FOUNDER'S WISDOM.
I... YES. OF COURSE.
AS IF NOTHING HAS CHANGED. DO YOU UNDER-STAND?
WHAT DOES HE DO?
BUILDS WHAT NEELAN DESIGNS. I WILL NEED HIM FOR THE WALLS.
IN THE MEAN-TIME... *WATCHMAN!*
YES, MY LORD.
YOU HAVE FAILED ME.
W-WHAT?

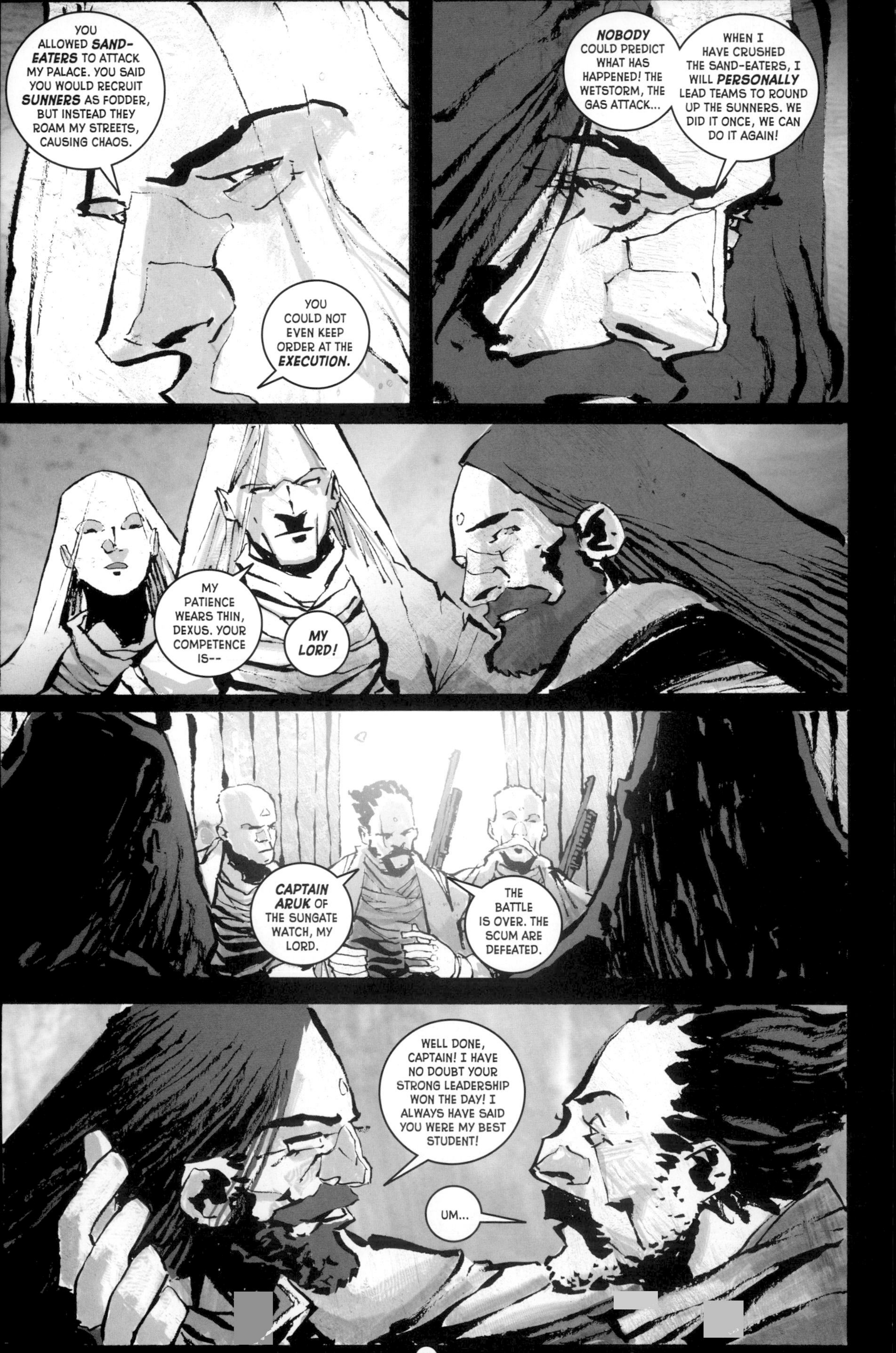
YOU ALLOWED **SAND-EATERS** TO ATTACK MY PALACE. YOU SAID YOU WOULD RECRUIT **SUNNERS** AS FODDER, BUT INSTEAD THEY ROAM MY STREETS, CAUSING CHAOS.
YOU COULD NOT EVEN KEEP ORDER AT THE **EXECUTION.**
NOBODY COULD PREDICT WHAT HAS HAPPENED! THE WETSTORM, THE GAS ATTACK...
WHEN I HAVE CRUSHED THE SAND-EATERS, I WILL **PERSONALLY** LEAD TEAMS TO ROUND UP THE SUNNERS. WE DID IT ONCE, WE CAN DO IT AGAIN!
MY PATIENCE WEARS THIN, DEXUS. YOUR COMPETENCE IS--
MY LORD!
CAPTAIN ARUK OF THE SUNGATE WATCH, MY LORD.
THE BATTLE IS OVER. THE SCUM ARE DEFEATED.
WELL DONE, CAPTAIN! I HAVE NO DOUBT YOUR STRONG LEADERSHIP WON THE DAY! I ALWAYS HAVE SAID YOU WERE MY BEST STUDENT!
UM...

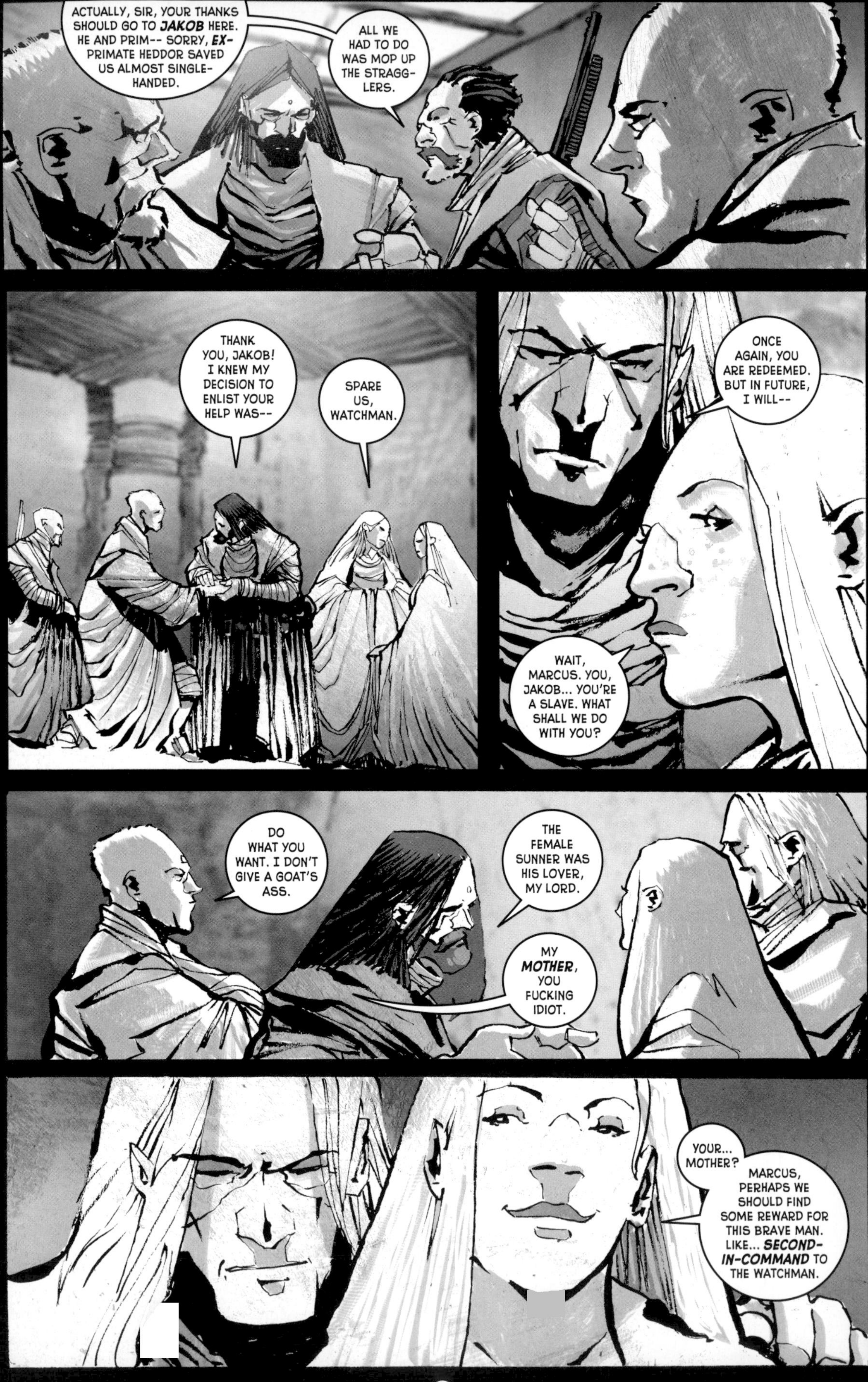
ACTUALLY, SIR, YOUR THANKS SHOULD GO TO **JAKOB** HERE. HE AND PRIM-- SORRY, **EX**-PRIMATE HEDDOR SAVED US ALMOST SINGLE-HANDED.
ALL WE HAD TO DO WAS MOP UP THE STRAGG-LERS.
THANK YOU, JAKOB! I KNEW MY DECISION TO ENLIST YOUR HELP WAS--
SPARE US, WATCHMAN.
ONCE AGAIN, YOU ARE REDEEMED. BUT IN FUTURE, I WILL--
WAIT, MARCUS. YOU, JAKOB... YOU'RE A SLAVE. WHAT SHALL WE DO WITH YOU?
DO WHAT YOU WANT. I DON'T GIVE A GOAT'S ASS.
THE FEMALE SUNNER WAS HIS LOVER, MY LORD.
MY ***MOTHER***, YOU FUCKING IDIOT.
YOUR... MOTHER?
MARCUS, PERHAPS WE SHOULD FIND SOME REWARD FOR THIS BRAVE MAN. LIKE... ***SECOND-IN-COMMAND*** TO THE WATCHMAN.

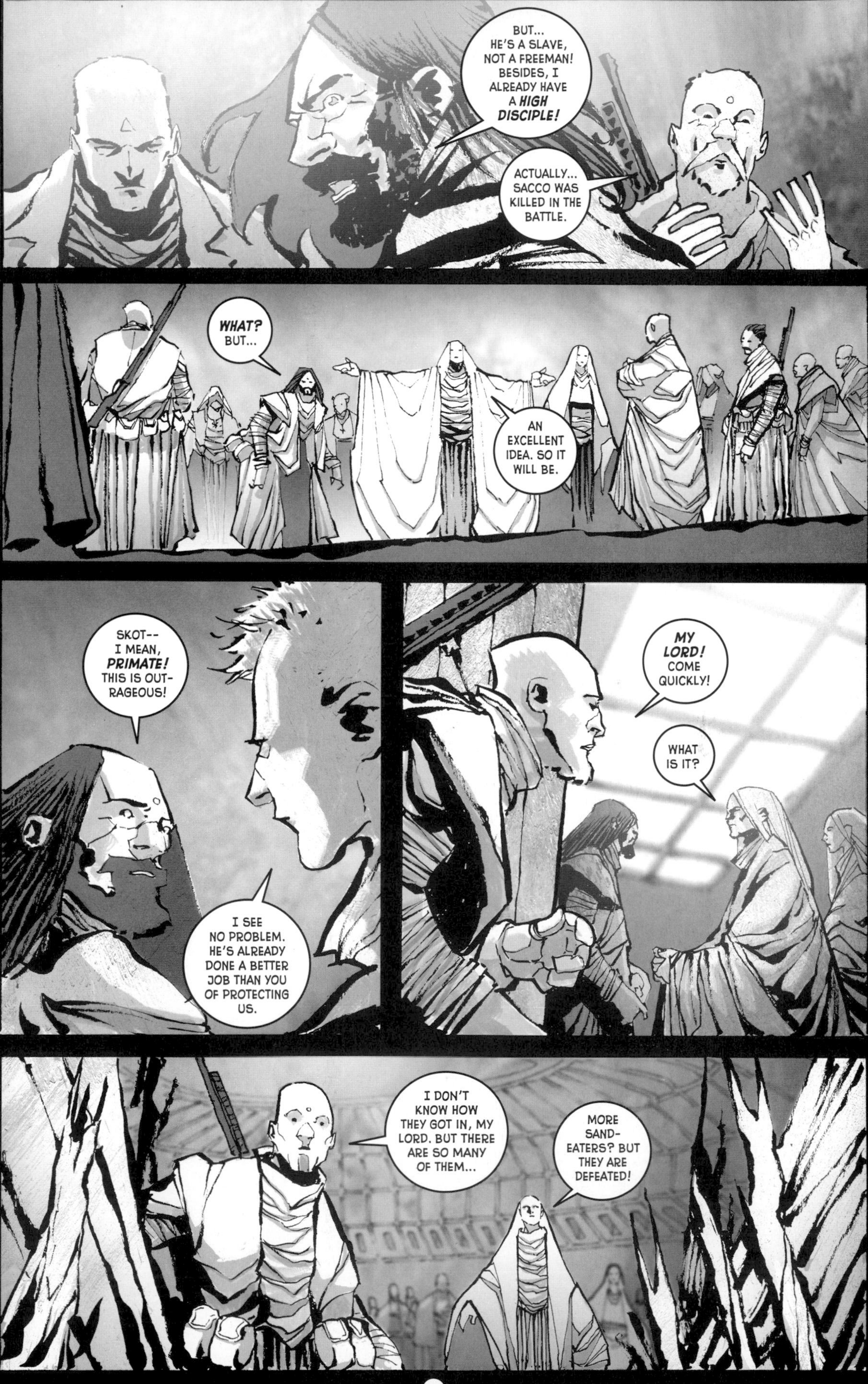
BUT... HE'S A SLAVE, NOT A FREEMAN! BESIDES, I ALREADY HAVE A HIGH DISCIPLE!
ACTUALLY... SACCO WAS KILLED IN THE BATTLE.
WHAT? BUT...
AN EXCELLENT IDEA. SO IT WILL BE.
SKOT-- I MEAN, PRIMATE! THIS IS OUTRAGEOUS!
I SEE NO PROBLEM. HE'S ALREADY DONE A BETTER JOB THAN YOU OF PROTECTING US.
MY LORD! COME QUICKLY!
WHAT IS IT?
I DON'T KNOW HOW THEY GOT IN, MY LORD. BUT THERE ARE SO MANY OF THEM...
MORE SAND-EATERS? BUT THEY ARE DEFEATED!

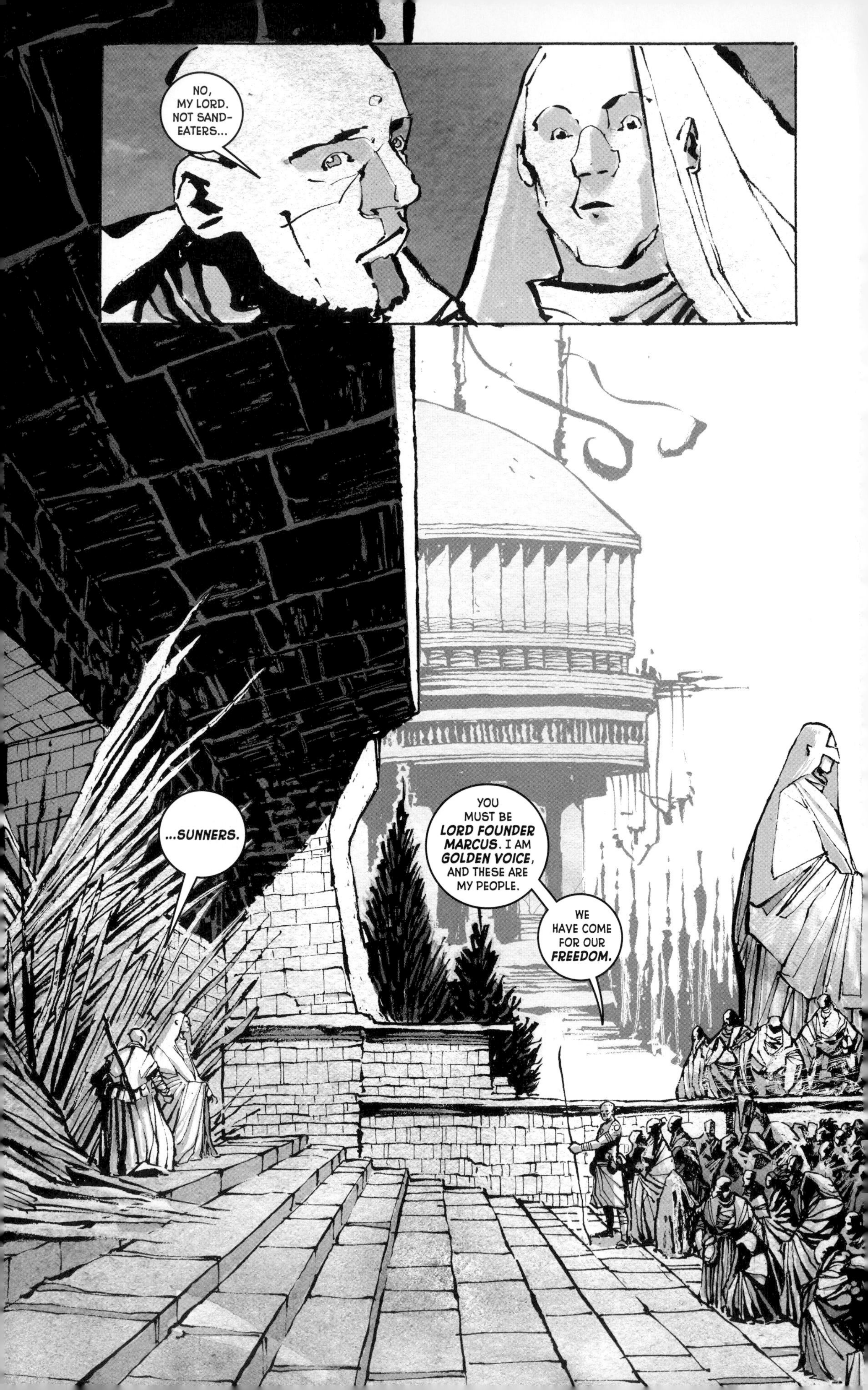
NO, MY LORD. NOT SAND-EATERS...
...SUNNERS.
YOU MUST BE LORD FOUNDER MARCUS. I AM GOLDEN VOICE, AND THESE ARE MY PEOPLE.
WE HAVE COME FOR OUR FREEDOM.

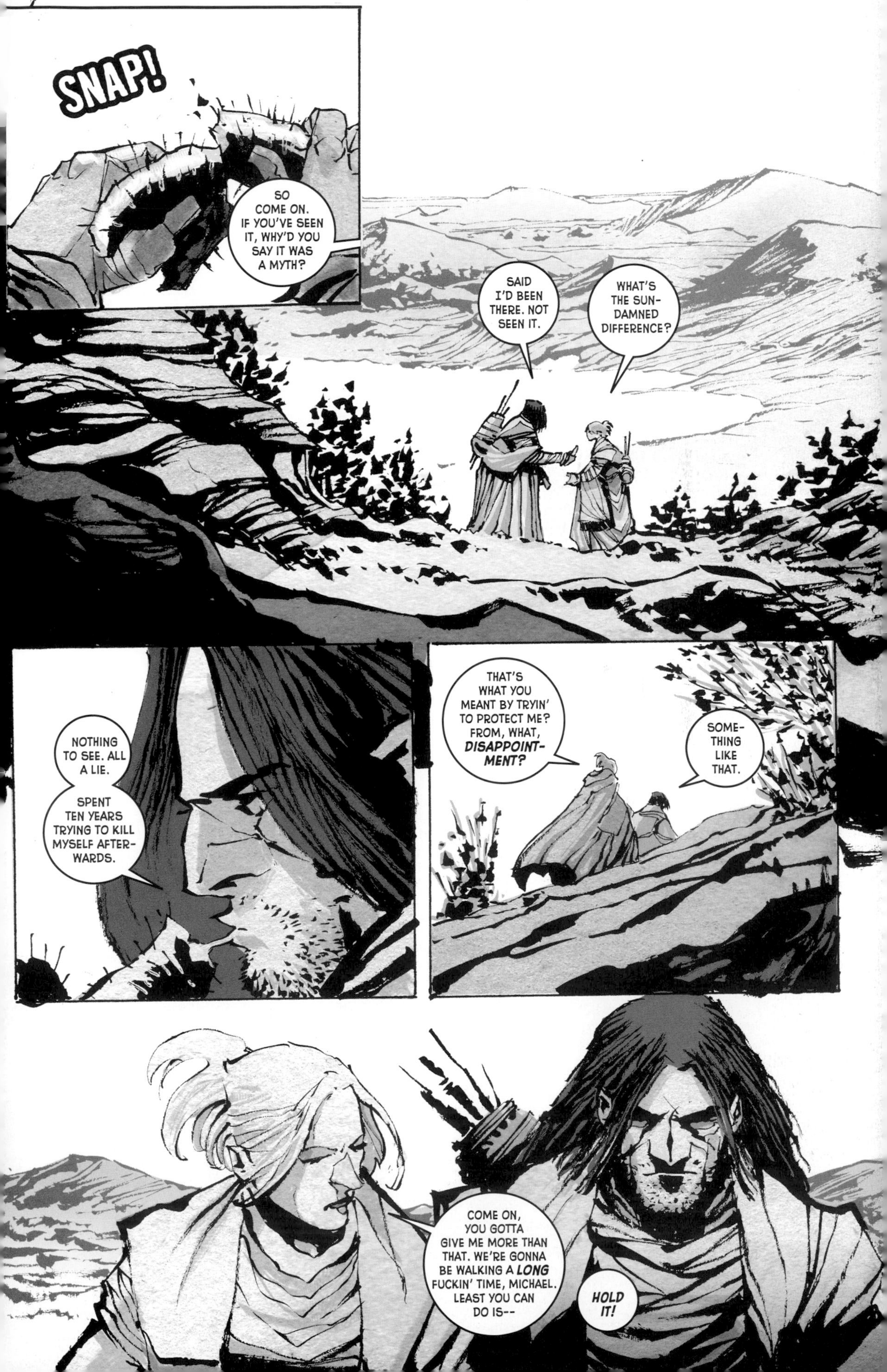
SNAP!
SO COME ON. IF YOU'VE SEEN IT, WHY'D YOU SAY IT WAS A MYTH?
SAID I'D BEEN THERE. NOT SEEN IT.
WHAT'S THE SUN-DAMNED DIFFERENCE?
NOTHING TO SEE. ALL A LIE.
SPENT TEN YEARS TRYING TO KILL MYSELF AFTER-WARDS.
THAT'S WHAT YOU MEANT BY TRYIN' TO PROTECT ME? FROM, WHAT, DISAPPOINT-MENT?
SOME-THING LIKE THAT.
COME ON, YOU GOTTA GIVE ME MORE THAN THAT. WE'RE GONNA BE WALKING A LONG FUCKIN' TIME, MICHAEL. LEAST YOU CAN DO IS--
HOLD IT!

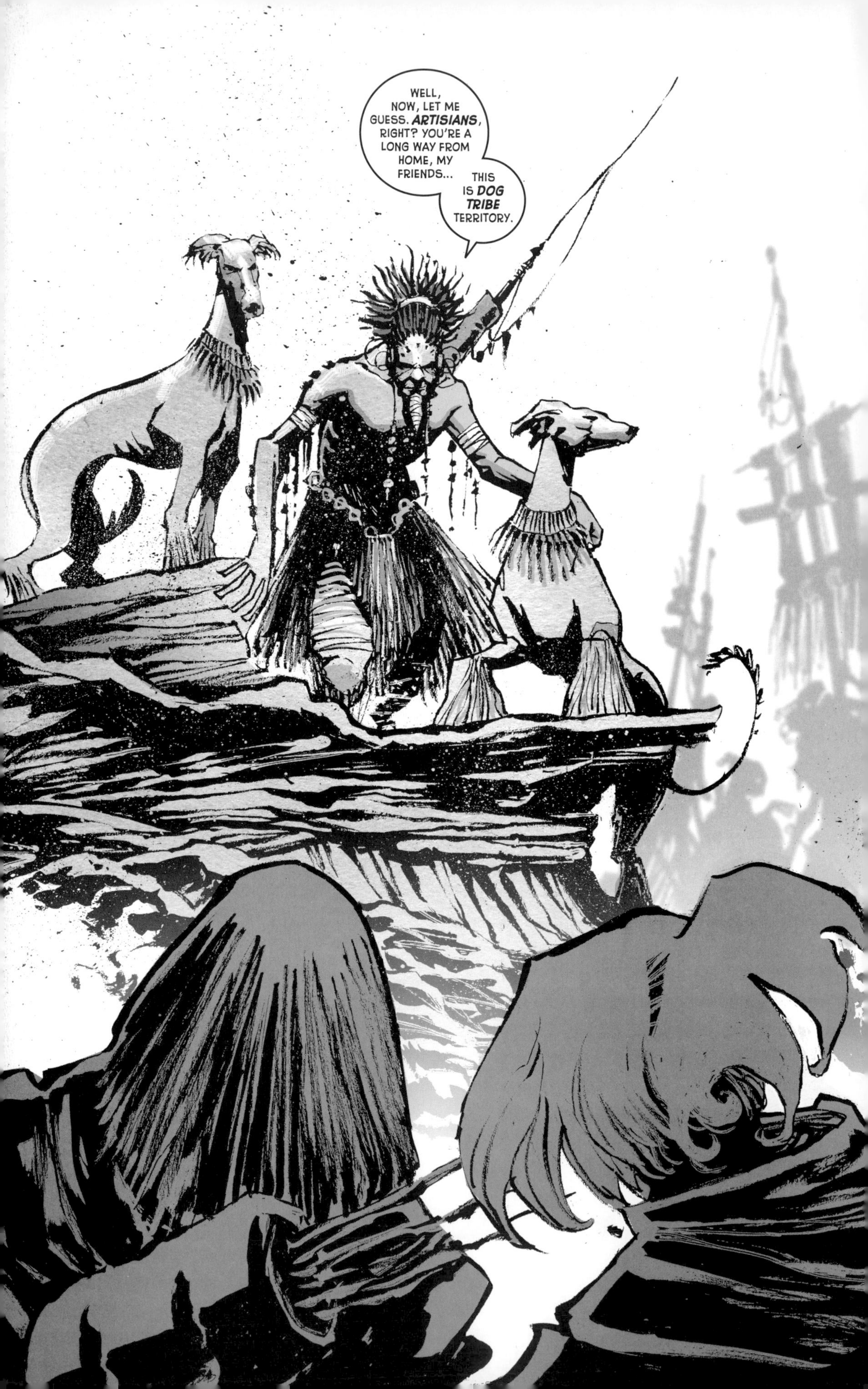
WELL, NOW, LET ME GUESS. ARTISIANS, RIGHT? YOU'RE A LONG WAY FROM HOME, MY FRIENDS...
THIS IS DOG TRIBE TERRITORY.

TO BE **CONTINUED**

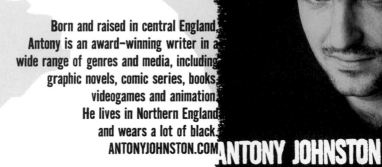

Born and raised in central England, Antony is an award-winning writer in a wide range of genres and media, including graphic novels, comic series, books, videogames and animation. He lives in Northern England and wears a lot of black.
ANTONYJOHNSTON.COM

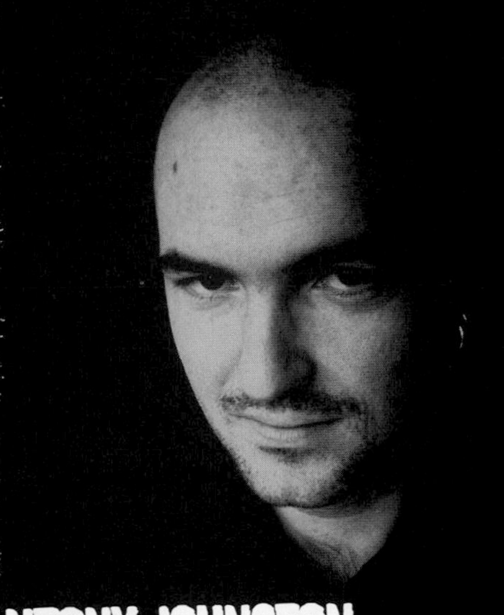

ANTONY JOHNSTON

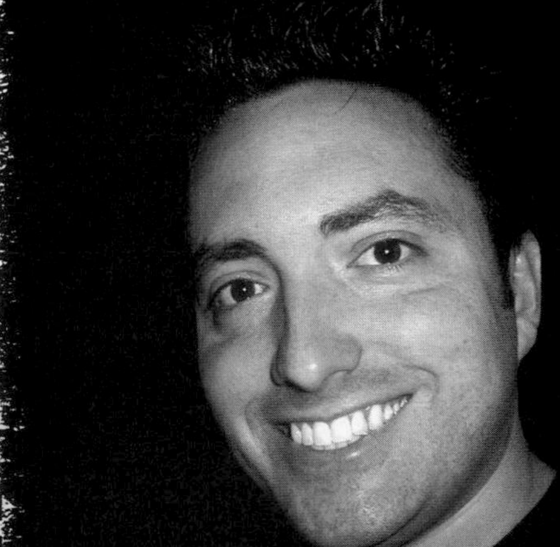

CHRISTOPHER MITTEN

Originally from the cow-dappled expanse of southern Wisconsin, Christopher now roams the misty wilds of suburban Chicago, drawing little people in little boxes. In addition to WASTELAND, he's illustrated graphic novels such as PAST LIES and LAST EXIT BEFORE TOLL (also from Oni Press), and contributed to the COMIC BOOK TATTOO anthology from Image Comics.
CHRISTOPHERMITTEN.COM

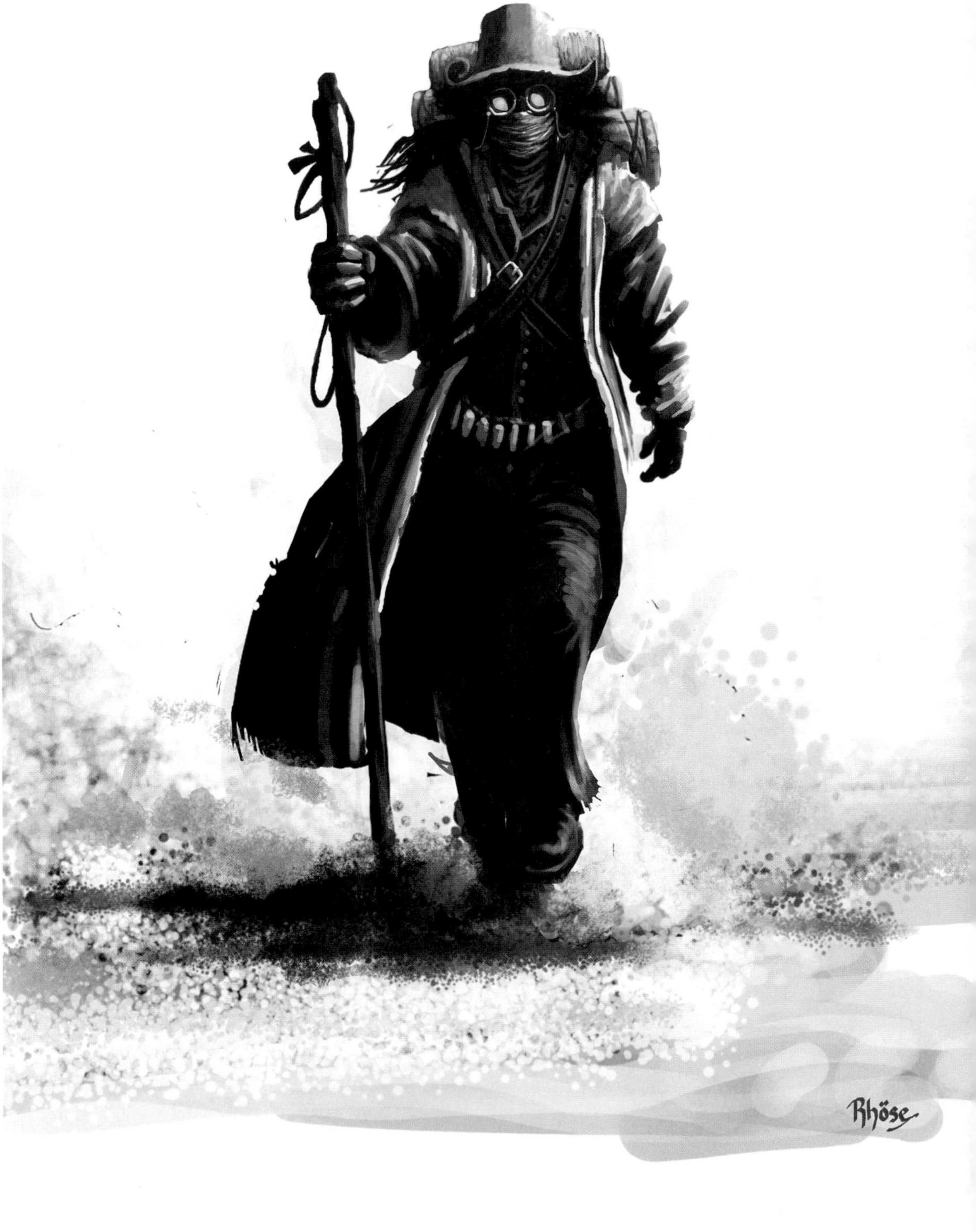
Rhöse

Niklas Rhöse
neostate.net

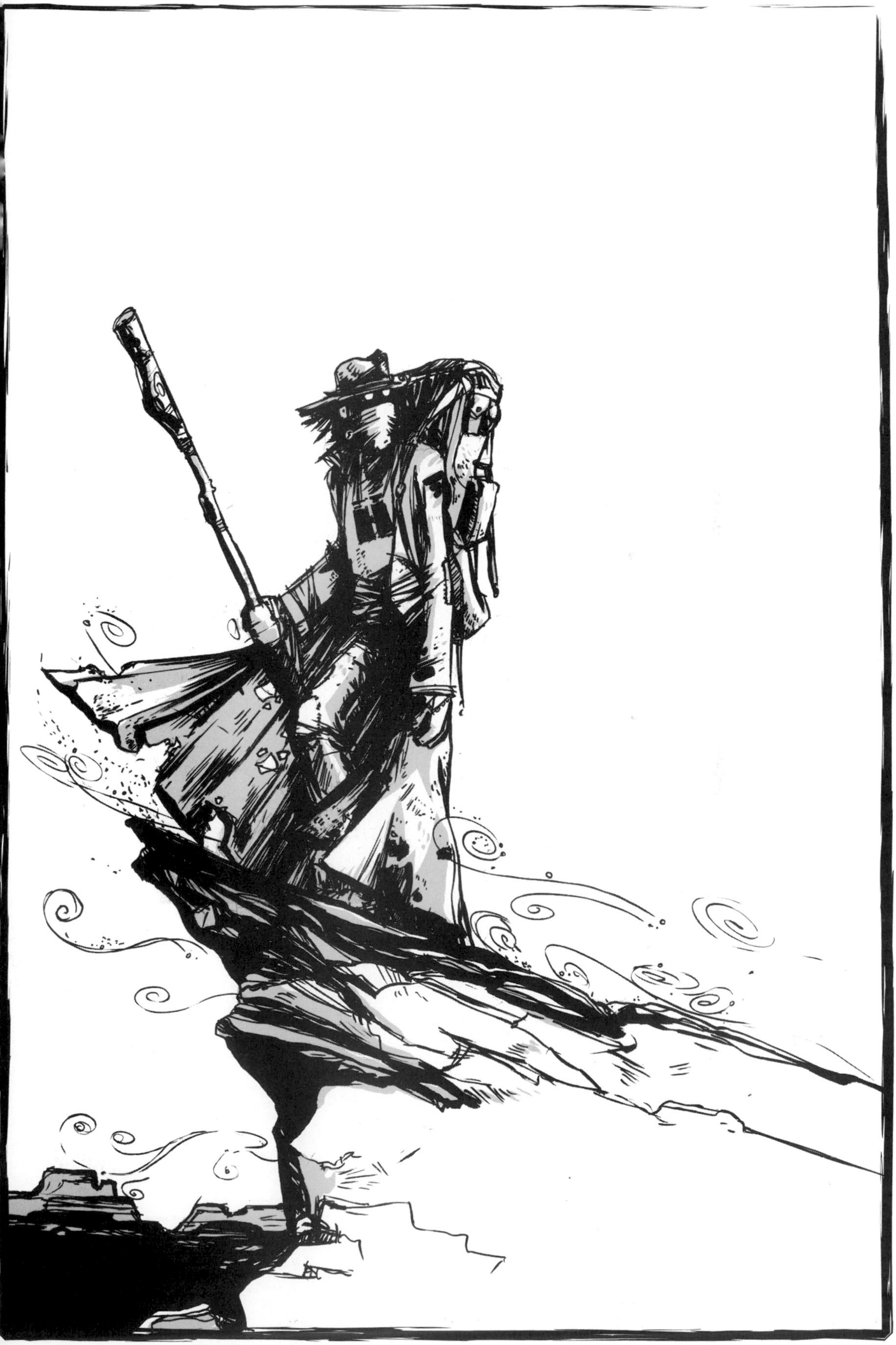

Mal Jones
maljones.com

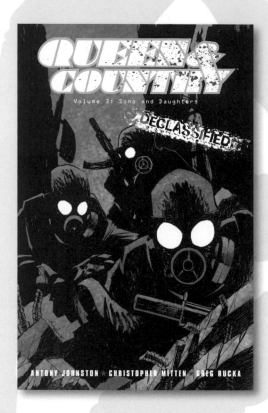

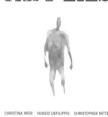

AND CHRISTOPHER MITTEN

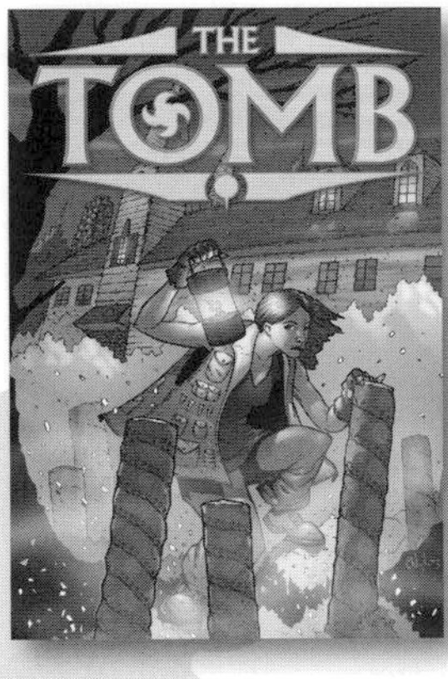
THE
TOMB

THE TOMB
CHRIS MITTEN,
NUNZIO DeFILIPPIS
& CHRISTINA WEIR

160 PAGES • $14.95 US
ISBN 978-1-929998-95-1

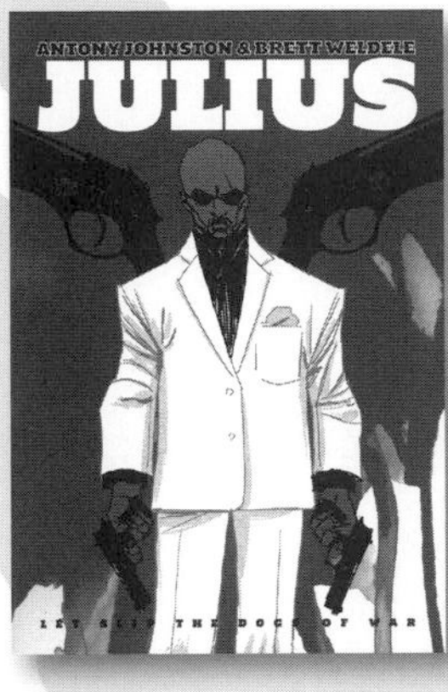
ANTONY JOHNSTON & BRETT WELDELE
JULIUS

JULIUS
ANTONY JOHNSTON
& BRETT WELDELE

160 PAGES • $14.95 US
ISBN 978-1-929998-80-7

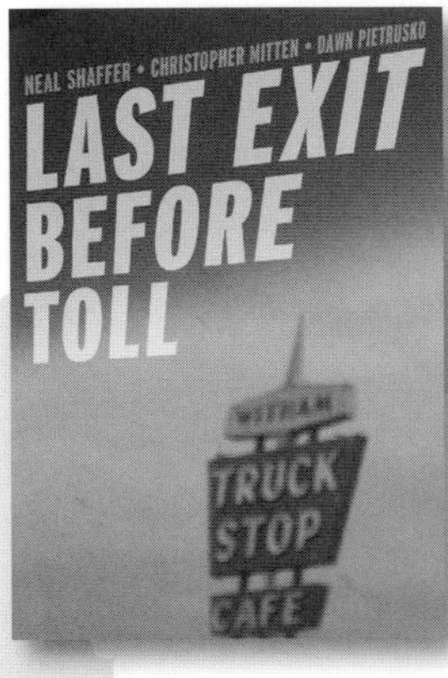
NEAL SHAFFER • CHRISTOPHER MITTEN • DAWN PIETRUSKO
LAST EXIT BEFORE TOLL
TRUCK STOP
CAFE

LAST EXIT BEFORE TOLL
NEAL SHAFFER,
CHRISTOPHER MITTEN
& DAWN PIETRUSKO

96 PAGES • $9.95 US
ISBN 978-1-929998-70-8

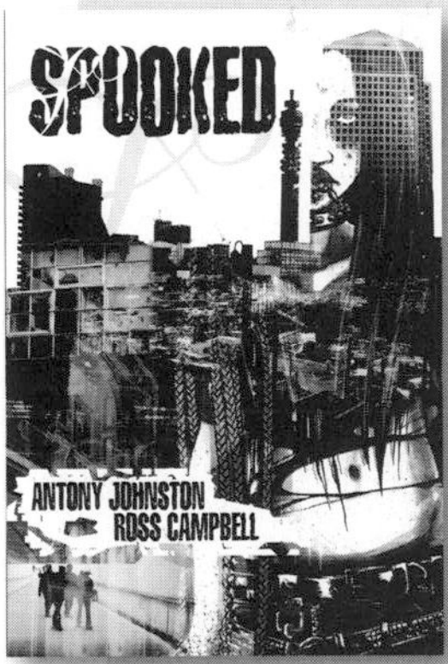
SPOOKED
ANTONY JOHNSTON
ROSS CAMPBELL

SPOOKED
ANTONY JOHNSTON
& ROSS CAMPBELL

168 PAGES • $14.95 US
ISBN 978-1-929998-79-1

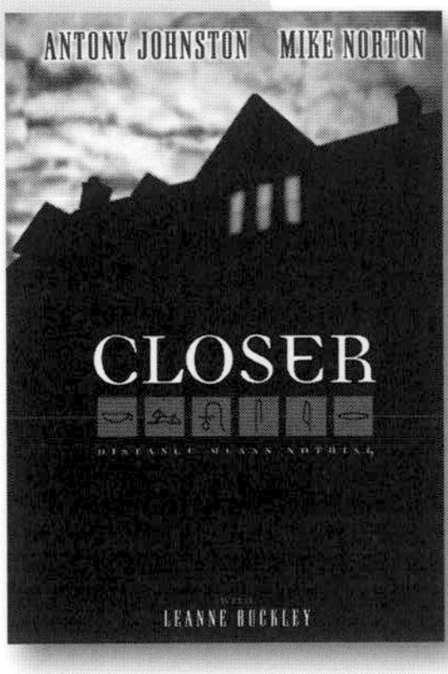
ANTONY JOHNSTON MIKE NORTON
CLOSER
LEANNE BUCKLEY

CLOSER
ANTONY JOHNSTON,
MIKE NORTON
& LEANNE BUCKLEY

160 PAGES • $14.95 US
ISBN 978-1-929998-81-4

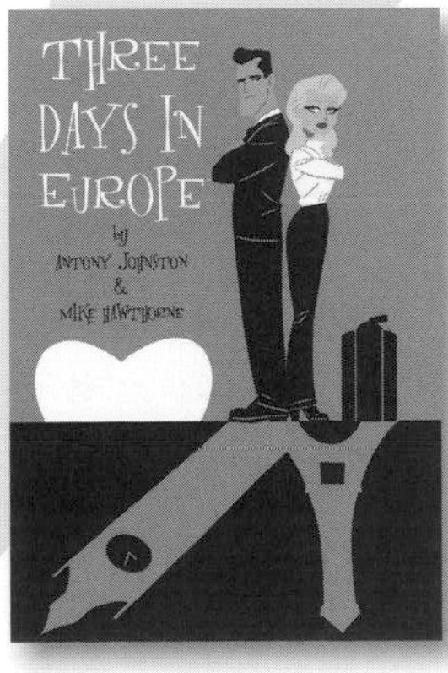
THREE DAYS IN EUROPE
by
ANTONY JOHNSTON
&
MIKE HAWTHORNE

THREE DAYS IN EUROPE
ANTONY JOHNSTON
& MIKE HAWTHORNE

144 PAGES • $14.95 US
ISBN 978-1-929998-72-2

CHRISTOPHERMITTEN.COM

MORE BOOKS FROM

CAPOTE IN KANSAS
A DRAWN NOVEL
ANDE PARKS
CHRIS SAMNEE

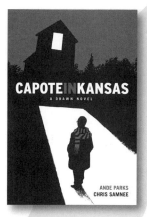

CAPOTE IN KANSAS
ANDE PARKS
& CHRIS SAMNEE

128 PAGES • $11.95 US
ISBN 978-1-932664-29-4

THE DAMNED
VOLUME ONE
"THREE DAYS DEAD"

THE DAMNED, VOL 1: THREE DAYS DEAD
CULLEN BUNN
& BRIAN HURTT

160 PAGES • $14.95 US
ISBN 978-1-932664-6-38

JUMPER
anywhere is possible.
JUMPSCARS

JUMPER: JUMPSCARS
NUNZIO DEFILIPPIS,
CHRISTINA WEIR
& BRIAN HURTT

96 PAGES • $14.95 US
FULL COLOR
ISBN 978-1-932664-93-5

Vasilis Lolos
THE LAST CALL

LAST CALL, VOL. 1
VASILIS LOLOS

136 PAGES • $11.95 US
ISBN 978-1-932664-69-0

NARCOLEPTIC SUNDAY
BY JEREMY HAUN & BRIAN KOSCHAK

NARCOLEPTIC SUNDAY
JEREMY HAUN
& BRIAN KOSCHAK

160 PAGES • $14.95 US
ISBN 978-1-932664-74-4

OJO
SAM KIETH
ALEX PARDEE CHRIS WISNIA

OJO
SAM KIETH,
CHRIS WISNIA
& ALEX PARDEE

144 PAGES • $14.95 US
ISBN 978-1-932664-13-3

AVAILABLE NOW FROM ALL GOOD COMIC & BOOK STORES • ONIPRESS.COM • JOIN US ONLINE AT

ONI PRESS

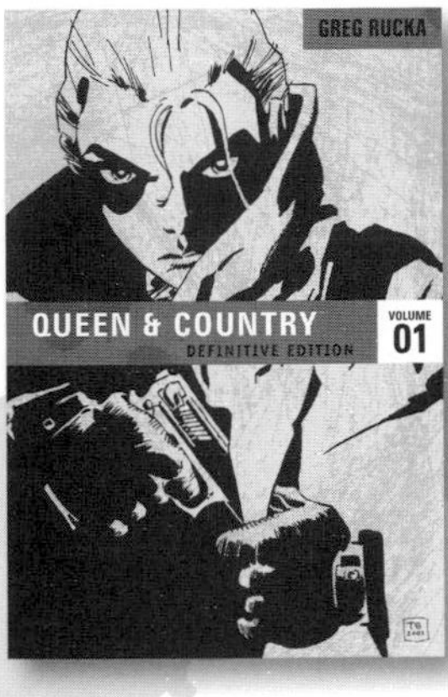
GREG RUCKA
QUEEN & COUNTRY
DEFINITIVE EDITION
VOLUME 01

QUEEN & COUNTRY: DEFINITIVE EDITION, VOL. 1
GREG RUCKA, STEVE ROLSTON, BRIAN HURTT & LEANDRO FERNANDEZ

376 PAGES • $19.95 US
ISBN 978-1-932664-87-4

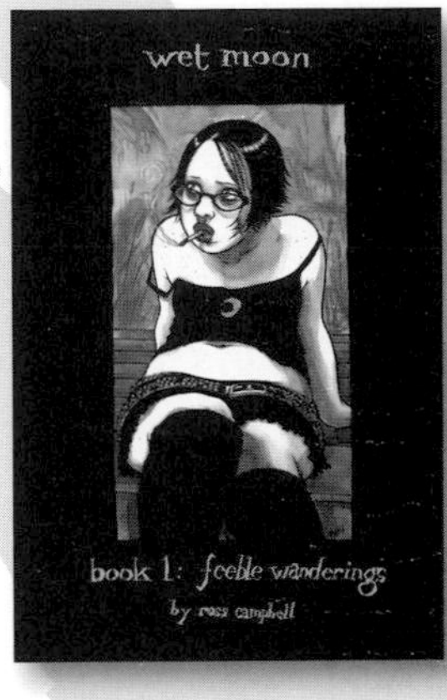
wet moon
book 1: feeble wanderings
by ross campbell

WET MOON, VOL. 1: FEEBLE WANDERINGS
ROSS CAMPBELL

168 PAGES • $14.95 US
ISBN 978-1-932664-07-2

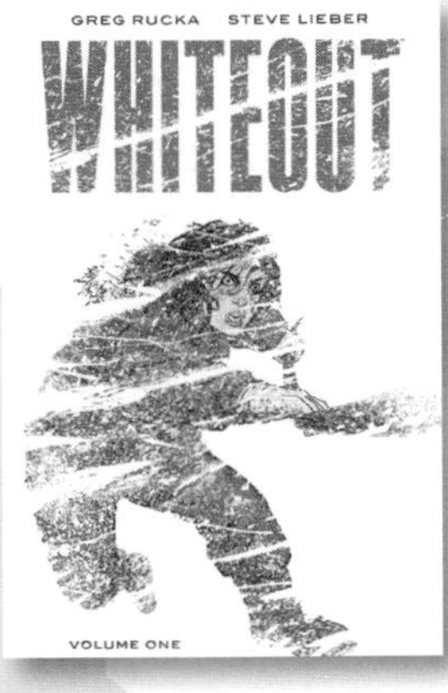
GREG RUCKA STEVE LIEBER
WHITEOUT
VOLUME ONE

WHITEOUT, VOL. 1: THE DEFINITIVE EDITION
GREG RUCKA & STEVE LIEBER

128 PAGES • $13.95 US
ISBN 978-1-932664-70-6

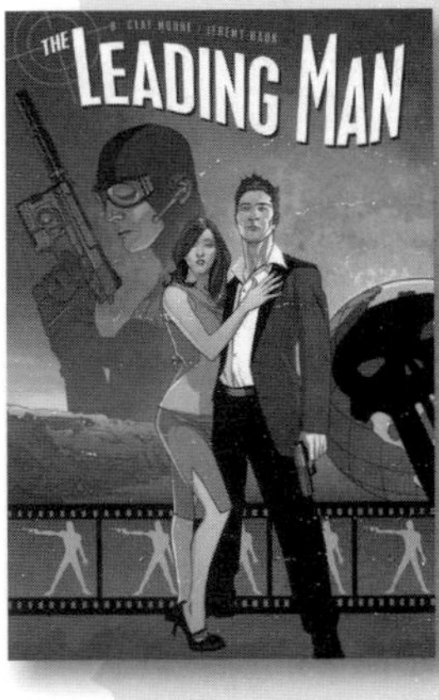
THE LEADING MAN

THE LEADING MAN
B. CLAY MOORE & JEREMY HAUN

136 PAGES • $14.95
FULL COLOR
ISBN 978-1-932664-57-7

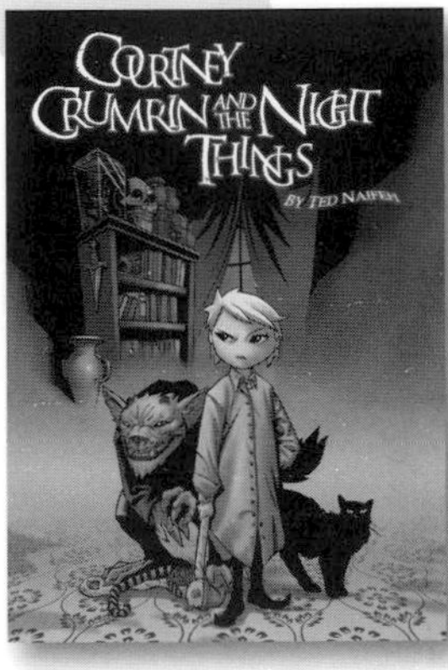
COURTNEY CRUMRIN AND THE NIGHT THINGS
BY TED NAIFEH

COURTNEY CRUMRIN, VOL. 1: THE NIGHT THINGS
TED NAIFEH

128 PAGES • $11.95
ISBN 978-1-929998-60-9

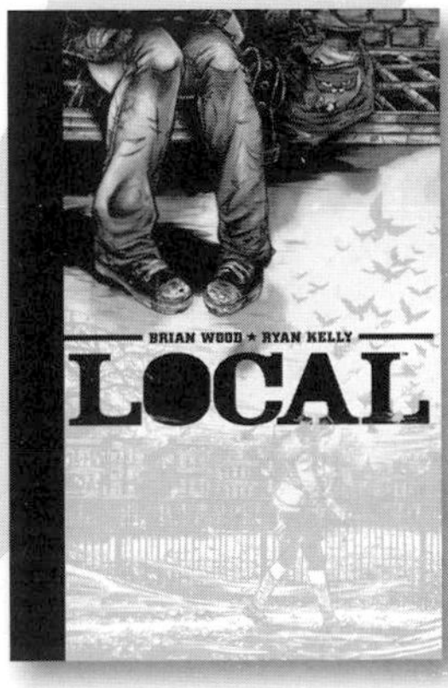
BRIAN WOOD ★ RYAN KELLY
LOCAL

LOCAL
BRIAN WOOD & RYAN KELLY

384 PAGES • $29.99
HARDCOVER
ISBN 978-1-934964-00-2

ONIPRESS.COM/FORUM